ROUTLEDGE LIBRARY EDITIONS: HISTORIOGRAPHY

Volume 35

GYULA SZEKFÜ

GYULA SZEKFÜ
A Study in the Political Basis of Hungarian Historiography

IRENE RAAB EPSTEIN

Routledge
Taylor & Francis Group
LONDON AND NEW YORK

First published in 1987 by Garland Publishing, Inc.

This edition first published in 2016
by Routledge
4 Park Square, Milton Park, Abingdon, Oxon OX14 4RN
605 Third Avenue, New York, NY 10017

Routledge is an imprint of the Taylor & Francis Group, an informa business

© 1987 Irene Raab Epstein

All rights reserved. No part of this book may be reprinted or reproduced or utilised in any form or by any electronic, mechanical, or other means, now known or hereafter invented, including photocopying and recording, or in any information storage or retrieval system, without permission in writing from the publishers.

Trademark notice: Product or corporate names may be trademarks or registered trademarks, and are used only for identification and explanation without intent to infringe.

British Library Cataloguing in Publication Data
A catalogue record for this book is available from the British Library

ISBN: 978-1-138-99958-9 (Set)
ISBN: 978-1-315-63745-7 (Set) (ebk)
ISBN: 978-1-138-64277-5 (Volume 35) (hbk)
ISBN: 978-1-138-64279-9 (Volume 35) (pbk)
ISBN: 978-1-315-62974-2 (Volume 35) (ebk)

Publisher's Note
The publisher has gone to great lengths to ensure the quality of this reprint but points out that some imperfections in the original copies may be apparent.

Disclaimer
The publisher has made every effort to trace copyright holders and would welcome correspondence from those they have been unable to trace.

Gyula Szekfü

A Study in the Political Basis of Hungarian Historiography

Irene Raab Epstein

Garland Publishing, Inc.
New York and London 1987

Copyright © 1987 Irene Raab Epstein
All rights reserved

Library of Congress Cataloging-in-Publication Data

Epstein, Irene Raab, 1925–
  Gyula Szekfü : a study in the political basis of Hungarian historiography / Irene Raab Epstein.
    p. cm.—(Modern European history)
  Thesis (Ph.D.)—Indiana University, 1974.
  Bibliography: p.
  ISBN 0-8240-8024-6 (alk. paper)
    1. Szekfü, Gyula, 1883–1955. 2. Historians—Hungary—Biography. 3. Hungary—Historiography. I. Title. II. Series.
DB923.7.S92E67   1987
943.9′0072024—dc19   87-25858

All volumes in this series are printed on acid-free, 250-year-life paper.

Printed in the United States of America

GYULA SZEKFŰ:

A STUDY IN THE POLITICAL BASIS
OF HUNGARIAN HISTORIOGRAPHY

by

Irene Raab Epstein

TABLE OF CONTENTS

Chapter		Page
	INTRODUCTION	1

PART ONE
THE DUALIST SZEKFŰ: 1904-1918

I.	Der Staat Ungarn and the Christian-German Cultural Community	8
II.	A Labanc View of Rákóczi	38
III.	Geistesgeschichte, Szekfű and Hungarian Historiography	53

PART TWO
THE CONSERVATIVE NATIONALIST: 1919-1933

IV.	After the Catastrophe: Assigning the Blame	74
V.	Széchenyi: The Touchstone of the Nation . .	92
VI.	Liberalism: Three Generations of Decline .	113
VII.	The Jews: The Bane of the Nation	146
VIII.	Nationalism and Nationalities: Historiography and the Revision of the Treaty of Trianon	178

PART THREE
THE REALIST SZEKFŰ: 1933-1955
FROM ST. STEPHEN'S STATE TO THE
HUNGARIAN PEOPLE'S REPUBLIC

IX.	The First Doubts: After Three Generations	217

Chapter		Page
X.	"Somewhere We Lost Our Way." Szekfű and the Popular Front	252
XI.	Volte Face: From West to East	273
	CONCLUSION: CONTINUITY AND CHANGE IN SZEKFŰ'S IDEAS	313
	BIBLIOGRAPHICAL ESSAY	325
	BIBLIOGRAPHY	326

PREFACE

The connection between historical scholarship and contemporary politics has been recently acknowledged by both Marxist and Western historians. The Hungarian Zoltán Horváth stated that

> small nations with a relatively short past have the greatest difficulty in developing a historiography that is independent of the state and its institutions, detached from party politics and the pressures of powerful groups. This being so, it tends to become a mere tool in their hands and a reflection rather of current interests than of actual conditions.[1]

The influence of politics on historiography is not peculiar to repressive societies and small nations. Historians living and working in authoritarian countries perhaps adhere to the official line prodded by their instinct of self-preservation, or, at least, by their ambition to succeed. But there are more subtle forces at work as well: scholars, like other people, share in the values of society underlying the political and social structure of the state. This is, of course, just as true in countries possessing a liberal democratic form of government and a capitalistic economy as it is in authoritarian, socialist nations. The Swiss historian Herbert Lüthy wrote that

---

[1] Zoltán Horváth, "Hungary: Recovering from the Past." In Contemporary History in Europe: Problems and Perspectives, ed. by Donald C. Watt, New York: Frederick A. Praeger, 1969, p. 219

> historical research . . . always contains an antinomy of truth and social utility, to a degree that is unknown to any other science; it can never be practiced in the same state of innocence customary with other sciences . . . .
>
> The science of history is indissolubly linked with the consciousness of history, which moves us to think and act in a historical, that is in a political fashion . . . . None of /the sciences/ has ever been so deeply and permanently at the mercy of political purposes.[2]

This study is an attempt to explore the connection between politics and historical scholarship in the case of a Hungarian historian, Gyula Szekfű, whose career spanned one of the most significant and eventful periods of Hungarian history. Because the changes in Szekfű's political and historical points of view paralleled the drastic changes which occurred in Hungary, his writing is particularly suited for an inquiry into the relationship between politics and historiography.

Except for the names of St. Stephen and Matthias Corvinus, which appear in that form in Western history books, all given names of Hungarians are used in their original, Magyar, form. The word Magyar, rather than Hungarian, is used throughout the study whenever the ethnic origin of the group or the person needs to be emphasized. All translations from the works of Szekfű and from other Hungarian sources are my own.

---

[2] Herbert Lüthy, "What is the Point of History?" *Journal of Contemporary History*, III (1968), p. 13.

I would like to express my sincere appreciation to the members of my doctoral committee for making their time available for the critical reading of this study. I am especially grateful to Professor Charles Jelavich whose courses and seminars in Austro-Hungarian and Balkan history taught me to put Hungarian problems into a larger historical framework. His generous counsel and assistance facilitated the completion of my dissertation.

PREFACE TO THE GARLAND EDITION

Hungarian historiography of the past three decades, since the death of Gyula Szekfű, reflects the gradually increasing intellectual freedom of the Hungarian society. Nevertheless, the writings of this illustrious scholar still await a comprehensive evaluation by a Hungarian historian.

In 1983, on the occasion of the centennial anniversary of the birth of Gyula Szekfű, the Hungarian Historical Association devoted a special commemorative session to his scholarship. The papers at this meeting, and the books and articles which have appeared so far, dealt mainly with Szekfű's early career and, especially, with the controversy surrounding the publication of one of his early books, published in 1913. No attempt has been made as yet to gain an insight into the reasons for the constantly changing views of this influential scholar, who, during his fifty-year career, traveled from the far right to the far left of the political spectrum, appearing sincere at every stage of his life. A study based on the voluminous correspondence of the historian (available in Hungarian archives but yet to be published) would surely yield an interesting character study as well as aid the understanding and evaluation of his oeuvre.

A fair amount of Hungarian historical scholarship is published in Western languages in Hungary today. Unfortunately, the historical writings of pre-World II Hungary are accessible only to scholars who can use Hungarian sources. Thus, in the United States, with the exception of the writings of S. B. Vardy, very little scholarship has been devoted to Hungarian historiography. The publication of this dissertation may serve to introduce the writings of Gyula Szekfű, whose work is too little known outside of Hungary.

INTRODUCTION

Less than a decade after the celebration of the Millenium, the one thousandth anniversary of the establishment of the Hungarian state, a young historian, Gyula Szekfű, completed the first of his many studies pertaining to Hungarian history. In those early years of the new century, in spite of tempestuous domestic politics, Hungary seemed to have a secure and stable future as a full-fledged partner in the Austro-Hungarian Monarchy. A young man of Szekfü's background, possessing a brilliant mind, a capacity for hard work and great ambitions, could not fail to achieve success in a teaching and writing career. Szekfű did, indeed, achieve distinction, but the course of his career was as unforeseen and as eventful as that of the next half century of Hungarian history.

Throughout the fifty-one year period between 1904 and 1955, the steady outpouring of scholarly and journalistic writing by Gyula Szekfű reflected both the changing fortunes of Hungary and the changing political orientation of the historian. For Szekfü began his career as a pro-Habsburg Dualist, turned to nationalism and anti-liberalism after the First World War only to change course in the 1930's when he recognized the folly of a pro-German foreign policy and abhorred the domestic degradation of the Hungarian state.

Szekfü was involved in the feeble anti-German resistance movement during the Second World War and he came to support the Communist regime in the years that remained him.

In spite of his constantly changing views, at all times, Szekfü appeared sincere rather than opportunistic. His books and monographs attested to his impeccable scholarship notwithstanding the biased interpretation, his journalism revealed strong opinions, and he was recognized by his detractors as well as his admirers as a man of creative literary talent as well as scholarly ability.

Gyula Szekfü started his career as an archivist in the <u>Haus- Hof- und Staatsarchiv</u> in Vienna. He became a professor of modern Hungarian history at the University of Budapest in 1924 and devoted the next twenty years to teaching, research and writing. In addition to his monographs, scholarly articles and a multi-volume history of Hungary, Szekfü was an editor and journalist of note and he also contributed to Catholic publications as one of the foremost Catholic laymen of Hungary.

During the Second World War, Szekfü turned to journalism revealing his opposition to the regime in thinly veiled allegorical articles. Because of his participation in the resistance movement, on March 19, 1944, the day of the German occupation of Hungary, Szekfü and his wife sought asylum with ecclesiastic friends and remained in hiding until the end of the war. In 1946, Szekfü became Hungary's first ambassador to the Soviet Union. Although he never became a member of the Communist Party and remained a devout Christian, at the time of his death in 1955, Gyula Szekfű was a member of the Presidium of the People's Republic of Hungary.

Because of the close relationship between Szekfü's work and fifty years of Hungarian history, an attempt will be made to put Szekfü's historiography into a political and intellectual context. This seems a proper method of examining Szekfü's oeuvre because of the reciprocal relationship between Szekfu and the political and intellectual community in Hungary. On the one hand, Szekfü's writing on past history and contemporary politics reflected the predominant view of the politically influential segment of Hungarian society, and, on the other, his books and articles exerted a strong influence on the Hungarian intellectual community.

Szekfű seldom expressed his political philosophy or ethical principles in the abstract; he made his statements by the interpretation of past events. His political ideas and his point of view can be evaluated only by the examination of his writing about events and personalities in Hungarian history. It is, therefore, necessary to discuss Hungarian history as it appears in Szekfü's historiography. His most important works, especially those which indicate and justify the changes in his views are examined in detail.

Following the major changes that occurred in Szekfü's political orientation, this study is divided into three parts. The first deals with the Dualist period and describes Szekfu's career and writings between 1904 and 1918. This was the period when his family traditions and Western, especially German, intellectual influences were manifested most strongly. Recognizable vestiges of these influences could be found even after Szekfű's politics had undergone drastic changes decades later.

The second and most important period of Szekfű's historiography began in 1920 and lasted until about 1933. The interwar period was one of reactionary nationalism in Hungary and Szekfű's writings in the 1920's provided much of the intellectual underpinnings of the first decade of the Horthy regime. Virtually all of Szekfű's important and scholarly writings appeared between 1920 and 1933, his political views were identical with those of Hungary's leadership and his intellectual influence was at its height. The emphasis of this study, therefore, is on Szekfű's conservative nationalist period. The chapters in Part Two are topically rather than chronologically arranged.

The 1934 edition of Három Nemzedék (Three Generations), Szekfű's seminal book originally published in 1920, carried a lengthy addition dealing with the postwar decade. This new material gave the first indication of a change in Szekfű's thinking concerning Hungarian politics. The third section of the study attempts to deal with this change and follow it to its conclusion: the volte-face of Szekfű's previous political and intellectual position.

It is not an exaggeration to say that never was there a closer relationship between the work of a man and the events of his times than in the case of Gyula Szekfű. To write about Szekfű's career is to write about a half a century of political and intellectual history of Hungary. To discuss Szekfű's point of view necessitates dealing with one thousand years of Magyar history. To evaluate his writings one must contend with the contradictions in the life of a man who started out in the service of the Habsburgs and ended in the service of Mátyás Rákosi, turning from a life-time of belief in Hungary's mission as a bulwark of the West against the barbarian East to support a government based on principles he previously considered evil and allied with a nation he previously considered uncivilized. And even when one does not view the entire course of Szekfű's career, it is necessary to come to terms with the inconsistencies in the system of values of a man who could be, at one and the same time, a whole-hearted Dualist and a Magyar patriot, a Christian moralist and a pragmatic realist, a champion of the welfare of the people and the supporter of a Stalinist state. It is no wonder that while the life and work of lesser historians have been evaluated in biographies and historiographical studies, Marxist historians shy away from writing about a man so difficult to evaluate "correctly." As one Hungarian intellectual put it: "We praise him and disparage him with an equally bad conscience."[1]

---

[1] László Bóka, Válogatott Tanulmányok, Magvető, Budapest, 1966, p. 1054.

The intriguing questions concerning the contradictions in Szekfü's character and the numerous inconsistencies in Szekfü's views cannot be reconciled without a great deal more personal information about Szekfü than was available to this writer. This study does not purport to deal with Szekfü the individual except to provide some basic information pertinent to his career; rather the purpose is to examine Szekfü's views on Hungarian history and Hungarian politics as they were revealed in his writings and to trace the connection between the historian's changing views and Hungarian politics in the twentieth century.

PART ONE

THE DUALIST SZEKFŰ: 1904-1918

CHAPTER I

DER STAAT UNGARN AND THE CHRISTIAN-GERMAN
CULTURAL COMMUNITY

Midway between the Hungarian capital and Lake Balaton lies the ancient Transdanubian city of Székesfehérvár. Built on the site of the Roman settlement of Herculia, it is a city with a double heritage. According to legend, when the Magyar tribe occupied the area of Transdanubia, the head of the tribe, Árpád, selected the site of Székesfehérvár as the seat of his permanent residence, probably in the last year of the ninth century.[1] It was, however, his descendant, St. Stephen (1000-1038), whose name was most closely associated with the city. The first king of Christian Hungary made Székesfehérvár the seat of Hungarian Christianity. In the year 1003, work had begun on the Romanesque basilica which became the scene of coronations and funerals of all the kings of the House of Árpád. A royal residence and numerous churches had been built by the successors of St. Stephen, and, until the Battle of Mohács in 1526, the yearly Országgyülés (National Assembly) had been held in Székesfehérvár.[2]

Nothing remained of the physical splendor of the Middle Ages except the small Gothic Chapel of St. Anna, built during the reign of Matthias Corvinus (1458-1490) in the fifteenth century. The monuments to the heritage of the medieval Magyar Kingdom had been completely obliterated during the century and a half of Turkish occupation.[3] Destroyed and depopulated, the almost purely Magyar city of Székesfehérvár was rebuilt and resettled in the Baroque style and in the Baroque spirit by the House of Habsburg in the beginning of the eighteenth century. Székesfehérvár again became the seat of a bishopric and regained its previous status as a Royal Free City. Religious orders--Jesuits, Franciscans and Cistercians--established monasteries and built churches there. The imposing Baroque Palace of the Bishop and the smaller building of the City Hall of similar architectural distinction dominate the center of the city to this day.[4] The majority of the new settlers were German who became Magyarized in the course of the nineteenth century. Both the German and the Magyar population of Székesfehérvár, like Transdanubians in general, had been overwhelmingly Catholic and Kaisertreu, and their tangible tradition of Roman Catholicism was the connecting link to the double historical heritage: the medieval Hungarian civilization and the culture of the Austrian Baroque.

Born in 1883, in the city of Székesfehérvár, Gyula Szekfü was a child of an upper middle class, comfortable, devoutly Catholic family. Unlike the overwhelming majority of urban people in nineteenth century Hungary, the Szekfü family was of Magyar origin. The son of a lawyer, Gyula Szekfü received a traditional upbringing and decided early on a scholarly career, while his brother chose the priesthood.[5]

In Hungary, the last two decades of the nineteenth century were years of a deceptive calm and an appearance of permanence. Szekfü's childhood and youth in the security of his family in a sleepy, provincial town sheltered him from an awareness of the contradictions within Hungarian society. The effects of a developing industrialization and the attendant social, and economic changes already visible in the capital were unknown to the students of the Catholic Gymnasium of Székesfehérvár. Truth and morality were uncomplicated, absolute concepts; Christian love for one's fellow men, faith in God and country, and work to the utmost of one's ability were values handed down to the young Szekfü by his family, his Church and the traditions of Székesfehérvár.

A childhood and youth in such an environment was likely to encourage a strong attachment to tradition and an interest in history. It was also natural that the historical point of view of a young man of Szekfü's background rested on a pro-Western and pro-Habsburg premise, but nevertheless it was based on Magyar traditions. Gyula Szekfü's upbringing, education and social position, his religious belief and respect for authority pointed to a vested interest in the old order and an orientation toward Vienna and the West.

After completing secondary school in his home town, Szekfü enrolled at the University of Budapest studying history and philology under the eminent German-trained historian Henrik Marczali. He received his doctorate in 1904, writing a dissertation on the sixteenth century historian István Szamosközy, who was Prince Bocskay's official historian in Transylvania.[6]

For nearly twenty years after receiving his degree, Szekfű worked as an archivist in Budapest and in Vienna. Very little is known about his years at the National Archives in Budapest; he worked there in quiet anonymity. In 1912, he moved to the Haus- Hof- und Staatsarchiv, finding his work and his life in Vienna stimulating and satisfying. There were several eminent Hungarian scholars working in the Staatsarchiv who were often joined by visiting Hungarian historians doing research on documents pertaining to Hungary.[7] Szekfű and his friends were dedicated scholars living in an intellectual and geographical milieu where they were in touch with the new currents of thought and became acquainted with the new methods of scholarship of Western historians. They had a certain disdain for the historians back home, for the "patriarchal" organization of the Hungarian Academy of Sciences and the backward state of Hungarian historical scholarship.[8]

The writing career of Gyula Szekfű can be divided into three distinct periods, each closely related to the historical and political realities of the time in which he had written. The first period included his writings until the end of World War One and the dissolution of the Austro-Hungarian Monarchy. During this time Szekfű was wholeheartedly a

Dualist, pro-Habsburg, pro-German but nevertheless patriotic Magyar, who, in an earlier age, would have been a Labanc.[9] The most important works of his Dualist period coincided with his career as an archivist in Vienna; they were reflections of his political and philosophical convictions and the historical-political reality of Hungary within the Dual Monarchy. "Szekfü became a historian in Vienna, in the shadow of St. Stephen's Cathedral," and this fact strongly influenced his view of life and history.[10]

During the years Szekfü worked as an archivist, he wrote a number of books on Hungarian history. Serviensek és Famíliárisok was published in 1909, a slim volume that became an important addition to the social history of the Middle Ages, in which he illuminated the little known existence of a social group between the nobles and the jobbágy (serf).[11] There followed a volume of the Hungarian correspondence of the Pashas of Buda during the Turkish occupation, which he edited with his fellow archivists Sándor Takács and Ferenc Eckhardt.[12] These books established Szekfü's reputation among historians but did not attain wide readership for the subjects were not of interest to the general public even in such a history-conscious country as Hungary.

Between 1913 and 1917, Szekfü published two books which constituted important landmarks in Hungarian historiography and in the development of Szekfü's career. In 1913, the controversial study of the Transylvanian Prince, Ferenc

Rákóczi II, A Száműzött Rákóczi (The Exiled Rákóczi), created
a furor in Hungarian public opinion and a trauma of possibly
permanent significance on its author. Three years later,
during World War One, Szekfű wrote a brief, comprehensive
history of Hungary for a German audience. Der Staat Ungarn
defined Szekfű's view of Hungarian history as he saw it
during his Dualist period. Because this book provides an
excellent starting point for the examination of Szekfű's
Dualist views and, at the same time, provides a historical
context for A Száműzött Rákóczi, it is necessary to disregard
the chronological order of publication and turn our attention
first to Szekfű's war-time book, Der Staat Ungarn: Eine
Geschichtsstudie.

"Politische Bücherei," a new venture of the German
publishing company which brought out Der Staat Ungarn, was
established to publish books of history and politics. It
attempted to fill the gap in the political education of the
German people who were "completely uninformed concerning the
nature of international political relationships."[13] Szekfű's
book was among the first of its publications; its purpose
was to provide a book about Hungarian history answering a
need to educate the German people about their ally during
World War One.

Der Staat Ungarn attempted to present a "biography"
of the Hungarian state. Szekfű intended to treat the history
of Hungary as an organic process, emphasizing those factors

which influenced its political and cultural development.[14] In the preface of the German edition Szekfű claimed that he had two fundamental positions: First, that the Hungarian state from its inception to his own day was the "product of a _single_ nation, the _Magyar_ nation," and, second, that the Hungarian state at the time of St. Stephen entered into the "Christian-German cultural community" and throughout the centuries it maintained a close political and cultural contact with the German states.[15] The book was, according to the author, modeled on Friedrich Meinecke's _Weltbürgertum und Nationalstaat_, which appeared ten years previously.[16]

The following are the salient points of Szekfű's views of the development of the Hungarian state from the time of the arrival of the Magyars to the Danube valley to the end of the eighteenth century.[17]

The most important factor in the early history of the Hungarian state was the manifestation of a political ability. Unlike the previous nomadic conquerors of the Danube-Tisza region, the Hungarians showed a realistic political sense when they decided to settle in what was previously the Roman Province of Pannonia in the Transdanubian region. This was the first of many events which brought Hungary to Western influences. As a former outpost of the Roman Empire and the more recent rule of Charlemagne, the Transdanubian region still possessed the traditions and influences of a culture which made a more stable basis for the establishment of a new state. The Moravian Slav population of the area was already Christian, a settled agricultural folk who, according to Szekfü, had no political talent. They enriched the Hungarian language with a vocabulary pertaining to the tilling of the soil and the Christian religion, and, in due time, the hard-working, steady Slav ethnic group assimilated into the Magyar culture, contributing a valuable element to the new ethnic mixture. But they themselves were incapable of forming and maintaining an independent state. Szekfü thought that the history of the Middle Ages showed that "in certain eras there were certain nationalities who possessed the power to establish and administer a state. The roots of this power . . . reach into the moral realm."[18] Szekfü referred to this talent as "political will." "In the Danubian basin, only the Magyars possessed political will."[19] The view of the innate ability of the Magyars to form a state while the other nationalities of Hungary were politically undeveloped was not original with Szekfü. It was often cited as a justification to deny political rights to non-Magyars in the nineteenth century.[20]

The nomadic federation of tribes was transformed into a medieval state by the descendants of Árpád without the help of any outside forces, a fact of decisive importance for the future development of the Hungarian state. Géza, the head of the Hungarian Confederacy from 972 to 997, reestablished authority by force over the chiefs who favored the Byzantine form of

Christianity or relapsed to Paganism. He led the people to the Western Christian community in order to prevent their reversion to the nomadic state. But it was St. Stephen (997-1038) who concluded the transformation of the Magyar people and state into the medieval Christian kingdom on a Roman-German model.[21]

Szekfü considered one of the gravest shortcomings of nineteenth century "romantico-liberal" historiography its total lack of appreciation of the overwhelming significance and greatness of St. Stephen. The historians of the nineteenth century depicted the founder of the Hungarian state and Hungarian Christianity as a colorless, shadowy figure, not the giant of Hungarian history, the source of all subsequent development of the nation.[22] Szekfü intended to correct this view and devoted a large portion of the book to St. Stephen and the early Middle Ages.

St. Stephen resolved the conflict between the pagan, conservative East and Western civilization by defeating the tribal chiefs. For the survival of the Magyar nation depended on its becoming a Christian state and being associated with the West. Stephen himself converted to the new faith as an adult, yet he became a convinced and devout Christian, determined to keep his nation on the Christian path. Because he whole-heartedly accepted the "Christian-German view of life," he chose the Carolingian Monarchy as a model for his state. He did not become a vassal of the Holy Roman

Emperor; he took the Carolingian precept: "all power comes from God," and turned to the Pope for his crown as a representative of an independent Christian nation.[23]

Szekfű emphasized that St. Stephen chose to use the German feudal institutions in his administration, rather than the Slav models that were closer at hand. He eliminated the tradition of tribal landholdings and instituted private ownership. New, large landholdings were awarded to his Magyar supporters, to German knights and ecclesiastic organizations. The old military organization, in which all soldiers were of equal rights, was abolished and each landholder or senior was responsible for keeping soldiers who were subordinate to him. In turn, the seniors owed their allegiance to the king. Thus, the concept of nomad freedom gave way to the German principle of hierarchical allegiance, and a free nomadic people was transformed into loyal subjects of the king.[24]

In the interest of the survival of the Hungarian state Stephen did not hesitate to suppress any opposition against the new way of life. Revolts were put down and their leaders exiled or killed. "This was the first Hungarian tragedy, followed by a long series of similar tragedies. The cause of the conflict was always the same: to reconcile their Eastern origins with their Western mission."[25]

St. Stephen and his successors instituted the policy of bringing in German settlers, another of the many strands of beneficient relationship with the German people and the

German culture. The development of Hungarian cities were closely associated with the German settlers of the Middle Ages. The cities were the sources of money economy; they provided soldiers, taxes, tolls and dues. In turn, the domestic power and wealth which the German settlers helped to provide enabled the Hungarian kings to pursue an aggressive foreign policy.[26]

Szekfü implied that as long as Hungary's development closely paralleled that of the German lands Hungary prospered. A western type of feudalism never developed in Hungary, because St. Stephen created a strong centralized state. Nevertheless, as in Poland, a powerful nobility arose by the thirteenth century. To a limited extent, the social development of Hungary resembled those of the East European nations. For under weak kings the lords became so powerful that the kings had to get the aid of the lesser nobles (middle holders) in order to control them. This class later turned against the king and, in their successful demand of the "Golden Bull" in 1222, they attained equal power with the magnates, una edamque nobilitas and the right of jus resistendi.[27] After the extinction of the House of Árpád, the structure of the Hungarian society resembled more the Polish than the German development. The Hungarian feudal state was unmistakably the Eastern European type where the kings had to present an "inaugural diploma" which amounted to "capitulations" to the estates at their ascension to the throne.[28] In the case of foreign kings, this was a healthy development for the maintenance of Magyar administration, nevertheless, under weak rulers, the state became disorganized and chaotic. However, unlike the Polish nobility which "lacked the capacity for self-discipline," the Magyar nobles, even in possession of <u>jus</u> <u>resistendi</u>, considered their king the natural leader of the country. For the nomadic horseback riding Magyar people had been transformed, once and for all, into a <u>kaisertreu</u> nation by its first king, St. Stephen.[29]

The most important reason for the consistent loyalty of the powerful nobles to the crowned king was the legal concept of the Holy Crown. In feudal Hungary, the term "the body of the Holy Crown" (<u>totum</u> <u>corpus</u> <u>sacrae</u> <u>coronae</u>) came into usage, meaning not only the geographic extent of the state, but also the political factors that made up the state; first and foremost the king and the estates. The body of the Holy Crown included Croatia, Slavonia and Dalmatia as well as the area girded by the Carpathian mountains. The concept of the Crown meant the indivisibility of the Hungarian state, according to Istvan Verböczi's <u>Tripartitum</u>.[30] The power of the state resided with the political nation (the nobility) and the nation offered the Holy Crown to the king as a symbol of legality. The rights of the king resided with the Crown. The Crown symbolized the total power and content of the Hungarian state, given by the nation (estates) and worn (exercized) by the king. Thus, election of the king and loyalty to the king united into a harmonious whole.[31]

According to Szekfü, it was in the fifteenth century that "Hungary's fate and Hungary's mission" became apparent: the country had to become the bulwark of Western Christendom; it had to defend the West against the onslaught of the Turkish armies. The Turks were a different kind of enemy from the previous Eastern invaders threatening the West. They were not a loose federation of nomadic peoples, such as the Magyars themselves were before Géza and Stephen, but a powerful military monarchy with a superior organization centrally controlled, who fought in the name of God's command. In contrast, power in Hungary was divided between the King and the Estates who were slow to respond to the quick and powerful attacks of the enemy. Nor was there any outside help. The age of the Crusades were over and the popes did not succeed in uniting the Christian countries against the Turks. In time, Hungary was crushed under the heavy burden of the task.[32]

The rule of Matthias Corvinus (1458-1490), a strong king able to control the estates, was notable of much conflict with the German Emperor even though the purpose of both rulers was the same: to create a powerful Central-European Christian block in order to defeat the Turks. Both of these Rennaissance rulers, Maximillian I and Matthias, wanted the leadership to themselves. Matthias did not achieve his purpose but prevented the Habsburg ruler from taking control of Hungary and Bohemia. Nevertheless, Matthias' rule was a high-point in Hungary's political achievement in the Middle Ages; he was a ruler of strength who held the interest of the country more important than the interest of the narrow class of nobles. Upon his death, his opponents, the powerful lords were quick to select the Czech Vladislaus Jagiello (1490-1516) to the throne of Hungary, for he was a man they could control. The ensuing lack of strong central administration, a selfish disinterest in the country's welfare on the part of the once more powerful estates and personal and political factionalism between feudal lords led to a bloody peasant revolution, political chaos and disintegration "rivaling the saddest chapters in Polish history."[33] Under these circumstances the country could not resist the new Turkish onslaught in 1526 and suffered total defeat at Mohács. Szekfü consistently implied that disaster came when, in some ways, Hungary's history was connected with, or paralleled, that of the Slav East, while the country prospered whenever it was associated with the German West.

Of all the historical events of Hungary, one of the most significant was the effect of 150 years of Turkish occupation. As a result of the battles, thriving Magyar communities had been totally destroyed, entire regions depopulated and occupied by people of other nationalities. The old Magyar population, living in the Southern provinces since the tenth century, perished or fled and their places were taken by "Serbian guerillas who came, together with their families, along with the Turks and made their living out of robbing and looting."[34] In time, the previously Magyar areas of the Bácska and the Bánát became populated by Serbs and Romanians. In other Turkish occupied areas, while the landowners perished or fled, the peasants remained and survived. After the initial hardship of military action, under the Turkish system of occupation, there was little contact between the conquerors and the conquered: the peasants were relatively free. The new landowner was a military man who lived in a castle and seldom ventured into the Village. As long as the peasants paid their taxes, did the <u>robot</u> and other services, they could live in accordance with their own national and religious convictions. The larger towns in the area between the Danube and the Tisza were directly under imperial control; they grew and flourished under the Turks and retained their Magyar character. These were not the German-founded trading centers; they were large peasant communities, originating as market towns. The survival of the Magyar nation was due primarily to "the dogged, steady energy of the Magyar peasant, who . . . in the absence of the nobles, maintained the national character of his native land, for he was attached to the soil, spiritually conservative and physically tireless . . ."[35]

Of the two Christian-controlled areas, Transylvania remained nominally independent under the rule of a national prince, elected by the House of Representatives subject to the approval of the Sultan. This new state was far ahead of its time in religious toleration and national cooperation. The administration of the state was based on the so-called "Union of the Three Nations," meaning the Magyars, Székelys and Saxons, all of which sent representatives to the National Diet. The Saxons and Székelys were townspeople or free peasants; the Magyars constituted the nobility. Together they maintained their privileges against the prince, controlled his election and voted the taxes and military requirements. Religious conflicts were solved by the official recognition of four religions: Catholic, Lutheran, Calvinist and Unitarian.[36]

Szekfü strongly emphasized the Magyar character of Transylvania. Because of traditions and the strong personalities of most of the reigning princes, Magyar central administrative power remained strong in spite of the privileges of the "three nations" and "four religions." Thus, Transylvanian politics remained Hungarian.

> Transylvania remained essentially an independent state and it succeeded in preserving intact the heritage of the Árpád House, the continuity of the Magyar nation and the Magyar state until the time came for the liberation from Turkish suzerainty of the rest of Hungary; after that there ceased to be a historical reason for an independent Transylvania.[37]

Meanwhile the non-occupied part of Western Hungary became part of the Habsburg Kingdom. The Hungarian estates elected Ferdinand after Mohács in the hope of German help against the Turks. But the <u>Mitteleuropa</u> of the sixteenth and seventeenth centuries was helpless and ineffective in its defense against the Eastern invaders. The Habsburg capital was away from Hungary, and the absence of the wearer of the Holy Crown created new circumstances. The estates became more influential; power struggles between the estates and the king, national nobility and foreign ruler brought about constitutional conflicts. Hungary was a small weak sister in the union of Austria and Hungary. Power, therefore, gradually shifted to the king and his centralized administration.[38] However, the Magyars continued to exercize considerable power through the counties. The role of the Magyar nobility in the counties of Habsburg Hungary was as significant as that of the Magyar peasants under Turkish occupation: they maintained the Magyar character of the local administration with considerable autonomy.[39]

In the seventeenth century, religious conflicts were added to the national struggle. Large areas of Northern Hungary and the cities between the Danube and the Tisza became Lutheran or Calvinist and resisted the counter-reformationary efforts emanating from Vienna. Protestant Transylvania could not successfully challenge Habsburg Hungary for the Magyar Crown not only because it was under

Turkish suzerainty, but also because the majority of Western Hungarians remained Catholic and loyal to the Habsburgs. Yet Transylvania had been able to prevent a national disaster comparable to what the Czechs suffered at the Battle of the White Mountain.[40]

Nevertheless, a deep religious and political gulf developed between the Catholic, pro-Habsburg West and the Protestant, proudly Magyar, anti-Habsburg East. This gulf "tore the spiritual life of the nation asunder," laying the basis for the Kuruc-Labanc conflicts.[41] The Kuruc east of the River Tisza wanted an independent Hungarian state, while the Labanc of Western Hungary were content to live under Austrian rule as long as the Habsburg Emperor was also the rightful Hungarian King. Pro-Western Hungarians wanted national self-determination also, but they wanted it with the agreement and the approval of the King and the government of Vienna, and not by the use of their right of jus resistendi. Ridiculed and hated by the Protestant East, they were looked upon with suspicion by Austrians as well. "Rejected by both sides, they were the real 'great-Magyars' (nagymagyarok) for they strove to achieve a united Hungarian nation under their lawful king."[42]

The liberation of Hungary from the Turks coincided with the development of absolutism. Szekfü emphasized the importance of the fact that the new system was imposed upon Hungary by a foreign ruler. Leopold I (1640-1705) had little interest in Hungary; he ruled from Vienna and concerned himself with German and Italian politics. A strong Magyar king such as Matthias could have broken the power of the estates. Hungarian social and political development then would have paralleled that of the French or the Prussians. Under the Habsburg rule, absolutist ideas remained foreign and resulted in a protracted struggle between the Austrian king and the Magyar estates. It was a nationalistic struggle and it disrupted that German-Magyar harmony which Szekfü considered the prerequistie for Hungarian progress.[43] When the united energies of <u>Mitteleuropa</u> regained Hungary from the Turks, the absolutists of Austria and Germany exploited the situation by forcible Germanization and by the colonization of depopulated areas by non-Magyars. The German speaking Swabians and the Slovak peasants did not hinder the Hungarian national development; it was the Serbian migrants whose political separatism was based on a difference in religion and culture, who posed a serious obstruction to Hungarian development and boded ill for the future. Especially significant was the military role assumed by the Serbs. Henceforth, the defence of Hungary's southern border was in foreign hands.[44]

The purpose of the Germanizing and centralizing policy within Hungary was the strengthening of the Habsburg Monarchy. However, the policy backfired. Instead of creating a powerful unified state, it led the discontented Magyar segments into the arms of the French. The French were only too happy to exploit this discontent at the expense of their arch enemy, especially since the Turks were now too weak to pose a threat to the Habsburgs.[45] The efforts at Germanizing created a hatred of Germans among the Magyars. This German hatred was not seen by Szekfű as a dislike of one ethnic group against another, but a political defense against Vienna's absolutist, Germanizing policy.[46]

The ensuing Kuruc-Labanc struggle drained the energies of the nation. French perfidy prevented the success of the Rákóczi rebellion (1703-1711) just as the Turkish alliance failed to ensure the success of the revolt of Imre Thököly (1678-1682) a generation earlier.[47] It became evident that national progress could not be achieved by depending on foreign help, for the raison d'être of the state was based exclusively on the union of the nation and its king, the essence of the concept of the Holy Crown.[48] Under these circumstances compromise was the only way out. With the Peace of Szatmár in 1711 (characteristically signed by a Magyar on each side), Hungary returned to the Western cultural community, reconstruction of the country and reconciliation within the opposing Hungarian factions could begin. Hungary's leaders had to realize that their nation was an integral part of the German middle-powers and that they could do nothing to change it.

> Henceforth, Hungary's greatest statesmen were burdened with a double task: on the one hand to retain intact the nation's independence, on the other,

to reconcile the interest of the national independence with the realistic consequences of being part of the German-Austrian-Habsburg power bloc.[49]

The single most important development of the Hungarian state in the eighteenth century was the unilateral Hungarian action concerning the Pragmatic Sanction of 1713. The Emperor Charles VI (in Hungary Charles III, 1711-1740) promulgated this law, enabling the female line of the Habsburgs to become heir to the throne. The 1722-1723 National Diet of Hungary accepted the Pragmatic Sanction and, at the same time, proclaimed a "personal union" of Hungary and the Hereditary Provinces under the Habsburg King.[50] This "personal union" did not appear in the Austrian version of the law, but it became codified in the law books of Hungary, forming a legal basis for further constitutional developments.

According to Szekfü, the significance of the Hungarian version of the Pragmatic Sanction is two-fold. First, the new law codifed the *de facto* situation in Hungary since 1526, and, second, it proved the political sense and the political maturity of the nation. The first act of the unified, liberated Hungarian state aided the stability of the Monarchy and attested to the Hungarian intention to belong to the culture of the German middle-powers.[51]

At all times, Szekfü viewed as the greatest of virtues the achievement of a compromise; the highest form of statesmanship was to maintain the Hungarian constitution while being part of the Austrian Monarchy. To Szekfü, the greatest Magyars were not the men whose intransigence left no alternative but revolt and exile but those who remained and undertook the difficult work of the "double task:" to retain domestic independence while being part of the world of German politics and German culture. The Compromise of 1867 brought about what Szekfü viewed as the ideal political solution for Hungary. That the creation of the Austro-Hungarian Monarchy and the unification of Germany came about almost simultaneously was a proof of their historical community of fate, according to Szekfü. Freed from past conflicts, the historical and national powers of three independent states making up Mitteleuropa stood on the threshhold of further development.[52]

It is not quite clear what Szekfü meant by the Christian-German community of nations. His emphasis on the identification of the Hungarian state with the Magyar nation within the Christian German cultural community corresponded to the de facto situation of Hungary within the Austro-Hungarian Monarchy. Szekfü spent his life during a period of diplomatic cooperation between Germany and the Dual Monarchy; he approved of the Monarchy's foreign policy, and, no doubt, expected the cooperation between the two governments to continue. Nor was it unrealistic for him to expect that German cultural influences on educated Hungarians would continue to be exerted. Whether Szekfü, in 1916, envisioned any future economic and political arrangements with Germany is not known. However, it is noteworthy that <u>Der Staat Ungarn</u> was written for a German audience a year after the publication of <u>Mitteleuropa</u>, by Friedrich Naumann. There is at least a possibility that this was not a coincidence; the purpose of the publication of Szekfü's book might have been to inform the German people about a country whose future was thought to be closely associated with the German Empire. There is, however, no evidence to prove this.

None of Szekfü's critics pointed up the similarities and possible connection between the "Christian-German community of nations" and Naumann's <u>Mitteleuropa</u>. Yet a case can be made for the existence of such a connection, at least in an indirect form. Beginning with his student days, and especially during his ten-year residence in Vienna, German historians exercised the most important intellectual influences over Szekfü, the books of Friedrich Meinecke first and foremost among them. Szekfü repeatedly referred to Meinecke's scholarship and ideas with approval and modeled <u>Der Staat Ungarn</u> on Meinecke's <u>Weltbürgertum und Nationalstaat</u>. According to a recent monograph on Meinecke, Friedrich Naumann's ideas were instrumental in the development of Meinecke's views and continued to exert an influence on him until the end of the First World War.[53] Meinecke was a connecting link between the ideas of Naumann and Szekfü.

<u>Der Staat Ungarn</u> revealed that the concept of <u>Mitteleuropa</u>—or Christian-German community of nations—was not the

only similarity of ideas between Naumann and Meinecke on the one hand and Szekfű on the other. In Szekfű's view, the primacy of foreign policy over domestic arrangements was the cornerstone of the policy of the Magyar state from its inception, just as it appeared in German historiography from Ranke to Meinecke. Szekfű portrayed the original Magyar tribes as noble savages who were transformed by their saintly king into law-abiding, God-fearing Christian subjects following their ruler in their acceptance of the "Christian-German view of life." Thus, the internal arrangements of the state were secondary to the relationship of Hungary with her neighbors. This Christian-German view of life demanded a great deal of the Magyars. It necessitated the "reconciliation of their Eastern origin with their Western mission."

Szekfű returned to Hungary's mission in this and other books usually in connection with the defense of Western Christianity against Eastern invaders: in the thirteenth century against the Mongols and in the fifteenth and sixteenth against the Ottoman Turks. The question arises: what was the mission of the freshly Christianized Magyar state of the eleventh century which necessitated the "first of many subsequent tragedies," the killing and maiming of those leaders who refused to abandon their old traditions? The answer can be deduced from Szekfű's introduction to the Hungarian edition of this book.

Explaining that he followed Meinecke's terminology in connection with the development of the nation-state,

Szekfü used the term national autonomy by using the word önrendelkezés, the Magyar equivalent of self-determination instead of autonómia. "Self-determination of nations," of course, was a much-discussed term during the First World War and Szekfü wanted to make it clear that he did not have in mind Woodrow Wilson's concept applied to the non-Magyar nationalities within Hungary. He use it--as Meinecke did ten years previously--not as a right but as an ability to determine its own destiny, to form a sovereign state without any outside help.⁵³ To Szekfü national self-determination was not a right of a people but the might of a state. Beginning with the eleventh century, as the only people in the Danubian basin "possessing political will," the mission of the Magyars was to maintain the state, to rule over the politically undeveloped non-Magyar nationalities of the Lands of St. Stephen and to bring them also into the framework of the Christian-German cultural community.

The "Christian-German cultural community," the Dual Monarchy and the Lands of the Holy Crown of St. Stephen were all casualties of the First World War. Written in 1916, Der Staat Ungarn contained no indication that its author was aware of the imminence of their collapse.

FOOTNOTES

¹Erik Molnár, ed., Magyarország Története (The History of Hungary). Budapest: Gondolat Könyvkiadó, 1964, I, 45.

²Magyarország Vereckétől Napjainkig: Történelme, Földje, Népe, Élete, Gazdasága, Irodalma, Művészete (Hungary from Verecke to our own days: Its History, Geography, Demography, Life, Economy, Literature, Art). Budapest: Franklin Társulat, no date, III, 248.

³While most of Transdanubia remained under Habsburg rule during the sixteenth and seventeenth centuries, Székesfehérvár was within the area right of the Danube which fell to the Turks. Much of the city was destroyed in 1543. The Basilica and the Royal Palace were blown up by the retreating Turks in 1603, when the Imperial Army temporarily reoccupied the city. Ibid., III, 248-249.

⁴Ibid., III, 251.

⁵There are no biographies written as yet about Gyula Szekfű, and the few critical evaluations of his works contain very little information on Szekfű, the man. The meager biographical data of this study is based on Magyar Irodalmi Lexicon (Hungarian Literary Lexicon). Budapest: Akadémiai Kiadó, 1965, III, 179-181, and on conversations with Gyula Bisztray, a former professor of literature at the University of Budapest and a friend of Szekfű.

⁶Gyula Szekfű, Adatok Szamosközy István Történeti Munkájának Kritikájához, (Factors About the Evaluation of István Szamosközy's Historical Works). Budapest, 1904. For the abridged version, see "Szamosközy Műve az 1594 Év Eseményeiről," (Szamosközy's Work about the Events of the Year 1594), Századok, XLII (1908), 217-244.

⁷Dávid Angyal, Emlékezések (Recollections). London: Szepsi Csombor Kör, 1971, p. 132.

⁸Ágnes Várkonyi, Thaly Kálmán és Történetirása (Kálmán Thaly and his history writing). Budapest: Akadémiai Kiadó, 1961, p. 412.

[9] The Labanc were seventeenth and early eighteen century Hungarian supporters of the Habsburg kings, content to live under Austrian rule; they were usually Catholic and living in the Western half of Hungary, often in conflict with the anti-Austrian usually Protestant Kuruc who wanted an independent Hungary.

[10] Várkonyi, Thaly, p. 311.

[11] A reviewer called it one of the most significant new historical works. "The author is one of the best of our young historical scholars." László Erdélyi, "Szekfű Gyula: Serviensek és Familiárisok." Történeti Szemle, II (1913), 282.

[12] Domokos Kosáry, "A Történetiró," (The Historian), Magyar Szemle, XLIV (1943), 233.

[13] Gyula Szekfű, Der Staat Ungarn: Eine Geschichtsstudie. Stuttgart-Berlin: Deutsche Verlag Anstalt, 1917. Published in Hungary as A Magyar Állam Életrajza (The Biography of the Hungarian State). Budapest: Dick Manó Könyvkereskedése, 1918, p. 3. This and subsequent footnotes refer to the Hungarian edition.

[14] Ibid.

[15] Ibid., p. 17. Emphasis is Szekfű's.

[16] Ibid., p. 21.

[17] Szekfű's views about Hungarian history in the nineteenth and the twentieth century will be discussed in connection with his subsequent works.

[18] Ibid., p. 30.

[19] Ibid., p. 31. The similarity between Szekfű's view and Erich Marcks' idea that "the essence of the state is the will to power" shows the extent of the influence of German historians on Szekfű. G. M. Stewart, "Erich Marcks," Essays in Modern European Historiography, ed. by S. William Halperin. Chicago: The University of Chicago Press, 1970, p. 221. Erich Marcks was one of the editors of the "Politische Bücherei" series which brought out Der Staat Ungarn. Szekfű, A Magyar Állam, p. 3.

[20] For the Magyar claim of superior political ability see Ernő Baloghy, A Magyar Kultura és a Nemzetiségek (The Magyar Culture and the Nationalities). Budapest: Deutsch Zsigmond és Társa, 1908.

[21] Szekfü, A Magyar Állam, pp. 31-32.

[22] Ibid., pp. 13-14. Szekfü admitted that his view of St. Stephen was strongly influenced by his religious upbringing.

[23] Ibid., p. 35.

[24] Ibid., pp. 37-38.

[25] Ibid., p. 41.

[26] Ibid., p. 50.

[27] Ibid., p. 65.

[28] Ibid., p. 70.

[29] Ibid., p. 75.

[30] István Verböczi codified the Hungarian laws in the "Triple Book" (Hármaskönyv) in 1513. This book served as an authoritative source for Hungarian constitutional law until 1848. For the laws of Hungary in the Middle Ages, see László Erdélyi, Magyarország Törvényei Szent Istvántól Mohácsig (The Laws of Hungary from St. Stephen until Mohács). Budapest: Eggenberger Féle Könyvkereskedés, 1942.

[31] Szekfü, A Magyar Állam, pp. 76-77. For the concept of the Holy Crown, see Gyula Szekfü, "A Szentkorona Eszme" (The Concept of the Holy Crown), Állam és Nemzet (State and Nation). Budapest: A Magyar Szemle Társaság, 1942.

[32] Szekfü, A Magyar Állam, pp. 80-81.

[33] Ibid., p. 85.

[34] Ibid., p. 90.

[35] Ibid., p. 93.

[36] Ibid., p. 95.

[37] Ibid., p. 100.

[38] Ibid., pp. 100-108.

[39] Ibid., p. 111.

[40] Ibid., p. 114.

[41] Ibid., p. 116.

[42] Ibid. The compound word "nagymagyar" here has a double meaning. It means both a great Hungarian as a personal quality and a believer of the "great-Hungarian" concept, the Hungarian equivalent of Grossdeutsch.

[43] Ibid., p. 129. Hungarian historians up to the end of World War Two, whether their sympathies lay with Kuruc or Labanc, agreed that the Hungarian struggle against the Austrians or Turks was based on nationalism and patriotism. In the case of the Turks and other Eastern invaders there was the added burden of defending Christendom from the barbarians. The truth may be much more complicated. Peter F. Sugar wrote:

> Did Nicholas Zrinyi (also known as Zrinski) defend the Castle of Szigetvár in 1566 as a Hungarian (or Croatian) patriot, a Christian, a soldier obeying his king's orders, or simply as a great lord defending his domains? Did Francis Rákóczi II fight the Habsburgs from 1703 to 1711 as a Hungarian patriot . . . as a Transylvanian particularist, as a lord powerful enough to dream a little kingdom of his own . . . or simply as a mercenary in the pay of Louis XIV? The Hungarian answer to these and other questions is always the same: the great leaders of the nobility were patriots. Yet this unanimity proves very little, because it is based on very carefully selected documentation.

Peter F. Sugar, "The Nature of the Non-Germanic Societies under Habsburg Rule," Slavic Review, XXII (1963), 6.

⁴⁴Szekfü, A Magyar Állam, pp. 134-136.

⁴⁵The French were definitely not included when Szekfü talked about the desirability of association with the West. Because of the alliance of France with the Turks in the sixteenth century, with Polish and Hungarian revolutionaries in the seventeenth and eighteenth centuries and as a source of dangerous ideas harmful to Hungarian political developments, the French were portrayed as historical trouble-makers obstructing the peaceful development of Hungary within the Christian-German community of nations. By West Szekfü meant exclusively the German lands.

⁴⁶Szekfü, A Magyar Állam, p. 137.

⁴⁷Imre Thököly, a seventeenth century Kuruc leader and ruler of Transylvania, also died in Turkish exile, like his stepson Ferenc Rákóczi.

⁴⁸Szekfü, A Magyar Állam, p. 147.

⁴⁹Ibid., p. 149.

⁵⁰Ibid., p. 150.

⁵¹Ibid., pp. 150-151.

⁵²Ibid., p. 216.

⁵³Robert A. Pois, Friedrich Meinecke and German Politics in the Twentieth Century. Berkeley: University of California Press, 1972, p. 4.

⁵⁴Szekfü, A Magyar Állam, p. 6. There is an interesting parallel between Meinecke's and Szekfü's view of national self-determination as a capability to be independent and the psychoanalytical concept of autonomy as man's inner ability to govern himself. Just as there are similarities between the discredited Geistesgeschichte and the psychohistorical studies which are becoming fashionable.

CHAPTER II
A <u>LABANC</u> VIEW OF RÁKÓCZI

With the exception of Count István Széchenyi, no historical figure has received as much attention by Hungarian historians as Ferenc Rákóczi II(1676-1735). In nineteenth century Hungarian historiography, the leader of the Rákóczi Rebellion (1703-1711) became an idealized hero, fighting for independence against the absolute, oppressive and Germanizing rule of the Habsburgs. Much of the admiration was well deserved. Although a mediocre military leader, Rákóczi was a compassionate man and his devotion to Hungarian independence was genuine. A descendant of Transylvanian princes, Rákóczi had a genuine concern for the simple peasants as well as his fellow nobles and he possessed a tolerance toward creeds differing from his own Catholicism, a trait uncommon at the turn of the eighteenth century. But during the Dualist period he was celebrated less for his personal qualities than as a symbol of the Hungarian struggle for independence from Austria. Along with Lajos Kossuth, Rákóczi was the patron saint of the Party of Independence.[1]

In 1912, as an archivist in the <u>Haus- Hof- und Staatsarchiv</u> in Vienna, Gyula Szekfü was arranging source material pertaining to the Turkish occupation in Hungary.

Among the newly acquired sources were documents pertaining to Rákóczi's years in Turkish exile.[2] These documents were first discovered by Kálmán Thaly, the well-known historian and politician, but illness prevented Thaly from using them and adding yet another book to his voluminous output on the Age of Rákóczi. After Thaly's death the Hungarian Academy of Sciences called upon Gyula Szekfű to write a book about Rákóczi's exile on the basis of these documents. The Academy planned the book as a memorial to Kálmán Thaly, a founding member of the Hungarian Historical Society and long time editor of its journal, Századok (Centuries).[3]

At first, Szekfű was not enthusiastic about the assignment to write the history of Rákóczi's exile based upon the Vigoroux documents and the papers of the French ambassador to Constantinople. He thought that writing a book on Rákóczi dedicated to the memory of Thaly might be interpreted as an endorsement of Thaly the historian. The truth was that Szekfű had little respect for Thaly's historical scholarship and he considered the Hungarian Historical Society backward, patriarchal and weighted down with an "archaic spirit."[4] He undertook the job finally, because he realized that the publication of a book on Rákóczi would be a significant literary event; it would interest the general public as well as the professional historian. Furthermore, Szekfű thought that it might help him get the professorship which was becoming vacant at the University of Budapest.[5]

After putting down the condition that if he felt necessary he could disagree with Thaly's view of Rákóczi, he embarked on the job and completed it in five months of intense work during the summer and fall of 1913. The book appeared under the title of <u>A</u> <u>Száműzött</u> <u>Rákóczi</u> (The Exiled Rákóczi), and caused an instant sensation. Not only did Szekfű differ with previous concepts of Rákóczi's historical significance, but he also challenged the school of historical writing dominated by Kálmán Thaly.

<u>A</u> <u>Száműzött</u> <u>Rákóczi</u> was something new in Hungarian historiography: an extremely readable and fascinating book. There was no unanimity among historians and critics concerning the merits of Szekfű's interpretation of the role of Rákóczi, but they all agreed on two things: that the work was based on meticulous scholarship and that Szekfű's ability as a writer took no back seat to his scholarship.[6] The fact that the book differed from the usual dull, pedantic writing to which Hungarian historians were accustomed might have contributed to the mistrust and lack of acceptance of Szekfű's interpretation.[7]

One consistent feature of Szekfű's historical writing had been the discussion of a problem as part of a larger phenomenon which could be understood only by the presentation of the background, the roots of the problem and the factors that caused or influenced the events. Attempting to show the complexity of his character and motivations, Szekfű was far ahead of his time in examining Rákóczi's early life and experiences and depicting the larger world around him--both Hungarian and European--in order to put his actions in the proper context and provide an insight into his behavior. A Száműzött Rákóczi was a forerunner of a psycho-historical study.

In the process of examining Rákóczi's early life, Szekfű showed a side of Rákóczi unfamiliar to the Hungarian reading public and inconsistent with the reverence accorded to him by Hungarian politicians. In particular, there were two things wrong with Szekfű's Rákóczi. One was that the tragic hero of Hungarian history was shown to be, in his youth and middle age, rather too fond of the opposite sex and, the other, that in his Turkish exile, Rákóczi lacked the wisdom to judge his and Hungary's situation realistically. The first offended the Victorian sensibilities of the public and the second was acceptable neither to the politicians nor to the average patriotic citizen.

Rákóczi, like his contemporaries of equal rank, enjoyed a gay social life. He married early, but it was a marriage of convenience; he preferred the company of other women to that of his wife. Indeed, when his wife gave birth to his first child, Rákóczi took daily rides to see his mistress of the moment. He carried on a love affair for years with the wife of a Polish prince. The charge that more than once, in grave and important moments, he foresook Hungary for pleasure seeking in Poland was not without basis, according to Szekfű. When the revolution was over, Kuruc soldiers and Magyar peasants alike suffered untold hardships, while Rákóczi and his entourage made their carefree way through the Polish countryside in sleighs with gaily jingling bells.[8]

Szekfű did not fail to explain that only the nineteenth century sentimental-romantic sensibility would consider gaiety in time of adversity unsuitable behavior. Much that Hungarian public opinion found objectionable in the beginning of the twentieth century was commonplace behavior among European aristocrats two centuries previously. Thus, Rákóczi's marital infidelity, gambling and pleasure seeking was actually minimized by the description of life in the court of Louis XIV. Nevertheless, the card playing, womanizing courtier that emerged in Szekfű's book was far from the figure of reverence Hungarians were accustomed to encounter when reading about the former Kuruc leader.

Szekfű implied that toward the end, the Kuruc revolt was not so much a fight for Transylvanian independence but for Rákóczi's own position as a sovereign ruler. The plans and activities during the years of exile manifested not a thirst for power on Rákóczi's part, but rather they were motivated by vanity, for the title of Prince of Transylvania was more important to Rákóczi than the actual power. The "inner satisfaction" that this title, devoid of any content gave him was behind the futile and pathetic efforts to regain it.[9]

In the long years of exile, first in France, later in Turkey, Rákóczi was shown to have lost touch with Hungarian reality. Loneliness, lack of intellectual stimulation, unwillingness to discuss the problems of Transylvania with anyone, made him less and less aware of the real situation within Hungary. In reality, while Rákóczi idly made his plans to regain his power, the estates who elected him made their peace with Vienna; they would have been unpleasantly surprised, had Rákóczi been able to return.[10] Over the years, he became further and further removed from his country physically, intellectually and spiritually. The one-time Kuruc leader who had a deep psychological bond to the Magyar soil and its people became nothing but a pretender to the throne of a country whose inhabitants were no longer interested in his fate. At the same time, the achievement of sovereignty of Transylvania became no longer a means to achieve Hungarian freedom, it became an end in itself.[11] The interest of Hungary took second place to his own interest as a pretender.

In the postscript, summing up his interpretation of Rákóczi's exile, Szekfű made a statement which, looking back on his oeuvre, turned out to be a central thesis of his long and prolific career:

> The life of every exile is futile, useless for the interest of his country, for the reason he is exiled is precisely because the new order of his country cannot utilize adherents of the previous regime, and eases the situation by obliging them to leave.[12]

The new development of the Hungarian nation had no use for Transylvanian separatism. The age that gave rise to men like the Bethlens and the Rákóczis was concluded.[13] The age of the <u>Kuruc-Labanc</u> conflict gave way to the age of unity, the healing of the century-old wounds, the restoration of peace. Rákóczi's futile efforts to revive the old order had become anachronistic, his role insignificant. The need for reconciliation and adjustment to the new circumstances seemed to be Szekfű's early message.

The publication of <u>A Száműzött Rákóczi</u> caused a political and literary uproar that made the name of the young historian famous throughout the country. He became the subject of journalistic polemics, angry speeches in the Parliament and a major political issue between the Dualist Party and the Party of Independence. The charges against Szekfű ranged from being wrong in his interpretation to deliberately blackening the name of a revered Magyar hero, and even to being bribed by the Austrian government to write an anti-Hungarian book.[14] Many Hungarians, some historians among them, considered the writing of this book an act of treason. For the book differed radically from the historical writing of the previous generation of historians and the issue was not only the iconoclastic view of the historical significance of Rákóczi, but also the role of the historian and the removal of historical scholarship from the arena of politics. Szekfű challenged the entire school of history writing so long dominated by Thaly in a book that was to serve as a memorial to the late historian. In a lengthly footnote, Szekfü criticized Thaly's scholarship, historical method, accuracy and even his professional ethics, charging him with stopping valid criticism and preventing the healthy development of Hungarian historical scholarship.[15]

Hungarian historical writing of the nineteenth century expressed fierce nationalism and often served political purposes. In an editorial in <u>Századok</u> in 1884, answering a critic who stated that Hungarian historiography was backward and isolated from the new ideas of the West, Kálmán Thaly expressed a point of view, shared by many Hungarian historians at the end of the nineteenth century. He said that new ideas and trends such as positivism, democracy and socialism did not apply to Hungarian history.

> We do not concern ourselves with the history of the world, but that of our own dear country, and we follow the aristocratic point of view . . . we do not concern outselves with democracy . . . that is we do not glorify Dózsa and the burning, looting mob, instead we extoll the Hunyadis, the Zápolyas . . . Rákóczis and other proud oligarchs--without them the Hungarian nation would not even exist! . . . Without these men our small race would be absorbed before long by alien people.[16]

This had to be prevented by all means, even if Hungarian historiography was considered shortsighted, backward and aristocratic. Hungarian historians were proud to express nationalism, and their aim was to guide and train the youth of the nation to approach the aristocratic heroes "with reverence."[17] Those historians who adhered to this view found Szekfü's new book totally unacceptable. And Hungarian public opinion, unaccustomed to a realistic appraisal of historical personages, was similarly affronted.

The first scholarly reviews of <u>A Száműzött Rákóczi</u>, while stating disagreement with the interpretation of Rákóczi's historical significance, agreed with Szekfü on his evaluation of Thaly's historical scholarship. In fact, most of the initial reviews concentrated on the history writing of Thaly and his followers who succeeded in creating a Rákóczi-cult because it flattered the national vanity.[18] A healthy scholarly controversy might have ensued resulting in the reevaluation and revision of the <u>Kuruc-Labanc</u> struggle in Hungarian historiography and a beneficial, healthy movement toward more objectivity and less patriotic fervor in historical scholarship. However, this was not to be, for Hungarian historical writing has been intimately connected with Hungarian politics from the beginning to this day. In 1913, the figure of Rákóczi was a national demi-God whose description in human terms was more than a <u>lèse majesté</u>; it was heresy. Even his prophet, Kálmán Thaly, proved to be unassailable in the political climate of the times.

Kálmán Thaly was a member of the Party of Independence since 1874. He once stated that the object of his political program could be summarized in one word, one name: Rákóczi.

"My historical scholarship indicates my political credo."[19] That is to say, the Party of Independence had the same goals as that of the Kuruc movement: they opposed the Dualist Liberal Party and wanted complete independence from Austria. Their hero was Lajos Kossuth and their ideal was 1848 and the War of Independence. Rákóczi and the Kuruc wars were looked upon as an earlier manifestation of the same goals pursued by the Party of Independence in Dualist Hungary. To those who supported the Independence Party, the figure of Rákóczi and Kossuth were beyond criticism.

Kálmán Thaly the historian, who described himself as "Rákóczi's court-scribe" devoted his entire scholarly output to the Kuruc era. At the same time, he was the vice-president and most vocal parliamentary spokesman of the Independence Party at the turn of the century. A less than adulatory view of Rákóczi and an attack on Thaly was viewed by a great many Hungarians as a Dualist political attack in scholarly disguise.

Accordingly, the scholarly reviews were followed by shrill newspaper articles and noisy parliamentary debates attacking Szekfű for reviling Rákóczi in order to cast aspersions on the political opposition of the government. The articles were followed by meetings in provincial political clubs protesting against the book. Cultural and political organizations, high school and university students sent telegrams to the Hungarian Academy of Sciences asking them to withdraw the book from circulation. The Academy hastened to disassociate itself from Szekfű's interpretation professing no political bias. The pro-government newspapers restricted their comment to stating neutrality and innocence of government responsibility for Szekfű's point of view. Századok, the journal of the Hungarian Historical Society, was silent and the few historians and scholars who supported Szekfű on the basis of "sound historical scholarship," also hastened to declare their disagreement with Szekfű's interpretation. Besides, their quiet, civilized voices were submerged by the tumultous, shrill attacks of the more vocal political proponents of Thaly's Rákóczi. To them, Szekfű was a traitor to the national spirit.[20] Since books on Hungarian history were widely read by the general public and they were reviewed by the daily press as well as in literary and professional journals, attacks on A Száműzött Rákóczi and its author became a public scandal in the chauvinistic press. As a pro-Habsburg Catholic living in Vienna and working in the Haus-Hof- und Staatsarchiv, Szekfű was particularly vulnerable to the charge of being a traitor.

In the summer of 1914, Count Gyula Andrássy (1860-1929) came to Szekfű's defense. What he said was not very different from previous statements of historians: he did not agree with Szekfű's interpretation, but the book was based on sound scholarship. He added some words of admiration for Kálmán Thaly, although he "did not consider him an ideal historian."[21] Coming from an Andrássy, the statement helped put an end to Szekfű's status as whipping boy, but only the outbreak of World War One brought complete relief from harrassment to the unfortunate young historian.

Needless to say the publication of this book did not help to attain the university professorship for Gyula Szekfű. Nor was he selected as corresponding member of the National Academy of Sciences at the spring meeting of 1914, as he had hoped. But these were only temporary setbacks in his long career. More important, and probably lasting, was the psychological effect of being in the eye of a public storm, being called a traitor and finding himself a subject of what amounted to political persecution.[22]

The uproar over A Száműzött Rákóczi was overshadowed by historical events and soon forgotten. It had a significant impact at the time of its publication, but it was not the most influential or the best known of Szekfű's works. The book on Rákóczi was followed by four decades of fruitful historical scholarship and journalistic writing. Nevertheless, the book written in 1913, dealing with the narrow topic of the political and psychological development of an exiled prince in his declining years, is a key to the understanding of Szekfű's life-work. First, because the theme of this book, the need to adjust to new political circumstances rather than cling to old principles, was one that was central to Szekfű's historical writing during his entire writing career. And, second, because the reception of this book resulted in a trauma which affected his subsequent historical scholarship. There are historians who claim that the Rákóczi controversy had left a permanent mark on Szekfű's personality and on all his subsequent works.[23]

FOOTNOTES

[1] For the relationship between politics and historiography in Dualist Hungary see Ágnes R. Várkonyi, Thaly Kálmán és Történetirása (Kálmán Thaly and his historical writing). Budapest: Akadémiai Kiadó, 1961, pp. 193-336.

[2] Manuscripts of Jean Vigoroux, a French diplomat of Rodosto, Turkey, in the property of the Lastic Vigoroux family of Naxos. Ibid., p. 310.

[3] Ibid.

[4] Ibid., p. 312.

[5] Ibid., p. 310.

[6] Aladár Schöpflin, a critic and literary historian said that Szekfű had a fine, analytical mind, splendid writing ability, psychological insight and a strong sense of realism. "I read it straight through as if it were a novel." Aladár Schöpflin, Thaly Kálmán Reviziója," Nyugat, VII (1914), 184. "Szekfű is the most complex creative intellect in our literature today." Antal Szerb, A Magyar Irodalom Története (The History of Hungarian Literature). Kolozsvár: Erdélyi Szépmives Céh, 1937, II, 509.

[7] Ágnes Várkonyi, A Pozitivista Történetszemlélet a Magyar Történetirásban (The Positivist View of History in Hungarian Historiography). Budapest: Akadémiai Kiadó, 1973, I, 252.

[8] Gyula Szekfű, A Száműzött Rákóczi (The Exiled Rákóczi). Budapest: A Magyar Tudományos Akadémia Kiadása, 1913, p. 25.

[9] Ibid., pp. 52-55.

[10] Ibid., p. 59.

[11] Ibid., p. 303.

[12] Ibid., p. 336.

[13] Gábor Bethlen, Prince of Transylvania (1613-1629) ruled over Transylvania at the height of its independent development; György Rákóczi I (1630-1648) and his son György Rákóczi II (1648-1660) were two other princes associated with the "golden age of Transylvania." Ferenc Rákóczi II was the grandson of the latter.

[14] Dávid Angyal, Emlékezések, (Recollections). London: Szepsi Csombor Kőr, 1971, p. 128.

[15] Szekfű, Rákóczi, pp. 370-475.

[16] Kálmán Thaly, Századok, VIII (1874), 295-297. Thaly himself, like the majority of Magyar historians in the nineteenth century, was a lesser noble.

[17] Ibid., p. 297.

[18] Várkonyi, Thaly, pp. 315, 317.

[19] Ibid., p. 196.

[20] For the bibliography of the Szekfű debate see Árpád Hellebrandt, "A Magyar Történeti Irodalom," Századok, XLVII (1914), 17.

[21] Count Gyula Andrássy, parliamentary leader and last foreign minister of the Austro-Hungarian Monarchy was the son and namesake of the first prime-minister of Dualist Hungary and later foreign minister of the Monarchy. For Andrássy's defense of Szekfű, see "Szekfű és Andrássy Gyula gróf," Huszadik Század, 1914, pp. 686-687.

[22] In letters to his friends, Szekfű revealed his fear of being looked upon forever as a traitor. "The 70,000 readers of the Pesti Hirlap will be convinced to the end that I wrote the book on the order of the Kamarilla or that of István Tisza." Letter to Sándor Takács, August 7, 1914. "I wouldn't be surprised if even twenty or thirty years from now I would come across the ghost of the charge of treachery." Letter to Arthur Odeschalchi, September 3, 1917. Cited in Várkonyi, Thaly, p. 414.

[23] Ibid., p. 324; László Németh, Gyula Szekfű, Budapest: Bólyai Akadémia, 1940, p. 5.

CHAPTER III

GEISTESGESCHICHTE, SZEKFŰ AND
HUNGARIAN HISTORIOGRAPHY

The dissolution of the Austro-Hungarian Monarchy did not bring any immediate change in the life of Gyula Szekfű. He remained in Vienna until 1922 and continued to work at the Haus- Hof- und Staatsarchiv. Nevertheless, the Dualist phase of his history writing ended with A Magyar Állam Életrajza in 1917. His next book, Három Nemzedék (Three Generations) appeared in 1920 and signified a clear break with his previous works. Három Nemzedék is considered to be the first book in Hungarian historiography written in accordance with the concepts of Szellemtörténet, the Hungarian equivalent of the German Geistesgeschichte. Since Szellemtörténet was the standard theory and method of Hungarian historiography in the interwar period and Szekfű was considered its chief practitioner, it is necessary to examine the school of historical writing known by the German term Geistesgeschichte, evaluate the German intellectual influences on Szekfű's historical scholarship and the significance of the adoption of a new theory in the intellectual history of Hungary.

Living in Vienna in the years before the war, Szekfű was aware of the new ideas of historical scholarship emerging

in the wake of the critical reexamination of the theory of
history. His perfect knowledge of German, fluent French and
adequate English enabled him to read the new historical works
of the West; he was familiar with the intellectual currents
of the times. With the exception of a few of his colleagues,
he had nothing but contempt for his contemporaries among
Hungarian historians. For models and inspiration he looked
to Germany: Leopold Ranke (1795-1886) and Wilhelm Dilthey
(1833-1911) in the past, Friedrich Meinecke (1962-1954),
Erich Marcks (1861-1938) and Karl Lamprecht (1856-1915) in
the present. These men were writing "universal history,"
they turned against the excessive specialization, scientism
and positivism of their predecessors.[1] The new trend of
materialism did not interest a man of Szekfü's tradition and
world view. He was attracted to the German theory that emphasized a psychological insight into the culture and the
relationship between the cultural and the political in the
history of nations. He thought that the writing of a historian rested on the twin pillars of politics and psychology.[2]

    The term <u>Geistesgeschichte</u> was originated by the nineteenth century German philosopher Wilhelm Dilthey who thought
that history, along with law, economics, literary criticism
and sociology belonged to a group of studies he called the
sciences of the mind (<u>Geisteswissenschaften</u>). The difference
between the sciences of the mind and the natural sciences was
that the former, aside from studying the facts--the outward

manifestations of the events--could also be "lived through" or experienced from within. For history dealt with the thoughts, feelings, sensations and experiences of men. These mental experiences had external manifestations (e.g. thoughts were expressed by writing or speaking); interpreting the external expressions of internal experiences was the proper task of the historian. In the view of Dilthey, a psychological in-involvement of the historian was necessary in understanding the past because history was lacking in objective reality. Lacking the laws of natural science, history was no more than the sum total of individual and unique truths. The task of historians was to discern and recreate these historical truths. Each age had its own spirit of the times which manifested itself in every facet of human endeavor be it political, economic or cultural. One way to examine the spirit of the age was through the examination of intellectual currents and the ideas of the leading statesmen and thinkers.[4]

The German historian Friedrich Meinecke, Szekfü's contemporary, followed the tradition of Ranke, which he sought to combine and enlarge by the theories of Dilthey.[5] His book, Weltbürgertum und Nationalstaat, served as an acknowledged model for Szekfü for A Magyar Állam Életrajza. Like Ranke and Meinecke, Szekfü emphasized the primacy of external factors: the deciding influence of foreign policy, and the overriding interest of the state within the domestic realm. According to a recent interpretation, Staatsnotwendigkeit was the touchstone of Meinecke's political thinking up to the end of the First World War.[6] Szekfű retained this belief throughout his life and agreed with Meinecke also on the spiritual and moral quality of the state.[7] Like Ranke, Meinecke believed that "the individual in history--whether this be a person, institution or a state--justified itself through its immediate and concrete relationship to general historical forces and trends."[8] Szekfű, too, adhered to the "Rankean solution" to the relationship of the individual to the general, and attempted to write just that kind of history in depicting Rákóczi in the larger context of Hungarian and European history. The Rankean "universal history" was the model for the five-volume history of Hungary co-authored by Szekfű in the late 1920's.

In Hungary, the description of this new theory and method of historical writing was not attempted until 1932, more than a decade after its almost exclusive use in Hungarian historical scholarship.[9] A Magyar Történetirás Új Útjai (New Paths in Hungarian Historiography) contained a collection of essays by leading Hungarian scholars explaining the use of Szellemtörténet in social and economic history, church history, legal and constitutional history, art history, history of literature, archaeology and philology. All these disciplines were to be utilized in the writing of "universal history." The last chapter of the book on "Political History," was contributed by Gyula Szekfű. The introductory essay, written by Bálint Hóman (1885-1953), the editor of the book, provided a general discussion of Szellemtörténet. Since Hóman collaborated with Szekfü on the multi-volume history of Hungary about the same time the book on historiography was in preparation, it is not unreasonable to assume that Szekfü shared Hóman's view on this "new path in history writing."

According to Hóman, Szellemtörténet was a concept in historical method; it did not change the aim or the content of a historical work. It attempted an intensive examination of cultural factors: the effects of the religious, philosophical and social ideas on individual acts and mass movements, as well as the political, economic and more easily observable materialistic manifestations of history. Szellemtörténet brought together all factors: material and ideological, cultural, economic, political and social, singular and typical, individual and collective into a synthesis of the whole.[10] The aim in Szellemtörténet was to examine the manifestations of the human soul. The historical method of Szellemtörténet required subjective intuition as well as the objective inductive method, for historical interpretation was possible only through beleélés and átérzés.[11] These two Hungarian words literally mean to "live into" and to "feel through;" the two terms together can be roughly translated as to know from within, to have an insight. This insight together with the knowledge of the facts enabled the historian to arrive at a synthesis concerning any historical problem. By examining the manifestations of the human soul, the historian "relived" the past events and this <u>quasi</u> experiencing of the past enabled him to look at the historical period in the spirit of the past age. Still Hóman acknowledged that while complete objectivity was the ideal, most historians could not entirely divorce themselves from the ideas and values of their own age. Because of this subjective element in the works of historians and the hypothetical value in historical truth, periodic reevaluation of historical events were necessary which could also incorporate any available new material.[12]

In the chapter on the writing of political history, Gyula Szekfű emphasized the importance of putting events in a proper historical context: providing a thorough background, showing the roots of events, giving the political and intellectual influences coming from abroad and relating the external influences to internal events in historical writing. Accordingly, before discussing Hungarian historiography, he reviewed some aspects of French and German historical scholarship and their influence on the Hungarian historians of the nineteenth century.

Szekfű thought that nineteenth century French liberal history lacked objectivity and did not progress much beyond the political historical writing of an earlier age. He saw a primitive, clannish view in the belief that France was the only "Kultur-nation," which had a mission to spread the great human ideas of freedom and culture to other European states "to rescue them from the medieval darkness." French historians expected the other nations' enthusiastic acceptance of French ideas and felt justified to spread them by force if necessary.[13] "The mantle of humanism given to them by the Enlightenment did not camouflage the original clannish political interests which it tried to cover up."[14]

The most important and, to Szekfü, the most unfortunate aspect of French historical writing was its glorification of the idea of liberty. The French Revolution was the raison d'être of the state, the central focus of the French view of history. It was beyond any criticism. Szekfü considered Jules Michelet (1798-1874) a highly cultured, noble-spirited man, but "the blind enthusiasm with which he found humanistic value even in the lowliest participants of the Revolution" was beyond understanding and detracted from his scholarship. In idealizing and glorifying the revolution on which nineteenth century France was founded, Michelet and his fellow French historians were motivated by the same political self-interest as the court historians of the Middle Ages.[15]

Szekfü turned to nineteenth century German historiography for contrast and credited Leopold von Ranke with "the highest achievement in political history writing." Ranke was the first "universal spirit:" his interest transcended his native land and searched not only for causality, but also for the leading ideas of an age. These ideas manifested themselves in identifiable forms and trends of a period. The recognition and selective use of the leading ideas, often beyond rational explanation, were more important than the mere recital of political events. Freed from the overwhelming flood of facts about petty and work-a-day political events, the historian could be far more objective.[16]

Szekfü claimed that Ranke's achievement in the writing of political history was the result of his religious belief. He attributed to divine providence the leading ideas of the age and the chain of political events in which they were manifested. Szekfü thought that the reason that his students, such as Heinrich von Sybell and Heinrich von Treitschke, did not retain Ranke's objectivity was that they lacked Ranke's relationship between beliefs and achievement. The second generation of historians following Ranke, Friedrich Meinecke and Erich Marcks, were more objective, but Szekfü lamented the fact that they left political history to others while they devoted their works to the history of political ideas such as nationalism, cosmopolitanism and raison d'état. These were only aspects of political history; the synthesis which characterized Ranke's achievement was lacking.[17]

Unfortunately--in Szekfü's view--the nineteenth century Hungarian historians chose the French, rather than the German model of history writing. Mihály Horváth (1809-1878) --whom Szekfü considered the best among them--made the ideas of liberty and revolution the yardstick by which to measure the significance of historical events. To him and his fellows, the maintenance of national, political and religious freedom was the historic purpose of the Magyars. They simplified Hungarian history to the history of freedom.

Szekfü thought it absurd to take an idea which originated in the eighteenth century and make it valid for preceding periods. It would be ahistorical to examine the centuries of feudalism, religous-patriarchal royal power, later absolutist rule and the Baroque Age and evaluate them in accordance whether or not they would reveal evidence of a search for liberty, at a time when the idea of national liberty had not yet existed. The result of such examination was a false view of history. Hungarian historiography and Hungarian political theory depicted national life as a conflict between good and evil, liberty and oppression and liberty became a political dogma of the opposition to the Dualist government.[18] This Kuruc view of history, because it was so convinced of its righteousness, considered any defeat or even opposition as a treachery or betrayal. The worst offenses of this liberal historiography were perpetrated by those historians who were also active in the Independence Party.[19]

Szekfü also showed the inconsistency of liberalism when it aligned itself with nationalism. Nationalistic liberals collided head-on with the idea of freedom of other nations. Liberalism lost its universal character; in pre-war

Hungary it became so interrelated with nationalism that criticizing liberalism became an unpatriotic act. Magyar liberal historians, writing about previous centuries, were not interested in the oppression of the jobbágy (serfs); individual and class freedom were disregarded in favor of constitutional liberties.[20]

The most favored topics of liberal historians consisted of uprisings and wars of independence as well as legal and constitutional questions. As a result, emphasis was put on Transylvania which was elevated to a symbol of liberty. Freedom of religion, as in Transylvania, became the ideal. This idealization of Transylvanian independence and the Kuruc movement by the liberal historians was considered by Szekfü the kismagyar view of history. The kismagyar, or small-Hungarian, view of history contrasted with the nagymagyar or great-Hungarian view. These concepts paralleled the Kleindeutsch and Grossdeutsch ideas of nineteenth century German historians. Szekfü thought that the analogy was apt because of the similarities in the development between Transylvania and Prussia:

> The existence and position of power of [Prussia and Transylvania] was the result of the dissolution of the Holy Roman Empire and that of Hungary; both defended its freedom against the remaining parts of the country in their efforts in reunification; . . . both were Protestants states opposing the Catholic Habsburgs. There is a similar analogy between the two historical points of view. The Kleindeutsch view was not interested in the manifestations of national

power beyond the greatness of Prussia, just as the
<u>kismagyar</u> concept overestimated the role of Tran-
sylvania and paid too little attention to the
achievements of the Western, anti-Transylvanian
Magyars; their quiet, uninterrupted efforts, their
self-sacrificing endurance between the Germans and
the Turks, their cautious political wisdom which always guarded them against extremism, these cannot
be included in a historical point of view extolling
ideas of liberty . . . . The <u>kismagyar</u> view of
history, because of its emphasis on national liberty, was closely associated with the tenets of the
Independence Party, and the latter saw in this historical view its own principles read into the past
. . . . This <u>kismagyar</u> point of view became exclusive both in historical scholarship and in public
opinion . . .[21]

The <u>kismagyar</u>, Protestant, Transylvanian nationalist expressed only one form of the Magyar spirit; without the other,
the West-Hungarian, pro-Habsburg, Catholic, the picture was
incomplete. A truly national point of view had to strive for
a synthesis of the two.[22]

There was another tradition in Hungarian history and
Hungarian nationalism, that of the statesmen István Széchenyi
(1791-1860) and Ferenc Deák (1803-1876) and the poets Ferenc
Kölcsey (1790-1838) and Mihály Vörösmarty (1800-1855). The
ideas of these great men should be the models for twentieth-
century historians, in Szekfü's view. When they looked at
Hungarian history they were not searching for ideas of liberty but for reflections of morality and culture in the past
of the nation. Historians who would learn nationalism from
them would obtain objectivity; from the heights of their
humanism they could look at history <u>sine ire et studio</u>.[23]

Finally, Szekfü considered political history alone insufficient. He thought that political and constitutional events were mere appendages to social, economic and cultural conditions. Without writing about the roots of the events and their material and spiritual manifestations, political history would be faulty and inadequate.

> Political history writing is the more likely to achieve its purpose the less it is political, the more it includes all aspects of national life, utilizing the newest methods of research and the point of view of Szellemtörténet--only then will it deserve to be called a truly national history.[24]

Although there was some skepticism about the validity of Geistesgeschichte among a few Hungarian scholars, it remained the most widely accepted theory of history until 1945.[25]

Hungarian historians today have some harsh things to say about Szellemtörténet. They point out that the use of this method had political aims and justify the view that the adoption of Szellemtörténet served the purpose of combating socialism by quoting Hóman:

> The path, direction and rhythm of historical developments are decided by the spiritual makeup and education of the people and their leaders. This recognition led to the adoption of the method of Szellemtörténet which is opposed to historical materialism on principle.[26]

According to the Marxist philosopher of history, József Szigeti (b. 1921) Szellemtörténet was the counterrevolutionary revision of Hungarian history. It came into use as a reaction to the Communist Revolution of 1919 and remained the most important method of historical writing throughout the Horthy era. <u>Szellemtörténet</u> filled the ideological need of the ruling class against the proletarian revolutionary movement and Marxist ideology. At the same time, it served as a proponent of nationalism and idealism, opposing historical materialism and Marxist internationalism.[27]

Claiming that history was nothing but the history of the human soul, Hungarian history became--naturally--the history of the Hungarian soul; concepts such as the "eternal Hungarian spirit" began to appear in the historical works of the interwar period. The denial of the existence of class conflict and the belief in the primacy of foreign policy over internal politics contributed to the nationalistic attitude of this school of thought. Conflicts among nations became emphasized as a motivating force in history. In the view of Marxist historians this emphasis on the spiritual and on the primacy of foreign policy served as a handy ideology to justify the brutal political repressions in the name of national interest or foreign danger. Similarly, the purpose of invoking irredentism was to distract the masses of people from the grave social and economic problems within the country.[28]

Marxist historians saw the interpretation of the entire Hungarian history as a defense of the West against the barbaric East as anti-Soviet views applied to the past. Interwar historians implied that just as the Habsburgs and the

German states provided Hungary with military assistance against the Turks in the past, Christian Europe should aid Horthy-Hungary in its fight against the Soviet Union or in its struggle against the socialist forces within Hungary. As part of the "Christian-German cultural community," Hungary showed her dependence on German imperialism, hoping that through this association her territorial claims will be attained.[29]

In spite of the faulty theories of <u>Szellemtörténet</u>, Marxist critics of Szekfü's interpretation of Hungarian history have words of praise for Szekfü as a teacher of the next generation of historians. A strict teacher but a kindly man, Szekfü demanded a great deal of work from his students and, interested in fledgling scholars, he was always willing to help them.

> He trained /his students/ to strict criticism of sources . . . never tired of repeating that the truth of the claims of a researcher is decided by facts and the quality of evidence he is providing for his interpretation, not by his official stature or his prestige in the scientific community. He was a strict judge of the works of his pupils, did not tolerate . . . unproved theses, superficial evidence or interpretation based on mere analogy. He taught them the theory and method of <u>Szellemtörténet</u>, but he expected their first attempts at historical research to be factual, to familiarize themselves with the sources, examine and evaluate them . . . . He taught them those same philological critical methods that he learned in the seminars of /Henrik/ Marczali.[30]

However "unhistorical" and "unscientific" the Marxist philosophy of history considers the method of <u>Szellemtörténet</u> and however Hungarian historians today disapprove and disagree with Szekfü's interpretation of Hungarian history, their criticism is always qualified by praise of Szekfü's ability as a writer and as a historian.

> Szekfü's synthesis was refreshing after the dry, boring, detailed narratives . . . . His extraordinary talent made him the master of historical synthesis. His comprehensive view which show the historical processes (though not always properly) in the complicated relationship of many interacting factors, colorful, masterly writing, . . . immense knowledge of the subject, the use of philological source criticism and the utilization of the results of the social sciences, in other words the complex methods of historical research and history writing: these were the factors that made Szekfü's work so satisfying for other historians and ordinary readers.[51]

The view of Marxist historians today that the need for an ideological underpinning of the reaction to socialism and revolution was the reason for Szekfü's adoption of the point of view of <u>Szellemtörténet</u> cannot be accepted. The interpretation of Hungarian history as a bulwark of Western Christendom defending Europe against the barbarian East originated in the Middle Ages. Hóman's statement that "<u>Szellemtörténet</u> . . . is opposed to historical materialism on principle" notwithstanding, there is no indication that in 1919, Szekfü consciously adopted a new historical method for political purposes. We have seen that he was influenced by German historians and German historical scholarship long before the Hungarian Revolutions of 1918-1919. The two major books of his Dualist period, A Száműzött Rákóczi and Der Staat Ungarn, are clear indication that Szellemtörténet in Hungary preceded the Horthy era.

What distinguished Szekfű's writing in the interwar period from that of the Dualist period was substance rather than method, especially in the books and articles which dealt with contemporary events rather than history. The method of his historical scholarship, his historical point of view and his emphasis on the primacy of foreign policy over domestic developments--these were surprisingly constant in Szekfű's scholarship in spite of his changing politics. Instead of a "counter-revolutionary revision of Hungarian history," Szellemtörténet was an anti-liberal revision, aimed against the nineteenth century liberal historians who "simplified Hungarian history to the history of freedom." It was a Labanc, nagymagyar revision of Hungarian history and it began with A Száműzött Rákóczi by Gyula Szekfű. Szekfű was attracted to the method of synthesis which allowed him to make "the past come alive." It enabled him to put Hungarian history into the context of European history. Finally, Szellemtörténet suited Szekfű because it was consistent with his devout Catholicism: he believed that Divine Will was manifested in the historical process.

Seemingly, a method of historical investigation which calls for intuition and subjective evaluation could not produce accurate and dependable scholarship. Yet experienced and highly respected historians, such as Benedetto Croce (1866-1952) in Italy, R. G. Collingwood (1889-1943) in England, Dilthey and Meinecke in Germany and Gyula Szekfű in Hungary used this method successfully. One hazard in achieving objectivity is that "one wishes to see the spiritual goals one feels to be one's own confirmed by revelations in the world."[32] But that is not peculiar to the method of Geistesgeschichte. Edward Hallett Carr suggested that when we take up a work of history our first concern should be with the historian.

> The facts are like fish swimming about in a vast . . . ocean; and what the historian catches will depend partly on chance but mainly on what part of the ocean he chooses to fish in, and what tackle he chooses to use; these two factors being determined by the kind of fish he wants to catch . . . . The historian will get the kind of facts he wants.[33]

Perhaps, then, Szellemtörténet was no more and no less reliable than any other theory and method of historical research.

FOOTNOTES

[1] Gyula Szekfű, A Magyar Állam Életrajza (The Biography of the Hungarian State). Budapest: Dick Manó Könyvkereskedése, 1918, pp. 7-9.

[2] Gyula Szekfű, "Az Osztrák Központi Kormányszervek Történetének Irodalma" (The Literature of the History of the Austrian Central Administrative Organization), Történeti Szemle, I (1912), p. 185.

[3] Several articles about Wilhelm Dilthey's theories appeared in Hungary in 1911 and 1912. The young philosopher György Lukács (1885-1971) dismissed Dilthey's views stating that the central idea was a "psychological concept . . . /which was/ confused and inadequate for the creation of a system of thought." Cited in Ágnes Várkonyi, A Pozitivista Történet-Szemlélet a Magyar Történetirásban (The Positivist View of History in Hungarian Historical Writing). Budapest: Akadémiai Kiadó, 1973, I, 227. The historian Gyula Korniss, on the other hand, hailed Dilthey's method as one which would serve as the answer to the problems of Hungarian historiography. Gyula Korniss, "Dilthey's Történetszemlélete" (Dilthey's View of History), Történeti Szemle, I (1912), 480-527.

[4] Summary of Dilthey's views based on Wilhelm Dilthey Gesammelte Schriften, vol. IV cited in Gyula Mérei, "Szekfű Gyula Történetszemléletének Birálatához" (About the evaluation of the Historical Views of Gyula Szekfű), Századok, XCIV (1960), 187. See also H. P. Rickman, ed., Pattern and Meaning in History; Wilhelm Dilthey: Thoughts on History and Society. New York: Harper and Brothers, 1961.

[5] Fritz Stern, The Varieties of History. Cleveland: The World Publishing Company, 1965, p. 267.

[6] Robert A. Pois, Friedrich Meinecke and German Politics of the Twentieth Century. Berkeley: The University of California Press, 1972, p. 13.

[7] Ibid., p. 50. cf. Szekfű, A Magyar Állam, p. 30.

[8] Pois, Meinecke, p. 52.

[9] Although the Hungarian version of Geistesgeschichte was the most widespread philosophical and methodological orientation of historical scholarship during the interwar period, there were others. The traditional Romantic school survived the First World War and the new Ethnohistory school also had its adherents. See Stephen Béla Vardy, Hungarian Historiography and the Geistesgeschichte School. Cleveland: An Árpád Academy Publication, 1974.

[10] Bálint Hóman, "A Történelem Útja" (The Path of History), A Magyar Történetirás Új Útjai (New Paths in Hungarian Historiography). Budapest: A Magyar Szemle Társaság, 1932, p. 43-44.

[11] Ibid., p. 27.

[12] Ibid., pp. 46-47.

[13] Gyula Szekfű, "A Politikai Történetirás" (The Writing of Political History) in Bálint Hóman, A Magyar Történetirás, p. 406.

[14] Ibid., p. 407.

[15] Ibid.

[16] Ibid., p. 410.

[17] Ibid., p. 411. By 1932, Meinecke changed many of his previous ideas about the power of the state while Szekfű retained his previous beliefs. This may account for the difference in Szekfű's view. Meinecke was no longer his model.

[18] Ibid., p. 429.

[19] Ibid., p. 432. Clearly, the reference was to Kálmán Thaly and Szekfű's own unhappy experience in connection with the publication of A Száműzött Rákóczi twenty years previously.

[20] Ibid., p. 438.

[21] Ibid., pp. 439-440.

[22] Ibid., p. 444.

[23] Ibid., p. 443.

[24] Ibid., p. 444.

[25] One critic said that a "subjective and unique" view of history was too close to "arbitrary." The historian who uses such a method "can be likened to a sailor who, instead of the stars, uses the clouds as a guide." Mihály Babits, "Szellemtörténet," Nyugat, XXIV (1931), 333.

[26] Bálint Hóman, Történettudomány és Politika (Historical scholarship and Politics), p. 15, cited in József Szigeti, A Magyar Szellemtörténet Bírálatához (About Evaluating Hungarian Geistesgeschichte), Kossuth Könyvkiadó, 1964, p. 87. This was written in 1943; by that time Hóman moved to the far right from his previously moderate political position, eventually becoming a Nazi collaborator, while Szekfű was active in an anti-German resistance movement. Both historians were far removed from the impartial apolitical scholarship they professed when they collaborated on Magyar Történet and A Magyar Történetirás Új Útjai.

[27] Szigeti, Szellemtörténet, p. 48.

[28] Erzsébet Andics, A Magyar Nacionalizmus Kialakulása és Története (The History and Development of Hungarian Nationalism). Budapest: Kossuth Kiadó, 1964, pp. 342-345.

[29] Ibid., pp. 346-348.

[30] Mérei, "Szekfű," p. 180.

[31] Ibid., p. 192.

[32] Friedrich Meinecke, Die Entstehung des Historismus, cited in Stern, The Varieties of History, p. 274.

[33] Edward Hallett Carr, What is History? New York: Random House, 1961, p. 26.

PART TWO

THE CONSERVATIVE NATIONALIST: 1919-1933

CHAPTER IV

AFTER THE CATASTROPHE: ASSIGNING THE BLAME

The historian brings to his history writing not only his own personality, his religious, social and political views, but the conditions of the society in which he lives and the historical events which affect the society and the historian. "The historian is part of history. The point in the procession at which he finds himself determines his angle of vision over the past."[1] Before we turn to Szekfű's most important and most influential work, Három Nemzedék (Three Generations), let us examine the factors that determined his angle of vision in 1919.

Between the publication of A Magyar Állam Életrajza (Der Staat Ungarn), in 1917, and that of Három Nemzedék (Three Generations) in 1920, radical changes had taken place in Europe. Outside of Russia, perhaps the most profoundly affected country in all Europe was Hungary.[2] At long last Hungary was completely independent but at a price of losing two-thirds of the territory that was considered the Lands of the Holy Crown of St. Stephen for nearly ten centuries. In addition, two revolutions, a democratic and a communist, followed by a counter-revolution and white terror, had taken place between the end of the war in 1918 and the appearance of Három Nemzedék in 1920. With the counter-revolution

Hungary moved to the far right in politics. The country remained a land of large holdings, little industrial development and a state bureaucracy which was enlarged manifold to give jobs to those Magyar petty-noble county and municipal officers who chose to go to Hungary from Slovakia, Transylvania and Croatia. Socially and economically, Hungary became the most backward country in Central-Eastern Europe.

The impact of Szekfü's new book can be explained only by the social, economic and cultural changes that took place in Hungary prior to World War One.[3] The essence of these changes was the decline of the class of lesser nobles who hitherto provided the intellectual and moral as well as the political and social leadership of the country. Toward the end of the nineteenth century, with the rise of capitalism, the emancipation of the Jews and the assimilation of the German and Jewish middle classes, the intellectual predominance of the lesser nobility began to disappear.

Hungarian literature of this period showed a marked change from that of the previous one: it reflected the social and economic changes that had taken place in Dualist Hungary. Until the last decade of the nineteenth century, with a few notable exceptions, Hungarian writers and poets were of noble origin. The rise of "bourgeois literature" in Hungary, as in other lands, coincided with the rise of capitalism. On the whole, it was written by urban people, the new middle class of non-Magyar--Jewish or German--descent. The literature of these urban intellectuals differed greatly from the traditionalists of lesser noble origin. The latter had looked backward for inspiration and found glory in the past; they were socially, politically and culturally conservative. The new writers considered themselves good Magyars, indeed, with their convert's zeal, many of them were nationalistic to the point of chauvinism, yet they did not dwell on the past. Not knowing anything but city life, they were inclined to live in the present, focusing on the current problems that attended the beginnings of industrialization, looking at these problems realistically and searching for answers. Realism and naturalism in Hungarian literature began with these authors.[4]

The quarter-century preceding the appearance of Három Nemzedék saw the birth of the Hungarian Social Democratic Party, the trade union movement, the growth of cities and the problems resulting from industrialization. There was an increasing skepticism and loss of faith in the traditional values; they were replaced by a naive optimism, a faith in science, in progress and in the perfectibility of man and society. A new literary magazine, Nyugat (West) was the forum of the urban modern literature and the mouthpiece of the new criticism. The journal, Huszadik Század (Twentieth Century), gave expression to the new science of sociology; it contained political, philosophical and sociological articles and expressed a democratic radicalism new to

Hungarian letters and Hungarian politics. The editors and many of the contributors of these journals were Jews, and the leadership of the Social Democratic Party and the political leaders representing the ideas of the new urban intelligentsia tended to be of Jewish origin. It is not surprising, then, that when the political and intellectual turmoil during World War I culminated in the two revolutions, the Jews were heavily represented among the revolutionaries.[5]

The white terror that followed the defeat of the Communist Revolution consisted of violent repression and open season on Socialists and Jews. The persecution of all the Jews was justified by the preponderance of Jews among the revolutionaries. The ensuing reaction was not just a political one; in the realm of literature, and all phases of culture, an attempt was made to set the clock back. The word Christian began to appear more and more frequently in political and literary slogans. It meant not only an attempt to restore the traditional values but, most of all, to regain intellectual leadership for the ethnically Magyar. For Hungarians blamed Jews and liberals for the political disasters of the country and historians and publicists as well as writers of fiction set out to prove that the Christian and Magyar ways were irreconcilable with the Western ideas carried and advocated by the Jews. Gyula Szekfű's <u>Három Nemzedék</u> reflected this view and the prestige of the historian conferred a mantle of respectability on popularly held opinions.

Három Nemzedék was the most influential book of the decade of the 1920's. According to George Barany, "the great emphasis on the anti-liberal, Christian-conservative and ethnically oriented elements in Hungarian nationalism which dominated Hungarian historical writing between the two world wars was largely attributable to the influence of Szekfű's Three Generations . . ."[6]

Szekfű's influence was not restricted to historiography. Három Nemzedék appeared at a crucial time and attained wide readership. Hungarian intellectuals were trying to find some explanation to fix the blame for the rapid and drastic changes. They were groping for a blueprint that would lead the way out of the confusion of the years since 1914; this volume provided the answers. It has been said that "Szekfű's Három Nemzedék created a path that led the intellectuals toward the political platform of Horthy."[7] The influence of this book was all the more serious and lasting because it was not the work of a demagogue but that of a scholar. A serious, yet highly readable, volume offering a new interpretation of the recent past, Három Nemzedék was, ostensibly, not written for any political gain but a result of a scholar's search for truth.

According to the preface, Három Nemzedék was meant to be the second volume of Der Staat Ungarn which was published in Germany in 1917, covering the history of Hungary to 1867. Szekfű stated that during the war, he declined

the German publishing company's request to write a history
of Hungary from 1867 to 1914 because his views had been "diametrically opposed to the contemporary liberal view of history." Szekfü saw the Dualist period as a half-century of
decadence, but felt that, by saying so, he would divide the
nation at a time when there was a strong need for unity.
After the Treaty of Trianon, the views of the Hungarian people
about the period preceding the war came to be much closer to
that of Szekfü's than three years previously and the publication of a new historical interpretation could no longer be
considered contrary to the national interest.[8] Some critics
of Szekfü implied that the real reason for the delay in publishing the book could be found in the psychological effect
of the reception of his book on Rákóczi. Henceforth, Szekfü's
work did not contain any unpopular interpretation.[9] Others
thought that, contrary to his statement that he postponed
publishing his long held views in the interest of unity in
war time, after the war, he adjusted his views to the new
realities. How else could one account for the fact that liberalism and the role of the Jews, the two main factors accounting for the decline during the Dualist period in Három Nemzedék,
were never even mentioned in A Magyar Állam Életrajza. "As
usual," wrote the populist writer, László Németh, "Szekfü
justified those in power."[10]

The years between 1920 and 1933 were Gyula Szekfü's
most productive period. He returned from Vienna in 1922, and

devoted the next two years exclusively to his writing. In the early 1920's his articles appeared in Napkelet (Sunrise) and Keresztény Politika (Christian Politics), and the names of these periodicals were indicative of their political and intellectual point of view. Napkelet (also a poetic word for east) was a conservative magazine, established to counteract the influence of Nyugat (West), the liberal literary journal. Both Napkelet and Keresztény Politika (carried literary and historical articles written for the educated public. Szekfü at this time wrote with the avowed intention of educating his readers. "The historian came to realize that his own discipline has a role and a responsibility in the development of national identity."[11]

In 1921, the Minerva Society was founded by scholars and writers, Szekfü among them, and in the following year, the periodical Minerva appeared. The Society's aim was to publish articles on the cultural history of Hungary and to further the trend of Szellemtörténet in historical scholarship and literary criticism.[12] Szekfü was a frequent contributor. Most of his articles written in the early 1920's were eventually published as a collection of essays under the title of Történetpolitikai Tanulmányok (Historical-Political Studies). The title came from Leopold Ranke's Historisch-Politische Zeitschrift, on which these articles were modeled, with the aim of educating people by putting a current problem in the context of history, or as Szekfü put it, "doing historical research on the issues of the day."[13]

In spite of the drastic intellectual changes, as the decade wore on, Hungary returned to a measure of normalcy. The outpouring of anti-liberal literature notwithstanding, some of the liberal accouterments of the state remained in post-war Hungary. After a period of terror following the defeat of the Communist Revolution, the new conservative power was consolidated and, under Count István Bethlen as prime minister, the parliamentary system was reestablished. This system was even more of a sham than the one before the war; franchise was limited, elections were open and corruption abounded. The Communist Party was outlawed, but, with some restrictions, the Social Democratic Party was allowed to function.[14] In addition to the government's Unity Party, and the opposition Smallholder's Party, the members of the House of Representatives included a few Bourgeois Democrats and Socialists. Trade Unions were also functioning. And in spite of all the "Christian National" agitation, industry and commerce, the professions, theatre and journalism continued to be dominated by Jews. The articles and speeches on the need to reduce Jewish influence and to create a Christian culture were ineffective; few Hungarians found the careers of storekeepers or engineers to be attractive. For no economic or social change had taken place in Hungary and, therefore, no change in the attitude of the people. The aristocrats were still immensely wealthy landowners, the gentry were still officials, and few of the peasants and laboring people had any chance to become educated and rise to the middle class. And when they did, they tended to study law and become officials because that had far more prestige than becoming a bank clerk or an entrepreneur.

Furthermore, in spite of the inflammatory rhetoric, there was a certain amount of cooperation between Jewish industrialists and the government. Friendships between Jewish and Christian writers were commonplace, "some of the best friends" of even the most anti-Semitic writers (including Szekfű) were Jews.[15] In the 1920's, after the initial terror had passed, the Magyars' bite was not as bad as their bark.

As everywhere in Europe, there was a certain amount of well-being in Hungary before 1929. The government was stable, agricultural products brought in a relatively good price and unemployment was limited. In spite of the dreary Christian-national moralizing, literature flourished, theatres were full and anti-Semitism was becoming less overt. It was a decade of fulfillment for Szekfű also. The historian received the long coveted university professorship in 1924. He continued to write "historical-political essays" but the bulk of his writing, from 1924 until the late 1930's, consisted of solid historical scholarship. His monographs dealt with Széchenyi, Gabriel Bethlen and the nationality problems of the nineteenth century. Between 1929 and 1933 he published the five-volume Magyar Történet (Hungarian History) in cooperation with Bálint Hóman (1885-1953), a medievalist who wrote the first two volumes, covering the period preceding 1458. The third edition of Három Nemzedék, containing a 150 page addition dealing with the decade of the 1920's, appeared in 1934.

In 1927, a new political journal, Magyar Szemle (Hungarian Review), was established and carried on its masthead a most prestigious name. The president of the editorial committee was the prime minister Count István Bethlen, who was instrumental in the founding of the journal and occasionally attended a planning session. The working editor was Gyula Szekfű. Although Magyar Szemle was a conservative journal with the views of the contributors coinciding with those of Bethlen and Szekfű, it was by no means an organ of the government. The stated aim of the journal was the education of the nation: the dissemination of Christian national principles. It contained articles on all aspects of the Hungarian society and on foreign affairs. Articles focusing on the nationality question of the past and on the problems of the Magyar minority in the succession states appeared frequently.[16]

Szekfű was an extremely consciencious editor. He gave attention to each issue from manuscript to final publication. He personally edited all articles and was interested in form and style as well as in content. He even inspected and approved advertisements. All this while he was professor of

modern Hungarian history at the University of Budapest and
engaged in research and writing of his books and articles.
He was aided by his puritanical life and working habits.
Szekfű was disciplined, punctual, adhered to a precise schedule
and worked systematically. He also had an ability to work and
concentrate in noisy, distracting environments. The research
for <u>Magyar</u> <u>Történet</u> was done in a busy room of the University
Library.[17] However, the influence Szekfű exerted with <u>Három</u>
<u>Nemzedék</u> on Hungarian intellectuals of the interwar period
was not equaled by any other of his subsequent publications
or activities.

<u>Három</u> <u>Nemzedék</u> was the examination of three generations
of politicians and statesmen who were responsible for the political and cultural developments in Hungary during the century
preceding 1914. The first of these generations was the contemporary of Count István Széchenyi (1791-1860), active in politics from about 1830 to 1849. The second generation, with two
illustrious survivors from the first, achieved the Compromise
of 1867, and provided the leadership of Hungary until the
last decade of the nineteenth century. The third generation
presided over the fate of Hungary during the illusory security and promise at the turn of the century and remained in
power until the last year of the First World War. The members
of all these generations called themselves, and were called
by Szekfű, liberal.

According to Wilhelm Dilthey's theory of <u>Geistes-</u>
<u>geschichte</u>, one way to examine the spirit of an age was through

the examination of the ideas of the leading statesmen and thinkers. Dilthey's theory, in a modified form, was carried out by Szekfű in <u>Három Nemzedék</u>. He began with a discussion of Széchenyi's character, ideas and achievements. Although only the first few chapters of the book deal directly with Széchenyi, in a very real sense this "greatest Hungarian" is the main character of the book. For Szekfű believed that the tragedy of Hungary was due to not living up to Széchenyi's political ideals and moral standards and not following his program of reform. In the rest of the book, Széchenyi served as a touchstone: to the extent that succeeding generations turned away from him, they caused the inevitable decline of the Magyar nation.

Szekfű's views on Széchenyi will be examined in detail later. Here it is necessary to mention only that the view that Széchenyi was a conservative rather than a liberal cannot be substantiated, and that the Magyar ruling classes of Dualist Hungary were liberal only in name. Szekfű considered one of the most fateful errors of doctrinaire liberalism to be the policy of allowing Jews of the other parts of the Monarchy to immigrate to Hungary, become assimilated and, eventually, dominant in commerce, industry, the professions and the arts. Szekfű made much of the destructive effect of the Independence Party's opposition to the Dualist government and disapproved of the policy of Magyarization as unwise and counterproductive.

Much of the criticism Szekfű heaped upon the Magyar leadership and the Jews was justified; the gentry was a declining class, liberalism, what there was of it, was responsible for the emancipation and immigration of the Jews who did play a dominant role in developing capitalism in Hungary. But the changes, dislocations, ills of society and that urban culture so abhorrent to Szekfű were no different in Hungary than in countries where industrialization was achieved by an ethnically indigenous segment of society. As a devoutly religious man whose sympathies were with the peasants and rural nobles, Szekfü viewed the new urban rationalist culture as alien to Magyar society.

The message of <u>Három Nemzedék</u> was clear: it was this newfangled foreign ideology of liberalism, leading inevitably to revolution, an alien urban culture, atheism and immorality, which had to be combatted by constant avowal of religion and nationalism. There were those, probably Szekfű among them, for whom these feelings were sincere. The majority of the people, however, mistook clericalism for Christian faith and chauvinism for true patriotic principles.

The Treaty of Trianon removed the nationalities and, with it, the nationality problems. Ironically, the Jews, who considered themselves Magyar and were so counted, thereby allowing the Magyars to claim a numerical majority in pre-war Hungary, were now almost the only aliens remaining. There was no attempt to rectify the economic and social ills of the country; no land reform such as had taken place in the succession states was enacted in Hungary. Instead, all the ills of the country were attributed to the injustice at Trianon and the pernicious effect of the Jews.

Before the Treaty of Trianon the Magyar gentry held the offices of the administration of the state and of the counties not only in the Magyar-speaking areas but in the nationality parts of the country as well. When two-thirds of the country joined the succession states, these Magyar officials were removed from office and flooded to Hungary. Most of them were absorbed in an enlarged civil service, but the insecurity remained. For them the loss of territory brought about an existential fear: their very livelihood had been endangered. Their sons, a dissatisfied youth who, after taking the time-honored legal course of studies, found nowhere near the opportunities of their fathers in careers as officials of the state, were subject to the ideologies of extreme political movements. Thus, when the precarious balance of the 1920's was followed by the economic hardships and political radicalization of the '30's, Hungary was headed for a disaster for the second time in the twentieth century.

In such a society, Három Nemzedék, the only demagogic work of Szekfü, had a far reaching effect. For here the blame was fixed: failure by omission on the part of the Magyar ruling classes and wrongdoing on the part of liberals and Jews were offered as explanation, and the readers were free to conjure up their own solution. Many right-wing radicals, future members of the Arrow-cross movement, got their ideas concerning the evilness of liberalism and the Jews from Szekfű's book and carried them far beyond the historian's original views. Years later, Szekfű complained to a friend that his most influential books were not the scholarly ones but rather those that had a journalistic appeal and that his views were distorted and misinterpreted.[18]

For the examination of Szekfű's views on Széchenyi, liberalism and the Jews in the following chapters, Három Nemzedék served as a major source not only because of the wide popular influence exerted by this book, but also because it expressed the official views of Hungary in the fifteen year period following World War One. Szekfű's articles in Magyar Szemle and the last three volumes of Magyar Történet constituted the sources for his views on nationalism and the problems of the nationalities.

FOOTNOTES

[1] Edward Hallett Carr, What is History? New York: Random House, 1961, p. 43.

[2] For the revolutionary years of 1918-1919, see Iván Völgyes ed., Hungary in Revolution, 1918-1919. Lincoln: The University of Nebraska Press, 1971.

[3] For the social, economic and intellectual changes in Hungary in the two decades preceding World War One, see Zoltán Horváth, Die Jahrhundertwende in Ungarn: Geschichte der Zweiten Reform Generation, 1896-1914. Leuchterhand: Neuwied, 1966.

[4] Miklós Béládi and György Bodnár, ed., A Magyar Irodalom Története (The History of Hungarian Literature), Budapest: Gondolat Kiadó, 1967, Vol. III, pp. 52-252.

[5] Oscar Jászi, Revolution and Counter-revolution in Hungary, Westminster: P. S. King and Son, Ltd., 1924, See also Tibor Hajdu, Az 1918-as Magyarországi Polgári Demokratikus Forradalom (The Bourgeois Democratic Revolution of Hungary in 1918). Budapest: Kossuth Könyvkiadó, 1968.

[6] George Barany, Stephen Széchenyi and the Awakening of Hungarian Nationalism. Princeton, N.J.: Princeton University Press, 1968, p. 466. Hungarian historians today concur with this view, in spite of the fact that Szekfü's postwar views and activities made him a persona grata in the eyes of the new regime. On the occasion of the ninetieth anniversary of his birth on May 23, 1973, Népszabadság, the official newspaper of the Communist Party, carried a commemorative article. It heaped much praise on Szekfü for his activities in the forties and fifties but did not fail to mention that "he was personally responsible for the nadir in our history, the erroneous ideology of the Horthy era." E. Pál Fehér, Népszabadság, May 23, 1973, p. 7.

[7] László, Bóka, Válogatott Tanulmányok (Collected Studies). Budapest: Magvető, 1966, p. 1102.

[8] Gyula Szekfü, Három Nemzedék. Budapest: Királyi Magyar Egyetemi Nyomda, 1938, p. 5.

⁹In a letter to a friend in 1914, Szekfű indicated that he was planning to write a serious study showing that the pre-World War One period was an age of decline and the Kuruc view of history (espoused by the historians and politicians who attacked his book on Rákóczi) was part of that decadence. Várkonyi indicated that this may have been Szekfű's plan to get even with his tormentors. Ágnes Várkonyi, Thaly Kálmán és Történetirása (Kálmán Thaly and his Historical Writing). Budapest: Akadémiai Kiadó, 1961, p. 324.

¹⁰László Németh, Szekfű Gyula. Budapest: Bólyai Akadémia, 1940, p. 38.

¹¹Domokos Kosáry, "A Történetiró," (The Historian) Magyar Szemle, XLIV (1943), p. 235.

¹²For the periodical Minerva and its connection with Hungarian historical and literary scholarship, see Borbála Lukács, Szellemtörténet és Irodalomtudomány (Geistesgeschichte and Literary Scholarship). Budapest: Akadémiai Kiadó, 1971.

¹³Gyula Szekfű, Történetpolitikai Tanulmányok (Historical-Political Studies). Budapest: A Magyar Irodalmi Társaság, 1924, pp. 8-9. It is interesting to note that Erich Marcks, one of the German historians Szekfű admired, stated in the preface of a book published in 1920 that he sought to "connect the past with the present and illuminate the one with the other." Cited in Gordon M. Stewart, "Erich Marcks," in Essays in Modern European Historiography, ed., by S. William Halperin. Chicago: The University of Chicago Press, 1970, p. 208.

¹⁴For the relationship of the Social Democrat Party to the Hungarian establishment of the interwar period, see András Fehér, A Magyarországi Szocialdemokrata Párt és az Ellenforradalmi Rendszer (The Social Democratic Party of Hungary and the Counter-revolutionary Regime). Budapest: Akadémiai Kiadó, 1969.

¹⁵Two of the very few pre-war historians Szekfű respected, Henrik Marczali and Dávid Angyal, were of Jewish origin. Szekfű always differentiated between "our own Jewish Magyars," those whose ancestors lived in Hungary for

many generations, and those who were children or grandchildren of immigrants. One member of the editorial committee of <u>Magyar Szemle</u>, Baron Móricz Kornfeld, was an industrialist whose father was an apostate Jew.

[16] Gyula Bisztray, "A Magyar Szemle," <u>Magyar Szemle</u>, XLIV (1943), p. 260.

[17] <u>Ibid.</u>, p. 267. Also conversation with Bisztray in Budapest, October, 1972.

[18] "The evaluation of Hungarian liberalism was reduced to Heil Hitler." Cited in Bóka, <u>Tanulmányok</u>, p. 1058.

CHAPTER V
SZÉCHENYI: THE TOUCHSTONE OF THE NATION

Count Stephen Széchenyi was a Transdanubian aristocrat who, after a period as an officer in the Imperial Army of the Habsburg Monarchy and extensive travels in Western Europe, devoted the better part of his life to an attempt of changing the medieval economic and political institutions of Hungary. His diaries and books constituted an important contribution to the Hungarian literature of the Romantic and Reform Era of Hungary and his proposals for economic and political reforms, as well as his practical activities in quest of the modernization of his backward country made him one of the most significant historical figures of the first half of the nineteenth century.[1]

From the time Gyula Szekfű first treated the role and significance of Count István Széchenyi in Hungarian history in A Magyar Állam Életrajza, he returned again and again to the figure of Széchenyi.[2] His most important work concerning Széchenyi remained Három Nemzedék. In it Szekfű set out to prove that Széchenyi was not a liberal but a conservative Christian Romantic for whom Western political and intellectual concepts were irrelevant. According to Szekfű, Széchenyi's political activity had nothing whatsoever to do with such abstractions as "liberty, equality and fraternity." The fate of the fatherland was a personal matter to him: "His politics originated in his soul."[3]

While Szekfü considered Széchenyi a Christian Romantic, he also showed him to be a realist who perceived the faults and needs of his nation and saw him as the "first and only man in the history of Hungarian politics who would not flatter his countrymen."[4] In Széchenyi's word, Hungary was a parlag, or a fallow land which was in need of cultivation. The satisfaction of the realistic needs of the nation, however, were only the means to attain a moral end. Change was necessary because Hungarian conditions did not befit a nation of Christian immortal souls. This fallow land had to be cultivated by education to achieve a wider dissemination of the national culture. The combination of reason and nationalism was necessary for "great and glorious achievements."[5]

Szekfü's interpretation of the above statement was that "reason" to Széchenyi did not mean the eighteenth century rationalist or the nineteenth century liberal view of reason; instead Széchenyi meant the development of the moral potential of man.[6] Nationality, too, had a special meaning for Széchenyi. While the most important characteristic of nationality was language, it was not the only one. The moral and spiritual attitude of the nation had to be learned along with the language. Those who acquired this inner spiritual possession were truly assimilated and became part of the Magyar nation. Thus, Széchenyi was against Magyarization because he felt that knowledge of the language was not sufficient and because he understood that forcible Magyarization would result in reaction and conflict. According to Szekfü, the concept of nationality in Széchenyi's scheme of things was related to a spiritual-moral world view.[7]

Széchenyi enumerated a list of Magyar sins, which he thought obstructed the development of the nation. These included vanity, self-delusion, conceit, instant enthusiasm for programs soon forgotten (*szalmaláng*), procrastination and laziness in public affairs, envy, factionalism and thirst for power. He wondered: how can the Magyar love his nation, when he hates everyone?

> It is indeed sad . . . for the Magyar tendency of hatred is not exhausted by antipathy against the aristocracy, . . . he hates also the government, he hates the church, hates the army, he hates the Croats . . . the Slovaks . . . the Greeks . . . hates city people . . . merchants . . . has no great love for the peasants . . . does not live in peace with people of his own kind /lesser noble/, yet he loves the fatherland; but since he hates everybody living in it, what he really loves is his own self which he confuses with his nation.[8]

Szekfü did not think that Széchenyi wanted to change the Hungarian constitution or the social and economic system; he wanted to bring about an improvement in the Magyar "spiritual disposition," and the development and ennobling of the Hungarian national soul. He attacked Hungarian feudal institutions not because he believed in human rights, but because it was in the interest of the "Magyar race."[9]

On the constitutional question--uppermost in the mind of the Magyar nobility in every age--Szekfű admitted that Széchenyi had specific suggestions for reform. But, he stated, like all other proposals of Széchenyi, these reforms were meant to serve moral and ethical ends. Széchenyi wanted to abolish the legal differentiation between classes not because he was influenced by foreign ideology but rather because "his nobility of spirit" accounted for it. Széchenyi had a warm regard for the declining lesser nobility and he also considered the oppressed millions of serfs. He wanted to improve the lot of everyone. Széchenyi saw that feudalism had outlived its usefulness. The constitution was clearly outdated; even the few thousand privileged families were on the decline, and the millions of peasants lived little better than animals. It was unseemly as well as morally wrong and economically disadvantageous. Szekfű quoted Széchenyi:

> In the nineteenth century, when human dignity is becoming sacred, we dare to speak publicly, without embarrassment, in the hearing of all Europe, about *misera plebe contribuente*.[10]

Széchenyi provided specific, detailed suggestions for constitutional reforms, but Szekfű did not deal with them in *Három Nemzedék*. Szekfű emphasized that no abstract theory of philosophy of state interested Széchenyi. He wanted to change the constitution to bring it in accordance with the requirements of the age, to benefit all the people regardless of class and rank, so that "all could aspire to the virtuous life." To develop the "immortal soul of the people" was his purpose. Széchenyi's inspiration was neither a liberal constitutional nor an autocratic legitimist theory, merely his own common sense. His own conscience dictated that nine million people should not be excluded from the nation and the protection of the constitution.[11] The reforms were merely a means toward achievement of high moral ends.

> His system of reforms occasionally may appear economic or political; they may seem to deal with the rights of the individual, commercial codes or what not; these are merely the temporary outward manifestations of the constant moral purpose: the ennobling of the Hungarian soul.[12]

More important, in Szekfü's view, Széchenyi never proposed, probably never even considered, the constitutional change to include a change of Hungary's relationship with Austria. He recognized that while ex principio Hungary was an independent, federated part of the Austrian realm, de facto, politically and economically it was merely a province with some administrative autonomy and nothing more.[13] He was aware that, in spite of the nominal constitutional form, Hungary was subordinated to the interest of the Empire. He clearly perceived the Kuruc-Labanc struggles that erupted from time to time during the centuries of Hungary's connection with the Habsburg House to be caused by the conflict between the de jure and the de facto relationship with Austria.[14] The Labanc acquiesced in the de facto Habsburg domination, while the Kuruc may be termed the strict constructionists of the Hungarian constitution with respect to Austria. Titled aristocrats, Catholics and those living in the Western part of Hungary (all of which was true of Széchenyi and Szekfü) were likely to be Kaisertreu, while the lesser nobility, Protestants, and those further away from the Austrian border often struggled against Austrian domination and for the constitutional rights for which they felt entitled.

Széchenyi thought a break with Austria "would bring the greatest misfortune to Hungary."[15] He knew that a Hungarian attempt to achieve independence had no chance for success; it would be defeated by Austrian economic and military might and Hungary would inevitably lose its constitutional separateness and the special status it enjoyed in the Habsburg Empire. It was for that reason that in the 1840's Széchenyi, the father of reform, turned against his own followers, for by then the reformers were in clear opposition to the government in Vienna. At that point, he began to vacillate and, eventually, changed course.[16]

On one other issue, Széchenyi and a few others differed from the majority of the reformers. This was the nationality question. Széchenyi considered the development of Magyar nationality second only to economic reforms as a major means by which Hungary should be brought up to the level of the more developed European nations.

> Our Asian language has a masculine strength which enabled us to maintain our national existence . . . and the miracle . . . that the Magyar in spite of the struggles and a sea of misfortunes throughout the centuries had not been absorbed by other peoples . . . that is due to the strength of our language . . . .
>
> Those who nurture our language have the life of our nation in their hearts; those who are against using our language are--albeit unaware--carrying the death of the nation hidden in their bosom.[17]

But Széchenyi did not think that a nation or nationality can be developed by artificial means. Language alone was not sufficient. Nationality to him was a spiritual entity,"ingrained in the nation's soul, not painted on." Assimilation was possible, but it was a slow and complicated process; not just language but ethical and spiritual elements of a people, moral values, ways of thinking and feeling had to be acquired. The process would take several generations.[18]

By the development of Magyar language and Magyarization, Széchenyi did not mean the teaching of Magyar to the non-Magyar nationalities, much less the forced Magyarization of later decades. He wanted to Magyarize the Magyars. For the educated Hungarians of the first decades of the nineteenth century spoke Latin in the Diet, and French or German within their families and in their social contacts, speaking Hungarian only with their peasants. It was the Magyar who seldom spoke his native tongue who endangered the survival of the Magyar language. It was he who had "the death of the nation hidden in his bosom."[19]

Széchenyi understood that forced Magyarization would not succeed; it would be harmful because it was based on the belief that the Magyar culture was superior to that of the other nationalities of the country. He saw the danger for this Magyar tendency for delusion; he considered the over-confidence in their own worth an obstacle to progress. Széchenyi predicted that contempt of the language and traditions of the other nationalities of Hungary would bring about reaction and conflict. He feared that, if aroused, the nationalities would join forces against the Magyars. These realistic fears of Széchenyi were acknowledged by Szekfű, but what he emphasized in Széchenyi's nationality policy was not the realism or the wisdom of a far-sighted statesman but the moral quality in Széchenyi's views. Szekfű saw the question of nationality as part of Széchenyi's ethical system of thought: the highest achievement of universal education would lead to moral virtue; the development of the Magyar language and nationality was the means for the Magyars to achieve moral righteousness.[20]

Széchenyi did not believe in revolutions. Nor did he think that a backward country could be raised to a higher level of development by "cheap" political means such as a parliamentary form of government, according to Szekfű. He believed that equality before the law and other free institutions were premature. In principle, Széchenyi thought it was fine to have a free press, but Hungary was not ready for it. A more educated public, such as existed in England was a prerequisite for the freedom of expression. In Hungary, where "public opinion was based on hyperbole, hypothesis and fallacy," freedom of speech and press could be dangerous and harmful. Controls were necessary.[21]

According to Szekfű, Széchenyi was against the cult of liberty. In general, he did not approve of political and ideological abstractions. Moral principles were the basis and the goal of his political career. Liberty to Széchenyi was a spiritual quality, not a political ideal; he believed that without morality the freedom of man in society differed little from that of the wolf. It provided destructive rather than creative energy.[22]

Széchenyi's ideas and political views as expressed in his writings and manifested in his political activities definitely proved, according to Gyula Szekfű, that Széchenyi was not a liberal. In spite of his reform program, Szekfű considered Széchenyi a conservative who was against the adoption of foreign dogmas and institutions. For instance, Széchenyi admired the British economic system but did not want to emulate its political system because it was a specifically British development and could not take root in another country. Széchenyi wanted a gradual, slow transformation in Hungary for he thought that the state and the nation were like organisms which would be destroyed by the trauma of a revolution. On the other hand, he had little in common with those foreign conservatives, who looked to the past for inspiration and wanted to prolong the life of outdated institutions. Nor was he the type of conservative nationalist who was a representative of the vested interests of his own class.[23]

How to classify Széchenyi? He was neither wholly conservative, nor a nineteenth century liberal. Szekfü solved the dilemma by christening him a "conservative reformer" who wanted to bring about changes by peaceful, gradual and orderly means as opposed to a liberal reformer whose aims were constitutional liberty and economic change by drastic measures, including revolution.[24]

Szekfü stated that Széchenyi's "conservative reform" politics could be understood only in the light of his Christian world-view. In his personality, religious piety was the most important; his political energies were devoted to his own and to his countrymen's salvation. "The worth of a man depends upon his usefulness to others," was the motto of one of Széchenyi's books.[25] He saw his own "mission" as the leader of his nation on the true Christian path which would lead to a society of true Christians. This would not be an ecclesiastical state but one characterized by a Christian spirit, love and consideration for one's fellow man, where everyone would live in harmony and human dignity. According to Szekfű, "Széchenyi's political system was one where the ultimate task of the state is the achievement of Christian morality."[26] Széchenyi spent his whole life and genius in the service of the moral improvement of his nation. His was the only ideology and application of European romanticism: it was Hungary's gift to European history. It took the form of Széchenyi's work and Széchenyi's life. "In Széchenyi, a new branch grew out of the Christian-German trunk: the Christian Magyar."[27]

Examining Szekfű's interpretation of the life and work of Count István Széchenyi one tends to agree with the Marxist philosopher of history, József Szigeti, on his judgment on <u>Geistesgeschichte</u>. Instead of presenting the past and depicting man in the spirit of a bygone age, the historian takes the spirit of his own times and depicts and distorts history in the light of the present.[28] The Széchenyi of <u>Három Nemzedék</u> reveals more about Szekfű in the 1920's than about Széchenyi in the 1830's. What Szekfű chose to emphasize about Széchenyi was that which was closest to Szekfű's own beliefs. Szekfű seized upon the subjective, the obscure and the mystical in Széchenyi's writing. Admittedly these were not hard to find. Széchenyi tried to convince his readers by religious and philosophical allusions, assuring them that it was morally just as well as economically advantageous to follow his suggestions. Like a fire and brimstone preacher, he excoriated his readers by showing them how they strayed from the path of righteousness, enumerated their mistakes, the sins of their fathers and foretold a dire future unless they mended their ways. But this was not the essence of his writing, merely the method by which he tried to convince and influence his audience. To put the emphasis on the subjective, the obscure, the mystical--the means rather than the ends--was to diminish Széchenyi's stature as a man and as a political force in the Hungarian Vormärz. Szekfü made him a dreamer rather than a doer, an idealist rather than a realist, a Christian Utopian rather than an enlightened liberal reformer.

Nor was Széchenyi the unique phenomenon, the Christian Magyar social and political theorist whose ideas were sui generis and had nothing to do with foreign political philosophies. "Scientific research has established definitely," said Szekfü in Három Nemzedék, "that Széchenyi was only slightly influenced by foreign political writers /alig állott idegen politikai irók hatása alatt/ . . . . Most of his theories and all of his teachings were original, so that we can speak of a system /of thought/ which was unique to him."[29] This was, of course, nonsense. George Barany, an authority on Széchenyi and nineteenth century Hungarian nationalism, disagrees with Szekfü's view. "Széchenyi was an enlightened reformer," and he was influenced by Western standards and

Western thought. His liberalism was not negated by the romantic element in his patriotic feelings and by his devoutly religious nature. English constitutional liberalism and ideas of the French Enlightenment exerted a great influence over him and his view of the Hungarian feudal system was always expressed in comparative terms.[30]

Széchenyi was also realistic in the evaluation of the economic situation of Hungary. The idea of the parlag (fallow land), which Szekfű chose to interpret in the symbolic and spiritual sense, had a realistic meaning for Széchenyi: he meant by Magyar parlag that Hungary was an underdeveloped country living in medieval economic and political circumstances, using outdated agricultural methods, in know-nothing intellectual isolation not even conscious of its extreme backwardness. Széchenyi's aim was to bring Hungary up to the level of nineteenth century Europe. If he was a Christian moralist, that did not prevent him from advocating liberal reforms. In a reversal of the method of the early Christians who made use of pagan rites by giving them Christian meaning, Széchenyi provided Christian moral justifications for the abolishment of feudalism and the development of a liberal capitalistic economy. There was a connection in Széchenyi's thinking between free association, laissez faire and very practical economic measures and moral concepts of developing and educating the "nation's soul."[31] But there is nothing unusual about that. Most politicians in every age manage to convince themselves that the concepts and actions which they consider politic are also righteous.

In any case, "the ennobling of the Hungarian soul" as an ultimate goal would be preceded and, presumably, facilitated by economic measures. Széchenyi must have seen prosperity as an antidote to sin, for most of his specific and realistic proposals were designed to improve the economic lot of the nation.[32] He stressed the importance of a money economy instead of the agricultural subsistence economy based on the <u>robot</u> system. He told his readers that profit making was not immoral, that capitalism was a means of developing the nation and improving the lot of everyone. He wanted to abolish the law of entail, for centuries the major code of the Hungarian feudal system, showing that the system was inefficient and economically unsound as well as morally wrong. He advocated a modern mercantile code and a law of exchange; he showed the need for a national bank. He spoke up for the rights of creditors and merchants in a society where traditionally a gentleman had nothing but contempt for the merchant and financier. He criticized the inefficiency of the county administrations. He advocated the building of new roads and bridges, regulation of rivers, cultivation of more lands, education of more people, tolerance of differences in class and religion. His first book advocated a magnificent combination of specific measures, couched in the language of a preacher but designed to bring about the kind of society which could catch up with the nations of Western Europe.³³

In his third volume, <u>Stadium</u>, Széchenyi proposed twelve concrete laws to be enacted at the next Diet. Ten of these laws, if enacted and carried out, would have transformed the social, economic and, eventually, the political structure of the country. These included (1) a new commercial code and a court of justice to insure legal equality between nobles and non-nobles in credit operation; (2) abolishment of the law of entail; (3) termination of the exchequer's right to inherit the land of an extinct family; (4) the right of everyone to own property; (5) equality before the law: the privileges of the nobles to be extended to all; (6) two elected representatives to the administration of each county (one noble, one ordinary citizen); (7) proportional participation of all in the expenses of county administration; (8) tolls and tariffs to be set by the Diet and apply to all (including the nobles); (9) abolishing all monopolies, guilds, price limitations and all such institutions which would curtail the workings of a free market; (10) the introduction of public trials and conferences in the legal system.³⁴ Not without reason was <u>Stadium</u> once called the handbook of Hungarian radicalism.³⁵

This was the program of a man whom Szekfü considered not a liberal but a conservative Christian Romantic. In the Hungary of 1833, when it was written, this proposal must have appeared to the vast majority of Hungarian nobles as a truly revolutionary document indeed. It is true, however, that Széchenyi did not advocate revolution; he wanted to bring about these changes by the voluntary action of his fellow nobles.

In addition to writing, Széchenyi actively labored to carry out some of his ideas. He established the Hungarian Academy of Sciences, "a gesture that founded modern Hungary."[36] He introduced horse breeding and horse racing and established a National Casino to promote the exchange of ideas. He made plans for and personally supervised the regulation of the Lower Danube and worked toward establishing a steamship service between Vienna and Constantinople. He wanted the twin cities of Buda and Pest to become a commercial center on the river route connecting the Habsburg Monarchy and the Middle East. He envisioned a comprehensive plan for river regulation, flood control, irrigation, communication and commerce. Széchenyi advocated and eventually formed an association to construct a permanent bridge between Buda and Pest and he fought for and achieved the abolition of tax exemption for the nobility for the first time: the nobles as well as others had to pay tolls on the new bridge.[37]

Both the theoretical and the practical parts in Széchenyi's efforts showed English constitutional and utilitarian influences, as well as French and American ideas of natural rights and freedom. Széchenyi read widely and traveled abroad in a systematic attempt to familiarize himself with the political theories and practices of the West with the deliberate intention of adopting their ways.[38] Withall, he remained a devout Christian and his ideal of elevating the "immortal souls" of his countrymen was, no doubt, totally sincere. But that made him no less liberal.

Szekfü emphasized that, in the 1840's, beginning with the book, Kelet Népe, (People of the Orient), Széchenyi turned against Lajos Kossuth (1802-1894) and his followers, disagreeing with them on their attitude toward Vienna and the non-Magyar nationalities.[39] However, this had very little to do with ideological differences, it only showed that Széchenyi was more realistic and practical than his followers. Széchenyi opposed as utterly foolish any effort toward independence from Austria, not in the interest of any mystical Christian-German cultural community (the term was coined by Szekfü three generations later), but simply because he knew that there was no hope for success. Similarly, he opposed forceful Magyarization of the non-Magyars, first, because he knew that it was not possible and, second, because he foresaw that it would lead to dangerous conflicts between the Magyar, Slav and Romanian inhabitants of Hungary. The break with Austria and the policy of Magyarization were the two points on which Széchenyi differed from the Hungarian revolutionaries of 1848, and on that basis Szekfü considered Széchenyi's views as eternal verities, while Kossuth and

and his followers, as well as the two generations of Hungarian leaders between the enactment of the Compromise and the outbreak of the First World War, were branded as dogmatic liberals who caused the decline and disaster that befell Hungary. Thus, Szekfü's entire thesis in Három Nemzedék was based on questionable premises.

FOOTNOTES

¹Széchenyi's writings are available in Gróf Széchenyi István Összes Munkái (The Collected Works of Count István Széchenyi), 12 vols. Budapest: Magyar Történelmi Társulat, 1921-1939. For a literary evaluation of his writings, see Antal Szerb, Magyar Irodalmi Történet (History of Hungarian Literature). Budapest: Magvető Könyvkiadó, 1972, pp. 283-289. For an evaluation of his role in Hungarian history until 1842, see George Barany, Stephen Széchenyi and the Awakening of Hungarian Nationalism (1791-1841). Princeton, N.J.: Princeton University Press, 1968. For the Marxist view, see Gyula Ortutay, "The Living Széchenyi," New Hungarian Quarterly, I (1960), pp. 36-49.

²Gyula Szekfü's publications about Széchenyi included Széchenyi Igéi (Széchenyi's Ideas). Budapest: Pallas R. T., 1921; "Széchenyi Ünnepe" (Széchenyi's Memorial), Kelet Népe, VI (1925), pp. 347-351; A Mai Széchenyi (Széchenyi Today). Budapest: Révai Kiadás, 1935.

³Gyula Szekfü, Három Nemzedék (Three Generations). Budapest: Királyi Magyar Egyetemi Nyomda, 1938, p. 18.

⁴Ibid., p. 28.

⁵Ibid., p. 20.

⁶Ibid.

⁷Ibid., p. 45.

⁸Cited in Ibid., p. 25.

⁹Ibid.

¹⁰Ibid., p. 34.

¹¹Ibid., p. 33. Szekfü did include Széchenyi's proposals for constitutional reforms in a later book containing a selection of Széchenyi's writings. But that book, A Mai Széchenyi, edited and annotated by Szekfü, appeared in 1935, at a different phase of Szekfü's life and gave a slightly altered picture of Széchenyi.

[12] Ibid., p. 35.

[13] Ibid., p. 37.

[14] Ibid.

[15] Ibid., p. 40.

[16] Ibid., pp. 38-40.

[17] Ibid., pp. 44-45.

[18] Ibid., p. 45.

[19] Szekfű, A Mai Széchenyi, pp. 219-223.

[20] Szekfű, Három Nemzedék, pp. 45-46.

[21] Ibid., p. 51. These ideas of Széchenyi, however, were contrary to his previous, more liberal, views. They were formulated in the late 1840's when he took issue with Kossuth and his followers and "considered it his main task to put the brakes on." Gyula Ortutay, "The Living Széchenyi," New Hungarian Quarterly, I (1960), p. 37.

[22] Szekfű, Három Nemzedék, p. 52.

[23] Ibid.

[24] Ibid., p. 54.

[25] István Széchenyi, Stadium, Budapest, 1833. In Szekfű, A Mai Széchenyi, pp. 237-267.

[26] Szekfű, Három Nemzedék, pp. 54-55.

[27] Ibid., p. 57.

[28] József Szigeti, A Magyar Szellemtörténet Birálatához (About the Evaluation of Hungarian Geistesgeschichte): Budapest: Kossuth Könyvkiadó, 1964, p. 13.

[29] Szekfű, Három Nemzedék, pp. 16-17. Szekfű later changed his opinion about this. In volume five of Magyar Történet, published in 1932, Szekfű acknowledged that Széchenyi was influenced by his experiences in England and

wanted a more liberal constitution on the British model. Széchenyi thought that the power and wealth of England was due to the fact that society was based on freedom on the individual. Ownership of property, a free market, free press, energy and ambition of the people and equality before the law were interconnected and produced a people who were responsible members of society. But Szekfü added that although these may sound like the ideas of a French liberal, they were based on Széchenyi's profound religious belief. " . . . his religious soul deduced, that when a nation achieves a certain level of culture, its members can be as equal on earth as they are in the eyes of God." It was merely a coincidence that equality based on natural rights also happened to be a liberal doctrine. Bálint Hóman and Gyula Szekfü, Magyar Történet (Hungarian History). Budapest: Királyi Magyar Egyetemi Nyomda, 1938, V, p. 271.

[30] Barany, Széchenyi, pp. 101-102.

[31] Ibid., p. 181.

[32] For the social and economic condition of Hungary and especially for the deteriorating agrarian system which Széchenyi wanted to improve, see Ibid., pp. 184-202. See also, Erik Molnár, ed., Magyarország Története (The History of Hungary). Budapest: Gondolat Kiadó, 1967, I, pp. 422-438.

[33] István Széchenyi's first book was entitled Hitel (Credit), published in 1830. In Szekfü, A Mai Széchenyi, pp. 29-168.

[34] István Széchenyi, Stadium, in Szekfü, A Mai Széchenyi, pp. 241-243.

[35] Ibid., p. 237.

[36] A. J. P. Taylor, The Habsburg Monarchy. New York: Harper and Row, 1965, p. 45.

[37] For Széchenyi's practical activities to improve the material conditions of Hungary, see Barany, Széchenyi, pp. 244-317.

[38] Ibid., pp. 273-275.

[39] Szekfü, Három Nemzedék, p. 124.

CHAPTER VI

LIBERALISM: THREE GENERATIONS OF DECLINE

Három Nemzedék has been called a 400 page-long posthumous struggle against Hungarian Liberalism.[1] The first book of Gyula Szekfű's conservative nationalist period measured liberalism against Széchenyi's system and found it wanting. Szekfű's views on liberalism provides us with his interpretation of Hungarian history from 1825 to 1919. He provided a background by describing liberalism in Western Europe, attempting to show its basic flaws and harmful effects on all societies (with the possible exception of England which Szekfű considered a special case). He reviewed in detail the devastating results of the "liberal" policies in Hungary.

Szekfű explained that, in the beginning of the nineteenth century, romanticism was far more important than liberalism because the French Revolution and the Reign of Terror effectively disillusioned the educated segments of Western societies about violent revolutionary doctrine. When reaction to the Napoleonic repressions and to the Holy Alliance revived the ideas of individual, social and political freedom, they wanted change through reason and liberty as the means to a peaceful transformation of society. The goal was a parliamentary form of government, wide franchise and free trade and industry in place of tariffs and guilds. Liberals fighting against the power of absolutism espoused nationalism as the ideal because the old feudal and absolute states were basically supranational and territorial.[2]

Although liberalism was a progressive concept in the history of ideas, Szekfű thought that in practice it turned out to be disappointing: it did not bring about the hoped for results. Liberals tended to be rigidly formalistic. They wanted written constitutions, but when they got them, the rights remained on paper. In Szekfű's view, adherents of liberalism turned against all authority and their anti-Christian and anti-clerical stance alienated the great majority of the people. Economic formalism in liberalism opposed any controls on free enterprise and gave birth to the "capitalistic monster." In the name of freedom it enslaved masses of people who were ruthlessly exploited in shops and factories. Opposed from the right by the God-fearing agrarian population and from the left by the newly rising industrial proletariat, liberalism was a bankrupt ideology leading to radicalism everywhere. For "where would a movement stop when its leaders advocated freedom instead of work . . . , whetted the appetite of the masses for gratification and thus deprived the movement of moderation?"[3] In the name of liberty liberal leaders failed to lead even their own class. Leadership itself was inconsistent with _laissez faire_ in internal politics and non-intervention abroad. The idea of liberalism, when espoused by masses of people, was a destructive force everywhere but in England where liberalism was a result of a unique historical development and contained sufficient safety mechanisms. In all other countries, instead of liberty and humanism it resulted in revolution and terror.[4]

One of the significant differences in the development of Hungarian liberalism was that Hungary lacked a <u>tiers état</u> in the Western sense. In France and England, industrial developments brought about a prosperous middle class whose political power was based on economic and intellectual independence.[5] In Hungary, there was no industrialization in the first half of the nineteenth century. Trade and commerce was in the hands of non-Magyars: Jews, Greeks, Armenians and Serbs; they were outside of the framework of the constitution and, therefore, could not become instrumental in the development of a middle class. The intellectual class was very small, not much more than ten-thousand teachers, priests, officials, doctors and lawyers in the entire country. The only class of people which was educated enough and economically independent enough to be attracted to the liberal ideology was the class of untitled nobles. Any change, political or economic, had to come through them. In nineteenth century Hungary, the class of middle and lesser nobles assumed the role of the <u>tiers état</u>.

The class of untitled nobility was not a small closed caste in Hungary. Of a population of eleven million,

550,000 were noble with 136,000 heads of households. Szekfü pointed out that while nobles were the only ones possessing political rights under the feudal constitution, Hungary was not as far behind the West as that statement would imply. He cited the example of France where, out of thirty million people, 188,000 had the franchise after 1830.[6] The only peculiarity of the Hungarian system was that despite the fact that the Magyar population of Hungary numbered less than five millions out of thirteen million total population, more than eighty per cent of the nobles were ethnically Magyar. The non-Magyar nobles, because of their privileged status, tended to be pro-Magyar.[7]

The first adherents of liberalism were the sons of the educated middle nobility, who were born in the first and second decade of the nineteenth century, and came to political consciousness in the 1830's after Széchenyi's appearance in Hungarian politics. They were educated in French language and literature and many of them had travelled in France and Switzerland. The Protestants among them may have studied at the University of Göttingen. Their liberalism at first was no more than the yearning of the rich and educated for anything that was Western. Among the poorer nobles, there was also a rebellion against their conservative elders. They turned away from the trend of Romanticism of the previous generation of educated Hungarians: they felt that the concentration on the past, the bemoaning of the fate of Hungary was utterly senseless. There was an unprecedented "generation gap;" the "life-style" of the youth differed greatly from that of their parents. Instead of looking for past glory and despairing over the present, they believed in progress and the perfectibility of man.[8]

Unlike the aristocrats and the untitled wealthier nobles, who had a more cosmopolitan education and travelled widely abroad, most of the lesser nobles had provincial political roots and an education which consisted of the classics and the reading of the law. Many of them came from the Eastern part of Hungary and were Protestants; there was always something of a democratic (<u>Kuruc</u>) spirit among them and they were receptive to the slogans of individual rights, intellectual freedom and respect for human reason. They also tended to be inordinately proud of the Hungarian constitution and jealously guarded their political rights in the counties. And, paradoxically, the liberal respect for reason and intellect aroused a great deal of sentiment and passion. Men who hitherto lived in virtually medieval intellectual circumstances became part of a movement against authority. For this reason, the reforms initiated by Széchenyi got on the wrong track.[9]

The turning point came at the sessions of the Diet during the years of 1832-1836. The conflict between the Aulic Conservatives and Széchenyi's Reform Party began over Széchenyi's proposal concerning the improvement of the condition of the peasants and the abolishment of the tax-exemption of the nobility. It continued over the plans for erection of a chain bridge across the Danube and, especially, over the issue of the universal requirement of the payment of tolls. The conflict was finally exacerbated by the emotional debate by the Liberals (Széchenyi's Reform Party) who, according to Szekfü, were more interested in such issues as religious tolerance and freedom of the press than in economic reform. From then on, "Széchenyi's star was on the decline." He lost his hold on the Reform Party whose members, in Szekfü's view, succumbed completely to the liberal movement. Developing the Magyar nation took a back seat to such "burning issues" as prison reform.[10]

The liberals continued to support Széchenyi's reform measures dealing with economic problems. However, they differed with him on two crucial questions: Hungary's constitutional relationship with Austria and the problem of the nationalities. The two questions were interrelated, for the aim of Hungarian liberalism was to transform the feudal state into a Magyar nation state. This had the double implication of complete administrative autonomy of Hungary within the Austrian Empire and of Magyar domination within the multinational lands of the Crown of St. Stephen.

The struggle for administrative autonomy was restricted to a kind of sterile opposition to anything having to do with Vienna: it was the patriotic thing to do. In Szekfü's view, there was very little real difference between the government party and the opposition: the Conservatives and the Liberals. The Conservatives were not against peaceful reforms.[11] It was the tone of the Liberals, not the issues, which precluded cooperation. It was not the substance of the Party's program but the style of behavior of the Liberal Party that caused Szekfű to brand them as radicals also. Not the demands themselves but the shrill tone of the speeches and newspaper articles by such young hotheads as Lajos Kossuth (1802-1894) convinced the government that Magyar liberalism was a branch of the European revolutionary activity which would sooner or later bring about a political upheaval in the country. This prevented the peaceful enactment of reforms and the transformation of the economic and political structure of the nation.[12]

If Széchenyi was the hero of Három Nemzedék, Kossuth was its villain. Not only during the years of his active participation but also throughout his long life in exile, and even after his death in 1894, all the mistakes and evils in Hungarian public life were related by Szekfű to the personality and actions of Kossuth. Szekfű saw the conflict between Széchenyi and Kossuth as one between Labanc and Kuruc and there is no mistaking where Szekfű's sympathies lay.[13] In contrast to Széchenyi, Szekfű saw Kossuth as completely caught up in the European ideas. His rigid, dogmatically liberal attitude precluded the

consideration of the special needs of his own country.
Kossuth was convinced that

> every age has its own ideals . . . which cannot be
> resisted . . . . In spite of the Asian character
> and habits of our people, we could not withstand
> Christianity, feudalism, serfdom, reformation . . .
> individual freedom and freedom of land are the
> powerful ideals of our age . . . .[14]

Kossuth did not see that Hungarian feudalism and other Hungarian institutions of foreign origin were different from the English, French or German; they were adapted to the special needs of the Magyars. "Dogmatic liberals such as Kossuth could not perceive such distinctions."[15]

Nevertheless, Szekfü showed that liberalism moved toward radicalism not when it adhered strongly to liberal principles but when it was in opposition to the government in Vienna. Kossuth was not consistently dogmatic in his application of liberal principles because opposition to the government was more important to him. County self-government was clearly against the liberal dogma of strong central administration, yet Kossuth favored it because the counties were strongholds of opposition. Protective tariffs were against the liberal idea, yet Kossuth was against joining the <u>Zollverein</u>. Most of all, he and his fellow liberals came into conflict with liberal dogma on the question of the non-Magyar nationalities. Here, again, they moved toward radicalism. The demands concerned not rights for the people, but rights for the state; they expressed not human but national aspirations. In the process, they came into conflict not only with Vienna, but also with the non-Magyar majority of the population of Hungary.[16]

Ferenc Deák (1803-1876) was the only nineteenth century statesman beside Széchenyi for whom Szekfü expressed an unqualified admiration. Like Széchenyi, Deák was a Transdanubian Catholic, but he was a lesser noble of moderate means. This Transdanubian Magyar was clearly superior to his Trans-Tisza counterpart. Szekfü explained the difference between the two types of Magyars: It was not so much a difference in temperament, but in the way each reacted to his own feelings. The Transdanubian was more cautious, considered things carefully before acting. He was not given to sudden short spurts of enthusiasm like his opposite number in the eastern part of Hungary. He was a product of a different race mixture, better educated, more reserved and, for centuries, in more of a need to find a modus vivendi with the Habsburg neighbor. The Magyars of the eastern part of the country were Protestants, rebellious, poorly educated, impulsive and politically irresponsible.[17] This, of course, explained the difference between Kossuth and Deák. (And, he might have added, between Thaly and Szekfü.)

Ferenc Deák, too, was a liberal but with a difference. He, too, espoused liberty as an ideal, but wanted to achieve it through humanistic, moral means. Responsibility and hard work were the only means he trusted, not the enthusiasm of the masses. He disagreed with Kossuth on the issue of protective tariffs and on the attempts at Magyarization, but his sense of responsibility to his party was such that he would not oppose them openly. He stood by the liberals until they turned on an extremely radical path. But even then, out of patriotism, he would not follow Széchenyi's suggestion of forming a centrist party, but quietly retired to his estate in despair over the fate of the fatherland. "Despair was a national disease that afflicted the greatest of the nation."[18]

To Szekfű, the lesson of 1849 was that the liberal tenets of freedom and equality led to radicalism: a foreign poison rejected by the Hungarian body politic. Szekfű quoted Zsigmond Kemény (1814-1875) a contemporary Hungarian conservative:

> The Magyar people are not republicans, but royalists; /they are/ not democrats; the principles of equality is foreign to them; they are not revolutionary or conspiratorial, they have no talents for plots, intrigues and insurrection . . . how is it possible, then, that an aristocratic and <u>kaisertreu</u> nation created a democratic republic in Debrecen in 1849?[19]

The answer was simple. Again, Szekfű quoted Kemény, with whom he was in complete agreement: "It is not a question of ideas, but of one individual." The sole responsibility for the debacle of 1849 belonged to Kossuth.

The first liberal generation of Hungary represented the highest achievement, the flowering of the Magyar nation. In addition to Széchenyi, their members included the statesmen Deák, József Eötvös (1813-1871), Miklós Wesselényi (1796-1850) and Kossuth, the poets, Ferenc Kölcsey (1790-1838), Mihály Vörösmarty (1800-1855) and Sándor Petőfi (1823-1849) and the historians and intellectuals László Szalay (1813-1864), Antal Csengery (1822-1880) and Mihály Horváth (1809-1878). True, there was a tragic conflict between the followers of Széchenyi and those of Kossuth and the misguided ideas and policies of Kossuth's party led to revolution and disaster, nevertheless Szekfű considered this first liberal generation, whether aligned with Széchenyi or Kossuth, totally sincere, uncorruptible and admirable. It was the second generation of liberals who started that downward slide which led straight to the collapse of the Monarchy and the Revolutions of 1918 and 1919.

In the Revolution of 1848 and the ensuing War of Independence, one fourth of the political and intellectual leadership of Hungary perished. Another fourth went into exile and though most of them eventually returned, they were forever lost to the public weal of Hungary.[20] Of the remaining leaders, Deák, Eötvös and Count Gyula Andrássy (1823-1890) were instrumental in bringing about a reconciliation with Austria. They realized that Austria's great power status was an impassable obstacle to Hungary's independence. "It is a childish fantasy to count on foreign help when everyone in Europe, from free England to despotic Russia, agrees on the preservation of Austria as a great power."[21] The thing to do was to restore peace with Austria and, as an influential part of the Monarchy, exert a deciding influence over Austria's action. Szekfü cited Kemény:

> Our historical mission is to mediate between East and West . . . . We can influence Austria's policy toward the East in the peaceful service of civilization. Therefore, Hungary's greatness and power is in the interest of Austria . . . . as well as that of European civilization and humanism.[22]

This sentiment had been echoed by many throughout the Dualist period.

Events justified Széchenyi. The remnants of the first liberal generation, having learned their lesson, took steps to carry out Széchenyi's ideas. The result was the Compromise of 1867.[23] To Szekfü, "1867 was the zenith of our constitutional history." In the four-hundred years of association with Austria, "never was our independence so secure" as during the Dualist period.[24] The Compromise was the best solution of an age-old problem arising from the centralizing, unifying forces of Austria and the defense of the constitutional independence of the Hungarian state.

But the lessons learned in the crucible of 1848-1849 were forgotten soon after the generation of Deák and Eötvös were gone from the scene. The new generation of leaders who was in power from the 1870's to the 1890's had not had first hand experiences or had forgotten the absolutism of the fifties. Hungarian public opinion and the Magyar leadership were genuinely enthusiastic about the Compromise at the time of Francis Joseph's coronation, but the era of good feeling did not last. Just as the fathers of the new generation were misled by the charismatic personality and oratory of their idol, Lajos Kossuth, the cause of the first dissension among the political leadership of the country after 1867 was the absent hero of 1849. Living in Italy, Kossuth was still the personification of the Kuruc dream of independence and a very real presence in Hungarian politics throughout the Dualist era.

In an open letter to Deák, Kossuth protested against the Ausgleich, claiming that the achievements of 1848 were repudiated and betrayed by 1867.[25] Not so, said Szekfü. The Revolution of 1848 was carried to completion by the Compromise. What Kossuth really wanted was not 1848 but 1849, that is to say, not the liberal reforms voted by the Parliament of Pozsony in April 1848 and approved by Vienna, but the Declaration of Independence and the governorship of Hungary achieved by Kossuth in Debrecen in 1849. "By unfurling the flag of 1848, Kossuth ruined forever the adherents of 1867."[26] With one simple gesture, he deprived the new government of popularity and created an opposition within the Parliament. The annual Parliamentary debates on budget, defense and recruits (the common affairs) provided the occasions of conflict between the Deák Party and the opposition. The debates concentrated on the shortcomings of the Compromise. "Forty-eight" became the ideal but "forty-eight" was merely the acceptable term for "forty-nine." "Parliament became a theatre featuring the ancient morality play, the conflict between good and evil . . . in the form of '48 versus '67."[27] The members of the opposition party were mere stand-ins, spokesmen for the real hero of the play, the irresistable but irresponsible emigre genius, Lajos Kossuth. In his incessant open letters he demanded complete independence in foreign and defense affairs and complete equality of rights among the citizens of Hungary. "These became the utopian politics on which the realistic policies of the Dualist Party had faltered."[28]

There was no real ideological difference between the two parties. The leaders of the second generation, Dualists as well as Independents, claimed direct descendence from the pre-1848 liberal opposition. Accordingly, the government party named itself Liberal Party (<u>Szabadelvü</u> <u>Párt</u>) and it was just as doctrinaire liberal as the opposition which was based on Kossuth's ideas. The only difference between the two parties concerned the constitutional question of Hungary's relationship with Austria, but that was enough to threaten the stability of the Dualist system. Therefore, in Szekfü's view, once an effective opposition threatened the maintenance of power by the Party of 1867, the government party had to remain in power by any and all means.[29]

The supporters of the government party included most of the aristocracy, those of the gentry whose economic position was still based on the land, those Magyars who lived in areas of non-Magyar nationalities, the Catholic clergy, higher officials of the administration and prosperous Jews--all with vested interests in the status quo. They were not numerous enough to provide a parliamentary majority. This was the reason why corruption and the system of the so-called "protekció" became part of the political system. First used in the election of 1872, Prime Minister Count Menyhért Lónyay applied government pressure and used bribery to elect a majority to Parliament. He was considered the creator of this corruption. Szekfü thought this was unfair to Lónyay, since corruption was everywhere a necessary corollary to parliamentarianism. The problem was that the government did not have the support of the people. Therefore, in order to preserve Dualism, it was forced to maintain power by fair means or foul: corrupt election politics, nepotism in administration and the provision of economic gains to its adherents.[30] Critics who revealed the misconducts and outright illegal acts wanted to embarrass the government rather than to express moral outrage. The constant muckraking on the part of the opposition did not aim at purification; it was only a means of attack on the

Dualist system. Charges and countercharges brought about a
nearly constant confusion and disorder. Instead of two
parties, Parliament consisted of two enemy camps.[31]

The Dualist Party had the task of maintaining Dualism in spite of the disadvantage that the opposition had the
support of the people, for liberal parliamentary elections
would have resulted in an anti-Dualist majority. In Szekfű's
view, the government was compelled to oppose extension of
the franchise and apply political and economic pressures in
order to maintain power in the national interest.[32] The
past master of this sick form of parliamentarianism was
Kálmán Tisza. During his tenure corruption became institutionalized, and he was strong enough to maintain a smooth
functioning of the state. The members of his cabinet came
from his close friends and associates, and the parliamentary
machinery was run by the nobility of his own County Bihar.
The administration of the counties was in the hands of petty
nobles who would do his bidding in order to keep their jobs
and saw to it that the outcome of elections would bring to
Parliament people who would be the willing instruments of
Tisza.[33]

If political liberalism led, inevitably, to a corrupt
parliamentary system, Szekfü saw liberalism in economic and
cultural affairs as equally disastrous, bringing ruin to the
lesser nobles. During the years of absolutism, the emancipation of the jobbágy (serf)--one of the laws of 1848--went
into effect, bringing about changes in the system of

landholding in Hungary. The emancipation meant little change in the condition of the peasantry, because it was not accompanied by a land reform significant enough to provide more than tiny parcels of land for a small portion of the emancipated serfs. The rest, though nominally free, remained in economic servitude on large estates. The lands of the aristocrats were entailed and untouched by agrarian reform and their financial situation could weather the economic changes successfully. It was the lesser nobility, owners of medium-sized or small estates, who were most seriously affected. The laws of 1848 not only deprived them of feudal dues and the compulsory services of the serfs, but they also had to provide draught animals and farm implements previously supplied by the jobbágy. Furthermore, they were no longer exempt from land taxes.[34]

Adding to the hardship of the lesser nobility was the method by which the state paid indemnity for the loss of peasant labor. Ostensibly in a geographic, orderly design, the Transdanubian magnates, who happened to be loyal and reliable from the standpoint of the Bach administration, were paid first and the lesser nobility of the easternmost part of the country last, the latter being most numerous among the Kuruc type of revolutionaries. The process took several years and during that period large numbers of lesser noble families became impoverished and lost their land.[35]

But even more important than the economic decline was the intellectual and moral decline of the lesser nobles, or gentry as they became known, in the generation following 1867. Even those who did not lose their land became impoverished because of the lack of credit and banks and unjust tax assessments. The gentry, however, refused to acknowledge a change in their circumstances. They could no longer travel abroad and their field of interest--always relatively narrow --did not extend much beyond local politics, but within their own circle they continued to live the same as before: well beyond their means. Drinking, gambling, neglecting their lands, feuding with their neighbors and trying to keep up appearances of tradition and class absorbed their meager energies. Nevertheless, this declining class not only maintained its political influence, it even enlarged its role in politics. The gentry took up residence in the provincial towns and county seats and became officials of state, county and municipal administration. Their livelihood now depended on the state and they became the instruments of Tisza's corrupt system of insuring the parliamentary majority for the government party and carrying out the policies of the government.[36]

In this atmosphere of economic, political and moral decline, liberalism became a mere slogan, rather than a real value in society. "Bourgeois selfishness, political helplessness and spiritual inertia" characterized society. But here again, Szekfü considered this inevitable. Everywhere in Europe, the first adherents to liberalism were high-minded idealists, but the wider the ideas were disseminated, the lower the standards, until idealism and enthusiasm faded, disappeared or were transformed into shallow, dreary materialism. It was at this time also that nationalism turned into chauvinism and the intellectual decline manifested itself in the third rate literary output and lack of scholarly achievements.[37]

Toward the end of the nineteenth century, the problems became greatly intensified, but they remained below the surface. Dualism, domestic independence, liberalism and capitalism constituted only the outward form.

> Like clothing made on the English model by French tailors, worn by offsprings of an Eastern people . . . as if we were ashamed of being Magyars, we tried to transform ourselves into liberal and capitalist Westerners . . . .[38]

Underneath the facade, the reality was different. Bitter conflicts between King and Parliament, between political parties, between central government and county administration and, last but not least, between the Magyars and the non-Magyar nationalities. Not since the period before Mohács was there so much turmoil in Hungarian public life as in the decade and a half preceding World War One.[39]

To Szekfű, liberalism was the foremost cause of the disorder. Liberalism aggrevated, if it did not bring about, the nationality conflicts, and liberal policies prevented the exclusion of Jewish immigrants and allowed them to develop economic and cultural domination. Instead of inaugurating some state welfare measures (like Bismarck in Germany), a liberal government allowed the spread of the ideas of socialism, an anti-Christian, un-Hungarian system of thought whose basic principles were the apotheosis of human selfishness. Liberalism was responsible for the rise of democratic and radical parties whose extreme form of doctrinaire liberal program was modeled on the French equivalent of the <u>Kulturkampf</u> and wanted to eliminate all religious influence from the schools.[40] And this all pervasive liberalism existed side by side with the increasing power, function and faith in the state.

In spite of the grave problems, there was the illusion of grandeur, the belief that Hungary was destined to be an independent nation in which the Magyars would have hegemony over the peoples of the Dual Monarchy and perhaps those of the Balkan states. There was nothing unusual about such ideas, according to Szekfü. In the last twenty years before World War One, all peoples, big or little, were imperialistic. All, that is, except the Hungarians. The Magyars only talked about it; never was it an officially espoused ideology. This Magyar illusion helped instead of hindered the non-Magyars who pointed to the imperialist rhetoric as a threat to them and "turned half the world against us."[41]

At the turn of the century, the liberal rulers ruled over a sick society, one that suffered from and was fatally weakened by inner contradictions. It was a "liberal" form of government where equal rights of the individuals were subordinated to the rights of the state. This was so not only in the conflicts between the Magyars and the nationalities, but also between the various classes of Magyars as well. The estates disappeared, but there remained a caste-like division in Hungarian society.[42]

The situation of the gentry was characteristic of the contradiction in Hungarian society and illuminated the dilemma caused by liberalism. Most of the gentry professed liberalism, yet they could not share the power of administration because their livelihood depended on it. Szekfű thought that they should have broken with their liberal principles and returned to the land, settling perhaps on latifundia. They could have enacted the necessary laws, since parliamentary representatives came from among them. "But liberalism deprived them of their will power," and prevented them from saving themselves by agrarian social measures.[43] Gentrydom was also an illusion. Desperately holding on to their identity and prestige, they could neither return to the soil, nor melt into the middle class. In fact, they obstructed the development of a Magyar bourgeoisie, for in the attempt of the burghers to conform to the life-style of the gentry, the bourgeois virtues of the middle class disappeared. They were aping the gentry in chauvinism, in living above their means and in debauchery.[44]

With the exception of the Jews, Szekfü showed every segment of Hungarian society in economic, social and intellectual decline, while the state was pursuing disastrous policies. Szekfü's diagnosis was accurate, but the disease he described was attributed to the wrong cause. "The examination was prepared retroactively to fit the result."[45] The result was Trianon, therefore, the preceding "liberal" era was ruinous. Szekfü was not alone in blaming the ills of society on liberalism. His view was a species of what Fritz Stern called the ideology of cultural despair, used to justify nationalism and authoritarianism. "All the vast and undesirable changes in the lives and feelings of Western man /conservative revolutionaries/ blamed on liberalism."[46] Szekfü had many of the characteristics that Stern saw as those of cultural despair. He, too, was a moralist who attacked modernity and secularism, bemoaned the loss of faith and upheld authority and the old values.[47]

Strangely, Szekfü, the political historian, who emphasized the overriding importance of foreign policy over domestic affairs and the influence of the power of the state over cultural developments, failed to consider European and world events in the coming of World War One and the dissolution of the Austro-Hungarian Monarchy. Similarly, in blaming liberalism for the mistakes in social, economic and nationality policy, he failed to take into consideration the nationalism of the Slavs and Romanians as part of a

Europe-wide phenomenon which the Magyars managed to exacerbate but over which they had otherwise no control; nor did he point out the international nature of the rise of the trade union movement and class conflict which were feeble in Hungary compared to many other European nations. To blame the pseudo-liberal Magyar ruling classes for **all** the factors that led to the Treaty of Trianon was to make them seem omnipotent: it implied a presumption that with the right policies Hungarians could have removed themselves from the effects of twentieth century historical events. This was a Hungaro-centric view, the opposite of that "universal history" which Szekfü claimed to admire.

Even supposing that liberalism **per se** could be blamed for some of the ills of society, the Hungarian ruling class of the Dualist period could not be accused of being liberal. Unless there was a clear-cut advantage, as in the case of the Jews, where the favorable policy toward them yielded both economic and political advantages for the aristocrats and the lesser nobles, there was very little evidence of liberal policies on the part of the government. The Nationality Law of 1868 was never put into effect, the non-Magyar lower classes were not represented in Parliament, the administration was retained in the hands of the gentry and government opposition was restricted to obstructionism without ever having a chance of coming to power. Corrupt elections, nepotism and the use of the gendarmes were part of the

parliamentary system that perpetuated a one-party rule. The
Hungary of the Austro-Hungarian Monarchy was hardly a liberal
state.

Szekfű continually differentiated between liberalism
and dogmatic liberalism. Although it is difficult to determine where he placed the dividing line between the two, it
seems to this writer that wherever liberal concepts or policies coincided with ideas expressed by Széchenyi, they were
acceptable; whenever they differed from the views of the
"Greatest Hungarian," they were doctrinaire and led to ruin.
Before the Revolution of 1848, Szekfű thought the difference between Széchenyi's Reform Party and Kossuth's Liberal
followers was more of style and manner than content. The
policies of Magyarization of the nationalities and freedom
of immigration of the Jews from other parts of the Monarchy
were not included in Széchenyi's program. These Szekfű
considered the policies of doctrinaire liberals.

The greatest sin of "doctrinaire liberalism" was its
stand against the Church, in Szekfű's view. Liberalism was
anti-religious and, therefore, it attacked the fundamental
basis of society. Here is the way Szekfű saw the contrast
between a dogmatically liberal and a traditional society:

> In the one, a belief in the basic goodness and
> natural good sense, in the other, the Christian dogma
> of original sin; in the one, the idea of individual
> freedom and the social contract, in the other the
> admonition to give to Caesar what belongs to Caesar;

> here freedom, there authority; here reason, there
> morality; here the pitilessness of the law, there
> the love of one's neighbour. One cannot imagine
> a more profound contrast.[48]

Nevertheless, he thought that it was possible for social, political and individual freedom to coexist with Christianity. Separation of Church and State, as in the United States, freedom of religion and education were in the realm of possibility, but they should be done only "with the consent of the Church."[49] But this was not the case in Dualist Hungary where the "doctrinaire liberalism" was anti-Christian, anti-authoritarian and, therefore, led to radicalism and revolution.

Három Nemzedék contained no political proposals and offered no alternatives to the detested liberal state. Szekfü discussed what he considered the ideal form of government in articles published in Napkelet and Keresztény Politika in 1922 and 1923. He believed that instead of the parliamentary system the state should be based on Christian national principles, free from the cult of the representative government of the liberal democratic era.[50] Szekfü was against the free competition advocated by liberalism and he was pessimistic about the nineteenth century idea of progress. He believed in the original Christian view of natural rights. His ideal was a stable, conservative, authoritarian Christian welfare state.[51]

Szekfü thought that a state which would be governed according to Christian principles would not be subordinated to the interest of a powerful class and would not abandon the poor and the weak. The governing body would be free of the petty issues of the day (<u>napipolitikától mentes</u>) and the leadership would be left to a national elite "who would do the thinking for others" (<u>a többi helyett is gondolkozhatnak</u>).[52] Instead of liberalism and equality, the state would rest on Christian consideration.

Szekfű did not spell out the details of how such a government might work, but he did not think that his concept of a Christian national state was a utopian idea. Ironically, he found a parallel in the new Communist regime in Russia which had set up just such a government, albeit in an "Asian, primitive, repressive form." There was a new privileged class: one of the "estates," the workers, governed and suppressed the others. The elite of the workers, the party members, did the governing. Given a period of domestic and international peace, Szekfű had no doubt, there would develop a permanent ruling class in Soviet Russia, which would maintain its power through their Praetorian Guards over the millions of suppressed people.[53]

However, in the "Christian national estate state," no one would be suppressed. "Everyone will enjoy the fruits of his labor . . . although a person whose work is of a higher rank will receive a higher award."[54] Christian national politics will ensure spiritual values. It will raise up the poor and the persecuted, lessen the differences between rich and poor and preserve the national culture.

Although Szekfü considered the idea of a "Christian national estate state" as a realistic one, he was not optimistic about its future in Hungary. The Christian national society would have to supplant that alien Budapest culture which was strongly entrenched and dominated the intellectual life of Hungary. This was an almost impossible task because the forces of liberalism were so highly organized. To develop an intellectual middle class capable of taking over the cultural leadership of the nation Szekfü suggested a culture tax, like the war tax of old, to finance education, health measures and cultural activities.[55]

There was no indication that the "Christian national estate state" was ever seriously considered by anyone, and it is unlikely that Szekfü expected such a state to be established. He was not directly active in politics; his influence was intellectual rather than political. This essay originally appeared in a little read Catholic journal. The tone of the article was thoughtful, speculative, philosophical; it was not written as a proposal for a political program, nor was it an exercise in polemics.

Nevertheless, Szekfü's views on liberalism and his exaltation of Christian national principles were closely attuned to the purposes of the post-war regime, where a Christian national program was offered to replace liberalism and to help stabilize post-war Hungarian society. As a Christian program it wanted to restore the authority of

the Church and the belief in the traditional values. As a
national program it clamored for revisionism, substituted
chauvinism for social and political reform and, most of all,
wanted to reduce the economic and intellectual importance
of the Jews. Anti-Semitism was part of this program.

FOOTNOTES

[1] László Németh, Szekfű Gyula. Budapest: Bólyai Akadémia, 1940, p. 39.

[2] Gyula Szekfű, Három Nemzedék (Three Generations). Budapest: Királyi Magyar Egyetemi Nyomda, 1938, pp. 81-84.

[3] Ibid., p. 87.

[4] Ibid., p. 89.

[5] Szekfű thought that even the Viennese bourgeoisie lacked the political and economic power necessary for the tiers état, because they were economically dependent on the Habsburg court and, therefore, had a vested interest in the status quo. Ibid., p. 69.

[6] Ibid., p. 74.

[7] Ibid.

[8] Ibid., p. 96.

[9] Ibid., pp. 101-105.

[10] Ibid., p. 106. For the Age of Reform, see Mihály Horváth, Huszonöt Év Magyarország Történelméből (Twenty-five Years of Hungarian History). Budapest: Ráth Mór Kiadása, 1883. See also George Barany, Stephen Széchenyi and the Awakening of Hungarian Nationalism. Princeton, N.J.: Princeton University Press, 1968.

[11] Even Metternich, no longer as reactionary as previously, may have gone along with the reforms, Szekfű indicated. Ibid., p. 127.

[12] Ibid., p. 129.

[13] Szekfű was careful not to anger public opinion by going too far in his criticism of the still popular Kossuth. Each disapproving statement was carefully counterbalanced with praise. "Kossuth never said anything unpopular to the people," said Szekfű, but he added that because of the enthusiasm of the Magyars for Kossuth, he never had to compromise his principles to have a mass following. Ibid., p. 139.

[14] From Lajos Kossuth, *Iratai* (Documents), XII, 23 cited in Szekfű, *Három Nemzedék*, p. 130.

[15] *Ibid.*, p. 131.

[16] *Ibid.*, p. 137.

[17] *Ibid.*, p. 141.

[18] *Ibid.*, p. 145.

[19] Zsigmond Kemény, *Forradalom Után* (After the Revolution), Budapest, 1850, cited in Szekfű, *Három Nemzedék*, p. 180.

[20] Szekfű repeated his observation that the life of an exile is futile, useless for the country, first mentioned in his book on Rákóczi. *Ibid.*, p. 167, cf. *A Száműzött Rákóczi* (The Exiled Rákóczi). Budapest: A Magyar Tudományos Akadémia Kiadása, 1913, p. 336.

[21] Szekfű, *Három Nemzedék*, p. 185.

[22] *Ibid.*

[23] Szekfű failed to mention that it was not just the changed attitude of the Magyar leaders that was responsible for the Compromise. External events affecting Austria had more than a little to do with the Habsburg willingness to achieve a *modus vivendi* with the Magyars. For the Marxist view of the Compromise, see József Galántai, *Az 1867-es Kiegyezés* (The Compromise of 1867). Budapest: Kossuth Kiadó, 1965. See also Zsigmond Pál Pach, "A Dualizmus Első Évei Magyarországon" (The First Years of Dualism in Hungary), *Századok*, XCIII (1959), pp. 34-74.

[24] Szekfű, *Három Nemzedék*, p. 198.

[25] *Ibid.*, p. 215.

[26] *Ibid.*, p. 218.

[27] *Ibid.*, p. 222.

[28] *Ibid.*, p. 223.

[29]Ibid., p. 226.

[30]Ibid., p. 231. Most of the members of the gentry were employed by the state, county or municipal administrations. At the same time, officials were permitted, even encouraged to enter Parliament. More than 60% of the members of the Parliament were public officials. A considerable portion of the remainder were men who were related to officials of the government, a result of the system where civil service jobs were obtained by nomination and recommendation alone. Corruption and misgovernment of the counties were not mitigated by the central government, for local and state officials were intimately related by interest as well as family and marriage ties. For a still very useful account of the social and economic changes in Dualist Hungary, see C. A. Macartney, Hungary. London: Ernest Benn, Ltd., 1934. Reference to the above, on p. 193. See also, Erik Molnár, et al., Magyarország Története (History of Hungary). Budapest: Gondolat Könyvkiadó, 1967, II, p. 113.

[31]Ibid., p. 232.

[32]Ibid., pp. 235-236. Szekfű's reasoning sounds familiar to anyone listening to the Watergate hearings in the summer of 1973, as this is written: the end justified the means. And anyway, everybody did it. Szekfű cited the corruption in eighteenth century England and in more recent French, Italian and Austrian parliaments. Corruption was built into the system. Ibid.

[33]Ibid., p. 238.

[34]Ibid., p. 173.

[35]Ibid., p. 175. Ironically, the emancipation of the serfs not only did not eliminate the feudal system, it reinforced it. For the aristocrats increased their landholdings; they were the ones who acquired the land of the lesser nobles.

[36]Ibid., pp. 176-178. Members of the gentry, who sat in the Lower House of the Parliament supported the big landed interests of the aristocrats on every important issue. According to Oszkár Jászi, the Lower House was no less a feudal body than the Upper House only "its voice was louder and its manner less aristocratic." Oszkár Jászi, The Dissolution

of the Habsburg Monarchy. Chicago: The University of Chicago Press, 1929, p. 227.

[37] Szekfü, Három Nemzedék, p. 261.

[38] Ibid., p. 272.

[39] Ibid., p. 294. For the period preceding World War One, see Jenö Horváth, A Milleniumtól Trianonig: Huszonöt Év Magyarország Történetéből, 1896-1920 (From the Millenium to Trianon: Twenty-five Years of Hungarian History, 1896-1920), and Zoltán Horváth, Die Jahrhundertwende in Ungarn; Geschichte der Zweiten Reform Generation. Luchterhand: Neuwied, 1966.

[40] Szekfü, Három Nemzedék, pp. 360-363. For the conflict of Church and State in Hungary, see Gábor Salacz, A Magyar Kultúrharc Története (The History of the Hungarian Kulturkampf). Pécs: Pécsi Egyetem Kiadása, 1938.

[41] Szekfü, Három Nemzedék, p. 309.

[42] Ibid., p. 312.

[43] Ibid., p. 319.

[44] Ibid., p. 321.

[45] Németh, Szekfü, p. 39.

[46] Fritz Stern, The Politics of Cultural Despair. Garden City, N.Y.: Anchor Book, Doubleday and Co., 1965, p. 10.

[47] Szekfü was famous for his pessimism. In an article written for the memorial issue of Magyar Szemle honoring Szekfü on his sixtieth birthday, an admirer said that Szekfü belonged to the finest of Hungarians who were always prophets of doom, nevertheless they worked feverishly to avert disaster and inspire the rest of the nation. Sándor Eckhardt, "Évfordulón," (On the Anniversary), Magyar Szemle, XLIV (1943), p. 229.

[48] Szekfü, Három Nemzedék, p. 86.

[49] Ibid.

[50] Szekfü expected the failure and demise of parliamentary systems everywhere in Europe within a century. Gyula Szekfü, "Állam és Nemzetfenntartás," Történetpolitikai Tanulmányok (Historical-Political Studies). Budapest: Magyar Irodalmi Társaság, 1924, p. 32.

[51] Lajos Gogolák, "Nemzetpolitika," Magyar Szemle, XLIV (1943), p. 246.

[52] Szekfü, Történetpolitikai Tanulmányok, p. 33.

[53] Ibid., p. 34.

[54] Ibid., p. 33.

[55] Ibid., p. 39.

CHAPTER VII

THE JEWS: THE BANE OF THE NATION

Reading Szekfű's assessment of the ills of the Dualist period, one could easily get the impression that the Jews arrived in Hungary in the nineteenth century thanks to the permissive immigration laws of the liberals, and, once there, the liberal policies allowed them to become dominant in the economic and intellectual life of the country. It is also noteworthy that, until the publication of <u>Három Nemzedék</u> in 1920, the historian had never mentioned the Jews in any of his publications. This book, written in the latter part of 1919 when reaction to the recently defeated Communist Revolution was manifested in violent anti-Semitism, presented the Jews, along with the liberals, as the major cause of decline and disaster culminating in the Treaty of Trianon. The best way to put Szekfű's treatment into historical perspective is to describe briefly the situation of the Jews in Hungary before the nineteenth century.

The history of the Jews in Hungary is as old as the Hungarian state.[1] During the rule of the Árpád Dynasty, from the tenth to the fourteenth century, they lived relatively undisturbed, their freedom of movement and activities hindered only as a result of papal intervention. That the kings were repeatedly threatened with excommunication and interdiction unless the Jews were dismissed from state offices shows that, in addition to trade and commerce, Jews had been employed in the service of the kings and the nobility. The Church forbade intermarriage in 1093, ordered the regulation of trade between Christians and Jews and the restriction of their residence to the seat of the bishops.[2] After the devastation of Hungary by the Mongols, King Béla IV (1206-1270) received special permission from the Church to give a charter of privileges allowing freedom of religion and providing royal protection to the Jews in return for their help in the reorganization and the rebuilding of the country.[3]

    The relatively good treatment of the Jews was not a selfless and disinterested policy on the part of the Árpád kings. The agricultural and transhumant economy of the Hungarian society lacked people to supply money and commodities to the royal and ecclesiastical courts and to the class of magnates. Furthermore, the Jews paid dearly for the royal protection in yearly special taxes.[4] Nevertheless, the condition of the Jews in Hungary before the fourteenth century was much better than their coreligionists' in other European countries. There is no doubt that the Magyars, only recently emerging from Paganism and often still relapsing to their old beliefs, tended to be more tolerant of foreign tongues and creeds than their more advanced neighbours.[5]

In spite of the tolerant attitude of the Magyars, the economic role of the Hungarian Jews differed little from that of the Jews in other Central-European countries. They were limited to commerce; the occasional state offices occupied by Jews were those dealing with finances. All other forms of economic activity were distributed under the tribal system. Only the position of the merchant remained to the foreigner. As long as the Jews were the only foreigners engaged in trade, their position was relatively secure. As soon as a Christian, albeit a foreign, trading class arose, the situation of the Jews became precarious. The German settlers of the towns of Hungary in the high Middle Ages found themselves in rivalry with the Jews and added to the pressure already exerted by the Church to restrict the economic activities and the geographic movements of the Jews.[6]

Life became extremely difficult for the Jews of Hungary under the Habsburgs. Physical persecution and economic hardship drove them away from the cities.[7] In the seventeenth and eighteenth centuries the Jews could count on neither the protection of the monarchs nor on the tolerance of the German and Greek bourgeoisie of the towns. Since they were completely deprived of legal rights in all the Habsburg lands, they depended solely on the protection and good will of the individual feudal lords, on whose estates (which included entire villages) they resided. The Magyar feudal lord tended to be more tolerant than his Austrian counterpart partly because of the greater religious diversity of Hungary and partly because, under the specific economic and social conditions of feudal Hungary, he had a need for the services of the Jews.[8]

The role of the Jews in the economic life of Hungary in the eighteenth century was not a significant one. They were excluded from the cities and the trade activities of the country were carried on by Germans, Greeks, Serbs and Armenians. The only occupations left for the Jews were those of the itinerant peddler, and the leaseholder of the village inn and the butchership from the owners of the estates. A few Jews were entrusted with the administration of the noblemen's finances. Jewish artisans were few for they could work only in Jewish communities; the guilds of the cities were closed to them. They were also excluded from the fairs of the cities.[9] On the eve of the Enlightenment, the Jews of Hungary were economically, socially and culturally separated from the rest of the population by a gulf which seemingly could not be bridged.

It was the reign of Joseph II which brought about a legal change in the condition of the Jews of the Habsburg lands. This practitioner of enlightened absolutism enacted a great many reforms in an effort to increase the efficiency of the state. Two of his reforms were of immediate concern to the Jews. The Edict of Toleration directly affected them;

no less important, though indirect, was the Emperor's attempt to Germanize the diverse lands within the Habsburg realm. The Magyar reaction to the policies of Joseph II is thought to have precipitated the Age of Reform in Hungary, and, in turn, enabled the favorable conditions to develop for the eventual emancipation of the Jews.

Along with the Edict of Toleration, which extended complete religious freedom for the Protestants and the Greek Orthodox peoples of the realm, the Emperor proposed a reform "Concerning the Betterment of the Condition of the Jews."[10] The purpose of the Emperor in framing this proposal was to make the Jewish population a more useful element of the state for he understood the reasons behind the Jews' concentration on business and finances. By providing a wider field of economic activity and opening a way for secular education, he loosened that strait-jacket which hemmed in the Jews of the Habsburg lands for so many centuries.

According to the terms of the Edict, the Emperor allowed the Jews a wide range of activities hitherto closed to them (including agriculture, arts and crafts and manufacturing), and opportunities for public higher education opened their way into the professions. At the same time, they could remove the special signs and discontinue the wearing of special clothes which had distinguished and humiliated them.[11]

It was up to the nobility of Hungary to execute the Emperor's edict of the change in the condition of the Jews in the beginning of the nineteenth century. Since this was the age of liberal reform, the Magyar nobles put no obstacles in the path of the order. Their magnanimity and cooperation could be extended all the more readily because the Jews represented neither an economic nor a political threat to them. The Magyar noble looked upon trade and money-making activity with something of a contempt. A gentleman could be either a landowner or an official, but never a merchant. He was willing to leave the activities of a middle class to foreigners, and, at this age of religious toleration, he was ready to accept a wider participation by the Jews. Indeed, the Jews had the advantage of not having any national loyalties to another state, as could be the case with the Germans and the Serb merchants who resided in the towns along the Danube.[12]

In the course of the nineteenth century, many of the townspeople of German and Slav origin became Magyarized and espoused Magyar nationalism. The sons of these Magyarized burghers often acquired, along with their new surnames, the Magyar aversion to business as well. Thus, as the non-Magyar Christian traders became Magyarized and turned away from business, the Jews found less opposition and more economic opportunities in the cities. They stepped into the vacuum.

According to Szekfű, liberals and conservatives alike agreed in the Reform Era that changes were necessary to provide more humane conditions for the Jews. However, while the liberals demanded equal rights and emancipation, conservatives urged caution, and, at the very least, a ban on further Jewish immigration from other parts of the Austrian Empire. For the number of the Jews increased greatly and the major reason for this large increase was the immigration of Galician Jews after the Partition of Poland made Galicia part of the Monarchy.[13] Doctrinaire liberals, following the example of France and the United States, insisted on emancipation of the Jews and <u>laissez faire</u> in immigration. While there was enough opposition to prevent complete emancipation in 1848, immigration continued unabated and the next generation of Magyar leaders could not stem the tide of the growth and development of the Jewish people.[14]

In the beginning of the nineteenth century, most of the Jews resided in small communities which were part of large feudal estates. There some of them rented the taverns from the landowners, some traded in grain and extended credit to the peasants. In an arrangement that was beneficial to both the Jew and the landowner, the Jew served as a middleman between the lord and the peasant. Szekfü quoted a contemporary landowner:

> [The Jew] lives almost exclusively on onions, is industrious, buys, sells, trades, if he has a horse, he uses it in a little moving-business for a small fee; he is satisfied with a small profit; though you have to watch him about the upkeep of the property because he is not very clean, but the income from the tavern is in good hands.[15]

Nevertheless Szekfü saw the role of the Jews as detrimental to society. He stated that the Jews exploited the peasants by buying wine from the lord cheap and selling it to the peasants at a profit. Because the Jew extended credit to the peasants, he was able to buy the grain of the poor villagers at a low price. Szekfü blamed the county administrators for allowing the Jew to extend credit to the peasants. The lord (who also held the county office or exercized an influence over it) allowed the Jew the use of the county apparatus to collect from the peasants, which, in turn, enabled him to pay his rent punctually to the lord. Nevertheless, it was the Jew Szekfü held responsible for the impoverishment and the alcoholism of the peasantry.[16]

The Jew began by renting the tavern rights and from there he moved on to the grain business. In the Napoleonic Wars the Jews supplied the army with grain.

> . . . without them the needs of the army would be difficult to meet, but they must not find out when the grain would be needed, otherwise they would buy up the grain ahead of time and create an artificial shortage in order to jack up the price.[17]

The Jew became rich in the war-time grain business and, after the war, made himself indispensable to the landowner. The rich merchant gave "green credit" to the noble for the growing crops. He became an agent between the landowner and the outside world. He took care of all the transactions: he bought the grain, rented rights to the tavern and sold

the wine and rented the forest to sell lumber; he alone knew
the market and foreign price of wool and skin which he bought
and sold. According to Szekfü after the Napoleonic wars,
the landlords were at the mercy of rich Jews.[18]

An enlarged role of the Jews dawned with the development of capitalism in Hungary in the second half of the nineteenth century. Szekfü understood and cogently explained the reasons for the economic predominance of the Jews in Dualist Hungary. Unlike the western countries, where capitalism, along with liberalism, developed in post-feudal conditions and in the presence of a politically powerful, prosperous middle class, in Hungary the beginnings of capitalism were added on to a completely unchanged agricultural society. The lesser nobility took on the political and intellectual roles that in other countries were assumed by the middle class, but they were not willing to take part in the development of capitalism because they considered trade and industry beneath their social status. Trade had been traditionally assigned to foreigners; when capitalism in the form of industry came to Hungary that, too, was left to aliens. "The impoverished lesser noble, in his shortsighted haste to secure himself a job in officialdom, irresponsibly left a vacuum which was filled by the Jews."[19]

By the 1870's practically all the trade, manufacturing and finance was in the hands of the Jews. The industrial development resulted in a change of their geographic position also: most of the Jews moved into the cities from the small towns and estates where they had previously resided. There was much financial cooperation and much movement between the "racially agile" Jews of Budapest and Vienna.[20]

In the absence of native ability, willingness and the necessary capital, Szekfü saw nothing wrong with allowing prosperous and well-connected Jews to participate in the industrialization of Hungary. He felt that Magyar elements would have been necessarily included and, eventually, would have taken over the leadership, since capitalism developed rapidly and the number of the native Jews were limited. This was prevented by the unwise liberal policy of allowing Jewish immigration from the East to continue. The leadership of business and industry was in the hands of Magyarized Jews, but the immigrants with their "alien culture and ethics" were immediately accommodated in the machinery of capitalism. The liberal Magyar leadership was blind to the danger of allowing Jewish immigration, for it considered Judaism a religion rather than a race. Thus, with the continued influx of Galician Jews, the economic life of Hungary assumed a Jewish character by the end of the century.[21] In the quarter of a century preceding the First World War the Jews became predominant in the intellectual life of Hungary as well.

The importance of the provincial cities and county administrations declined after 1867; Budapest became the focal point of Hungary. Politics, a centralized administration

and the development of a national press made the capital
city (Buda and Pest were officially united in 1872) the intellectual center of the nation. The traditional class of
lesser nobles still provided most of the writers and poets,
but they were not attracted to the strenuous discipline of
the daily press. Among the journalists, for the first
time, one could meet a fair number of writers of foreign
(German and Jewish) origin. These were Hungarian-born sons
of assimilated families, writing in Hungarian and using
Magyarized names. Szekfü approved of them.

> The first journalists of Jewish origin . . .
> were highly ethical and responsible. Their example
> shows that the Jews who have been living in Hungary
> for several generations would have been an invaluable addition to the Magyar people if their assimilation was not impeded by the ever increasing
> Galician tide of immigration.^{22}

Of the one million Jews in the Lands of St. Stephen (about
five per cent of the total population) just before the outbreak of World War One, almost a half were first or second
generation immigrants.^{23} For this was the period when masses of Jews left Russia, Poland and the Ukraine to escape
oppression and poverty. Part of them went to Western Europe
and the United States but most of them did not get that far
but "took advantage of the liberal civilized countries"
near-by which had no laws against immigration. Thus, in
Germany, Austria and Hungary identical situations developed:
among the Jews foreign immigrants equaled or outnumbered

those who had been living there for centuries and who had virtually melted into the local population. Therefore, said Szekfü,

> we should not be surprised that we have a Jewish problem in these three countries, and sooner or later we will have to face this problem, and when we do, it will not necessarily be an act of hostility against the Jews.[24]

Szekfü blamed the liberal Hungarian administration not only because they allowed the Jews to settle in Hungary, but also because they encouraged them to be Magyarized. These "uneducated, low-cultured" immigrants took advantage of the Magyar generosity and shortsightedness. The new-comers found that, once they crossed the Carpathian passes and settled in the Northern Highlands of Hungary, all they had to do was to change their outward appearance and learn Hungarian to be accepted. The Jew took advantage of the state-organized process of Magyarization, assumed a Magyar surname, opened a store, bought himself a little house and presto, there was one more Magyar in Hungary. That is why

> we were satisfied with a superficial transformation . . . confused language with nationality, Magyar values with the ability to speak Magyar.[25]

Once in Hungary, the next generation, the children of these storekeepers of the Slovak and Ruthene speaking Highlands, moved to Budapest or to the Magyar areas and entered into business or the intellectual fields. The Jews provided the manpower and the brains for capitalism and they received the profits as well. This meant that even first and second generation immigrants could rise to the middle class: "the Magyar middle class."[26]

The Jews rapidly took over the professions, for "they don't like manual labor and want to see their children in comfortable circumstances," preferably working in intellectual fields. They benefited from the attitude of the historical classes who wanted nothing but the time-honored officialdom and "they were practical enough not to attempt to compete with them in administrative jobs."[27] Instead, they became doctors, lawyers, engineers and journalists. "When we bragged about the cultural progress of modern Hungary," said Szekfü, "it was really nothing more than the move of the Jews from the economic to the intellectual fields."[28]

Yet the Jews, once Magyarized and superficially assimilated, took over the dominant views of liberalism, Magyar nationalism and illusions of Magyar superiority. Greatful for their opportunities, they faithfully adopted the official Magyar political views. They made Budapest their center; with their presence the capital became the center of capitalism and the center of national illusion. The greatest impact of the Jews was their domination of Budapest as the intellectual center of Hungary.[29]

Reading Szekfü further one surmises that the Jews did not move from the economic to intellectual fields, rather they combined the two. According to Szekfü, anything that required investment of capital became a Jewish enterprise. All the owners and operators of printing presses and publishing companies and most of the contributors of newspapers and periodicals were Jews. Jews provided the readers of books and the purchasers of art; literature and fine arts became cosmopolitan to please them. Jews were the audiences in theatres and musical productions. Therefore, the entire intellectual output of Budapest was adapted to their taste.[30]

The power of the Jews of Budapest rested on the press. No longer was the newspaper a tool for the edification, the political and moral enlightenment of the nation, as in the old days. The Jews made it into a business enterprise, requiring not education and character but business acumen. "The greed of big business is better assuaged by Jewish rather than Christian journalists," said Szekfü.[31] The more recent the immigrant Galician Jew, the better business sense he had:

> The more immigrants worked on the papers, the better the enterprise succeeded, . . . the bigger the profits of the entrepreneur; and the naive, pious Magyar, for whom the printed page was like a bible, was overpowered (alája gyűretett) by the Jewish-Magyar culture of Budapest.

Hungarian literature was in a decline at the end of the nineteenth century. At the same time, the press of Budapest became a national press. Szekfü found the "Jewish-Magyar" daily papers deplorable, and went into great length

in describing the evils and the deleterious effect of the
Jewish press on the "naive, pious Magyars." The press in
Jewish hands served Jewish ideology, according to Szekfü,
but a few paragraphs later he stated that the Jewish press
(i.e. the Magyar press) faithfully reflected the national
illusions, imperialism, intolerance and superiority over the
nationalities.[33] The Jewish press was to blame for the
political conflicts also: "Without the Jewish press of
Budapest the constitutional struggle and the national illusions could not have continued for decades."[34]

    The political destructiveness was only a part of the
evil effect of the press. The cultural destructiveness was
just as deadly. The Jews were ingenious; the press was
designed to be all things to all people. Only the core of
the papers were political. In addition to politics, the
Jewish journalists found it useful to include court-room
dramas and street events which would capture readers "by
catering to their base instincts." They included various
"columns" about any and all subjects, humorous pieces,
serial novels, news of the theatre and society and supple-
ments that were of interest to women and children. Szekfü
profoundly disapproved of such a popularized press, implying vaguely that there was some sort of conspiracy of evil
design to corrupt Magyar culture and morals. "The power
of the press over the souls of the Magyars was unlimited."[35]
The immediate aim was less diabolical: to sell more

newspapers by making any other reading matter superfluous. They achieved that purpose. "Our middle class, even our peasantry, got its education from the Jewish press." Around the turn of the century, only the French and the South American press compared in immorality and destructiveness to that of the Hungarian.[36]

Budapest was not alone in this predicament. "The culture of Budapest is a branch of the cosmopolitan culture of Berlin and Vienna." In each of the three capitals the intellectual climate was a product of Jewish capitalism and the "Jewish mentality." Its purpose was to satisfy big city Jews and those Christians who assimilated to them. The press, the theatre, concerts, opera, night clubs and cabarets all served the Jewish middle class. New-fangled ethical and philosophical subjects such as Buddhism, Freudianism and Bergsonianism were taken up by Jewish intellectuals; these shallow and useless fads were brought into vogue and substituted for the real spiritual needs of human beings.[37]

In Berlin and Vienna the Jewish culture had been elevated or, at least, counteracted by the high standards of the native intellectual environment, but Budapest was too weak and undeveloped to resist the low level of taste of the immigrant Jews. Nor was there any resistance from the provincial gentry, previously in the vanguard of the Magyar intellectual leadership. The average Magyar of the provinces was too naive to perceive the Janus-like character of the press: the politically assimilated, patriotic exterior covered a Jewish mentality manifested in subjects other than politics and covered inside the newspapers and periodicals. And so, the Budapest culture became a national culture.

> The good people of the provinces considered József Kiss a great Magyar poet and . . . short story writers of Budapest dealing with Jewish themes and similar urban subjects were looked upon as representatives of a modern Hungarian literature.[38]

Szekfü saw a close connection between this alien culture of Budapest and the moral and intellectual decline in Hungary. He went back to Széchenyi's term, explaining that the Jews succeeded in taking over the intellectual leadership of the country, because of the <u>parlag</u> condition of Hungarian society. This concept of the fallow land was used by Széchenyi in the literal as well as the symbolic sense. Szekfü used it to show that the Jewish economic and intellectual dominance was possible because of the failure of the traditional Magyar classes to provide a popular culture for the masses of Hungarians. In short, as in the economic sphere, the Jews filled an intellectual vacuum.

In addition to spreading their own popular culture, the Jews infiltrated the literary societies; there were even a few Jews admitted to the Academy of Sciences. Szekfü attributed the decline in the level of historical scholarship to the influence of the Jews. Szekfü recognized that Jewish historians faced a dilemma in their interpretation of Hungarian history. If they wrote objectively, without glorification, they would be considered alien critics if not traitors. Historians of lesser talent and integrity who received their position through the system of <u>protekció</u> would adjust to the expected norm in order that they would not provoke a reaction against their origin.[39]

Szekfü proved that insight was no deterrent to prejudice when he turned to the discussion of two dissenting parties. For if he considered assimilated Jews alien even when they echoed all the patriotic sentiments, Jewish criticism of Hungarian society was altogether more than he could tolerate. The possibility of valid criticism, based on principles and a realistic assessment of a backward feudal society, was not considered by Szekfü. He railed against illusions on every page of <u>Három Nemzedék</u>. Yet he saw those who criticized the illusions and suggested social and economic reforms as alien critics who contributed to the decline and prepared for revolution and ruin.

The Social Democratic Party was founded in the last decade of the nineteenth century. The leadership of the Party was predominantly Jewish while the rank and file members were mostly Christian. Szekfü had a neat explanation for this. The Jews were attracted to Marxism because it was anti-Christian and revolutionary. The workers, on the other hand, were following these Jewish elements because Magyar liberals were too short-sighted and doctrinaire to create state-organized welfare measures and alleviate their plight.[40]

The Social Democratic Party contained a dichotomy: the Christian members had morality but an undeveloped intellect, while the Jewish leaders had the intellect but lacked ethical principles.

> The amoral leadership could do whatever it wanted with the uneducated Magyar workers . . . thus, they became participants in the Bolshevik experiment /of 1919/; the necessary preconditions existed: workers like herds followed their aristocratic leaders, the intellectual proletariat who were mostly of Russian Jewish origin.[41]

Even more critical was Szekfű of the Bourgeois Radicals, a party of intellectuals with a small membership which had been compared to a head without a body.[42] The Party was founded by Oszkár Jászi, a man Szekfű singled out for the demagogic practice, much in vogue in the interwar period, of putting the original family name in parenthesis to remind readers that the man (or his ancestor) was a Jew. Thus, he referred to him as "Oszkár Jászi (Jakubovics)".[43] Jászi edited the periodical Huszadik Század (Twentieth Century), a journal of politics and sociology, devoted to the advocation of reform. The contributors came from among the progressive urban Jewish intelligentsia, many of them belonging to organizations highly critical of Hungarian society, bearing such names as the Freethinkers Organization of Hungary, League of General Franchise, Free University of the Social

Sciences and the Galilei Circle.[44] What galled Szekfü most of all was the fact that most of the Bourgeois Radicals were sons of assimilated, patriotic fathers.[45]

Jászi's attacks on Magyar national vanity, agrarian aristocrats, Jewish capitalists, the Catholic Church, Protestant pastors and the Party of Independence found eager listeners among the young intellectuals most, but not all, of whom were Jewish. Delivered in speeches or published in articles and books, the urging to needed reforms were seen by Szekfü to be

> coupled with unimaginable detestation of Hungarian life and institutions, and although Jászi, perhaps deluding himself, assigned the problems to the faulty structure of our society, behind the sociological pose one can continually detect an aversion to the Magyar character.[46]

To Szekfü, criticism of Hungarian society by Jewish intellectuals, even if they were members of families who had resided in Hungary for many generations, was not accepted as self-criticism: "They attacked the nation from the outside with their free-mason like world view, from the self-satisfied heights of Spencerian sociology."[47] Szekfü thought them dillettantes who lacked a sense of <u>real-politik</u> and experience and, most of all, the knowledge and understanding of Magyar life and Magyar needs.

Because they were critical of Magyar nationality policy, Szekfü thought that both the Social Democrats and

the Bourgeois Radicals sided with Francis Ferdinand and the
non-Magyar nationalities who "took orders from Belgrad,
Bucharest and Prague," implying that the two dissenting
parties verged on being traitors to the national cause. What
made Jászi especially dangerous in the eyes of Szekfü was his
exaggerated view of the nationality question. "His fuzzy
proposals for reforms . . . prepared the anti-national revolution."[48]

Here, then, is the indictment Szekfü brought against
the Jews:

(1) The newly assimilated but loyal and patriotic
Jews dominated first the economic, later the intellectual
life of the nation. Although they were politically loyal,
their Jewish mentality corrupted the Magyar spirit.

(2) A group of Jewish intellectual proletariat,
probably of Russian Jewish origin, seduced the Hungarian
working men and led them astray by organizing them in their
Marxist Social Democratic Party. They were responsible for
the Revolutions of 1918-1919.

(3) The highly educated Jewish intelligentsia, sons
of long-assimilated, patriotic fathers who were nevertheless
alien to the Magyar spirit, were clamoring for social reform;
their criticism of nationality policy encouraged the demands
of the non-Magyar nationalities of Hungary and, therefore,
they carried some of the responsibility for the dismemberment of Hungary at Trianon.

If a justification for the anti-Jewish outburst in 1920 was needed, Három Nemzedék and the rest of Szekfű's writings in the early 1920's could serve the purpose. Szekfű often compared Trianon and Mohács. One comparison he never made was the popular view of the responsibility of the Jews for the disaster, a charge that was made in 1526 as well as in 1920. There was an anti-Semitic outburst after the defeat at Mohács also, but no scholarly tome justified it by explaining the responsibility of the Jews for the disorder of Hungarian society and the weakness of the Magyars. After 1920, the emotional outburst found intellectual justification in the works of Szekfű and others.

Szekfű's arguments were full of contradictions and inconsistency. On the one hand, he accused the press of serving Jewish ideology, on the other hand, he stated that the Jewish press faithfully adopted the liberalism, nationalism and imperialistic national illusion of the gentry. It is questionable whether there was such a thing as Jewish ideology in Hungary before the First World War; few of the eagerly assimilating Hungarian Jews were attracted to Zionism before the 1920's.[49] Those who emigrated from Hungary went to Western Europe or the Americas not to Palestine.

Szekfű repeatedly referred to "uneducated" Jewish immigrants living in a "low level of culture," presumably in need of being uplifted by the superior Magyar civilization. His account of the role of the immigrant Jews was

inconsistent. On the one hand, he stated that the immigrant
Galician Jews remained in the North-eastern border areas,
and their children or grandchildren, the second and third
generation immigrants, moved to the inner part of the country
or to Budapest. On the other hand, Szekfü referred to the
Jewish press--by which he meant the Magyar press of Budapest
--as dominated by commercially oriented immigrant Jews who
superficially changed their mode of living and learned Hungarian.
The former statement is more likely to be true.
Hungarian is a difficult language and few immigrants, even
if well educated, could become journalists writing in Hungarian.
Like poor immigrants everywhere they did what they
could to find a job and make a living. It was their children,
or, most likely, their grandchildren, born in Hungary, well
educated, speaking and writing in Hungarian because it was
their native tongue, who succeeded in journalism and a few
of them achieved success as novelists and poets. József
Kiss, whom Szekfü dismissed so contemptuously, was a fine
Hungarian poet of the late nineteenth century, who spoke
and wrote his poems exclusively in Hungarian; he was a
grandson of an immigrant rabbi, about whom he wrote his
finest poetry. Szekfü took exception to the subject matter:
to write about "Jewish themes and urban types" meant a
corruption of Hungarian literature. He was appalled that
"the good people of the provinces considered József Kiss
a great Magyar poet."[50]

It is true that the Jews dominated the economic and, later, the intellectual life of Hungary. Szekfű understood that the role of the Jews in Dualist Hungary came about by default of the Magyar nobility. There was very little social mobility in pre-war Hungary. In the absence of the willingness and ability of the lesser nobles to interest themselves in anything other than officialdom, there was no other segment of society available for the task of modernizing Hungary. The social prestige and political power of the gentry exerted such a strong influence on the small segment of Christians who, by education or assimilation rose out of the lower classes, that they, too, shunned industry and commerce in favor of law and government offices. Szekfű's understanding of the reasons behind this development was not balanced by a similar understanding of the motivation of the Jews. His reasoning was emotional rather than intellectual and he tended to portray the Jews in terms of popular stereotypes.

The conventional Magyar view of anyone in Dualist Hungary who did not speak Hungarian was one of inferiority. The Magyars considered it their mission to bring the benefits of Western civilization to the non-Magyar speaking peoples of Hungary.[51] Thus, the immigrant Jews were considered in need of education. The fact was that the "low-cultured immigrant Jews" Szekfű spoke about with such disdain had a tradition of respect for learning and the pride of Jewish parents throughout the ages was in direct proportion to their children's intellectual achievement. While the Jews were separated from the rest of society by a hostile environment their education was restricted to Jewish religion and thought; as soon as they were given an opportunity for secular education, they availed themselves of it.[52]

In the century before World War one, as in previous centuries, the Jews of Hungary made the best of their circumstances. Hungarian Jews at all times occupied themselves with whatever field of activity was open to them. In the Late Middle Ages they were restricted to money lending; later they traded under the auspices of the Magnates, serving as their inn-keepers or village artisans. When their movement was not restricted they became itinerant peddlers; when allowed in the cities they opened a shop or learned a trade. When higher education was opened to them they entered intellectual professions. When they were given equal rights they became good, patriotic citizens, many of them eagerly changing their names and becoming assimilated in all but religion.[53]

Szekfü gave the impression that the Jews were either capitalists or socialists, with the balance being journalists and professionals. Further, they were either chauvinists or alien critics of Hungarian society. Nothing could be further from the truth. All the Jewish capitalists (owners of medium-sized and large enterprises), professionals and intellectuals added up to no more than five percent of the total Jewish population and most of the wealthy industrialists and intellectuals came from families who had been in Hungary for many generations. The rest of the Jews were neither capitalists nor socialists, neither chauvinists nor critics and would-be reformers.[54] Considering that the overwhelming majority of Dualist Hungary's one-million Jews were apolitical small shopkeepers, artisans, tenants on the land of aristocrats or the church and otherwise modestly occupied in the various roles of the petite bourgeoisie, Szekfű's treatment of the "Jewish problem" was highly distorted and misleading.

FOOTNOTES

[1] The first small Jewish settlement existed in Hungary in the year 960. Magyarország Története, Földje, Népe, Élete, Gazdasága, Irodalma Művészete, Vereckétől Napjainkig (The History, Georgraphy, Population, Life, Economy, Literature and Art of Hungary from Verecke to our own Day), 5 vols. Budapest, no date, I, p. 398. The ecclesiastical community of Esztergom contained the first sizable Jewish community in the middle of the eleventh century. Erik Molnár, et al., Magyarország Története (The History of Hungary). Budapest: Gondolat Könyvkiadó, 1967, I, p. 65.

[2] Miklós Asztalos and Sándor Pethö, A Magyar Nemzet Története Ősidöktöl Napjainkig (The History of the Hungarian Nation from Ancient Times to our own Day). Budapest: Dante Könyvkiadó, 1931, p. 40.

[3] Jüdisches Lexicon, Berlin, 1930, V, p. 1099.

[4] István Végházi, "The role of the Jews in the Economic Life of Hungary," Hungarian Jewish Studies, II (1969), p. 40.

[5] Raphael Strauss, "The Jews in the Economic Evolution of Central Europe," Jewish Social Studies, III (1941), p. 19.

[6] Végházi, "The Role of the Jews," p. 41.

[7] A wave of persecution spread across Hungarian towns in 1526 on the ground that the Jews were responsible for the defeat at Mohács. A ritual murder charge in 1529 caused the arrest of a large number of Jews. Special head tax and military taxes were levied on them in the sixteenth century. Jüdisches Lexicon, V, p. 1101.

[8] The basis of the feudal lord's protection of the Jews originated during the reign of Sigismund of Luxembourg (1387-1437) who premulgated the law, Jus Tenendi Judeos, in which he gave permission to some of the aristocrats to have Jews settled on their land. Végházi, "The Role of the Jews," p. 41.

[9] Ibid., p. 55.

[10] Henrik Marczali, Magyarország Története II. József Korában (The History of Hungary in the Age of Joseph II). Budapest: Pfeffer Ferdinánd Kiadása, 1888, II, p. 271.

[11] Ibid.

[12] Végházi, "The Role of the Jews," p. 57.

[13] Gyula Szekfü, Három Nemzedék (Three Generations), Budapest: Királyi Magyar Egyetemi Nyomda, 1938, p. 157. The number of the Jews increased from 75,000 in 1785 to 241,000 in 1840. Molnár, Magyarország Története, I, p. 451.

[14] Szekfü, Három Nemzedék, p. 160. Szekfü was mistaken. It was not the conservative segment of the Magyars who prevented the emancipation of the Jews before 1867 but the opposition of the German population of the cities who feared Jewish economic competition. Both Houses of the Hungarian Parliament voted in favor of full rights of citizenship for the Jews in 1840, stating that "we consider the Jews who live within our country not an alien people but a religious community, which is deprived of its civil rights because of its relgigion . . ." However, under the pressure of the Free Cities, the Crown refused to approve the proposal of the Parliament. Simon Dubnow, Weltgeschichte des Jüdischen Volkes. Berlin: Jüdischer Verlag, 1929, IX, p. 151.

[15] Bálint Hóman and Gyula Szekfü, Magyar Történet (Hungarian History). Budapest: Királyi Magyar Egyetemi Nyomda, 1938, V, p. 250. Volume five was written by Szekfü and first published in 1932.

[16] Ibid.

[17] Ibid. This stereotype portrayal of the profiteering Jew in wartime was a standard charge after World War One. Szekfü introduced it to the Napoleonic Wars in Hungary where it never existed. Szekfü stated this on the same page where he also quoted a contemporary who said that the Jew was an industrious man who was "satisfied with a small profit."

[18] Ibid., p. 251.

[19] Szekfü, Három Nemzedék, p. 246.

[20] Ibid., p. 249.

[21] Ibid., pp. 251-253.

[22] Ibid., p. 266.

[23] Ibid., p. 333.

[24] Ibid., p. 334.

[25] Ibid., p. 335.

[26] Ibid., p. 337.

[27] Not competing for civil service jobs with the gentry showed that the Jews were practical in a double sense. They understood that officialdom was reserved for the lesser nobles and did not want to alienate them by trying to compete with them and also because the Jews perferred the lucrative free professions. The latter was emphasized by Szekfű.

Between 1890 and 1900, the number of lawyers increased by 7.2%; at the same time the number of Jewish lawyers increased by 68%. 48% of all physicians were Jews at the turn of the century, while the Jewish population constituted only five per cent of the total. Ibid.

[28] Ibid.

[29] Ibid., p. 338.

[30] Ibid., p. 339.

[31] Ibid.

[32] Ibid., p. 340.

[33] Ibid.

[34] Ibid., p. 341.

[35] Ibid., p. 342.

[36] Ibid.

[37] Ibid., p. 343.

[38] Ibid.

[39] Ibid., p. 352. These were usually baptized Jews otherwise they would not have received university professorships.

[40] Ibid., p. 361.

[41] Ibid., p. 362.

[42] Gusztáv Grátz, A Dualizmus Kora. Magyarország Története 1867-1918 (The Age of Dualism. The History of Hungary 1867-1918). Budapest: A Magyar Szemle Társaság, 1934, p. 194.

[43] Since Jászi's physician father was also called Jászi, Jakubovics must have been a grandfather. This kind of identification was seldom done to an assimilated German or Slav and Szekfü had not generally practiced it even in the case of Jews.

For an analysis of Jászi's role and an interpretation of the ideas of the Bourgeois Radical Party, see György Fukász, A Magyarországi Polgári Radikalizmus Történetéhez: Jászi Oszkár Ideológiájának Birálata (On the History of the Bourgeois Radicalism in Hungary: A Critique of Oscar Jászi's Ideology). Budapest: Gondolat Könyvkiadó, 1960.

[44] For an interesting account of the Galilei Circle see Márta Tömöry, "Uj Vizeken Járok:" A Galilei Kör Története (I am Walking on Fresh Waters." The History of the Galilei Circle). Budapest: Gondolat Könyvkiadó, 1960.

[45] Hóman and Szekfü, Magyar Történet, V, p. 596. There is an interesting parallel between Bourgeois Radical sons of assimilated, prosperous, patriotic fathers in pre-World War One Hungary and anti-establishment, New Left children of patriotic American first or second generation immigrants of recent years.

[46] Ibid.

[47] Ibid., p. 597. The first page of the first issue of Huszadik Század contained a letter from Herbert Spencer to Oscar Jászi. Spencer wrote:

> I rejoice to learn that you propose to establish a periodical having for its special purpose the diffusion of rational ideas--that is to say scientific ideas--concerning social affairs. All the world over . . . , a society has been regarded

as a manufacture and not as an evolution . . . . it has been tacitly assumed that the order of social phenomena is determined by governmental action.

You will doubtless find it a hard task to undeceive your fellow countrymen on this matter. I . . . apploud the attempt . . . and wish that elsewhere the example you set may be followed.

Huszadik Század, I (1900), p. 1.

The lead article of the first issue of Huszadik Század closed with the words of Spencer: "No one can be perfectly free, till all are free; no one can be perfectly moral, till all are moral; no one can be perfectly happy, till all are happy."
Oszkár Jászi, "Tudományos Publicisztika" (Scientific Journalism), Huszadik Század, I (1900), pp. 2-12. See also, O. Jászi, "Emlékeimből: A Huszadik Század Elindul a Herbert Spencer Égisze Alatt" (From my Recollections: Huszadik Század Begins Under the Aegis of Herbert Spencer), Látóhatár, VIII (1957), pp. 135-139.

[48] Hóman and Szekfü, Magyar Történet, V, p. 597.

[49] "The Jews want exactly what the Magyar demands of a "nationality;" the fullest possible assimilation. Nothing pleases the Hungarian Jew so much as to be taken for a pure-blooded Magyar; no one carries the Magyar mentality to such extremes as the Magyarized Jew." C. A. Macartney, Hungary and her Successors. London: Oxford University Press, 1937, p. 459.

[50] Almost every Hungarian Jewish writer bore a Magyarized name and very few of them wrote about Jewish life. József Kiss was an exception. Unlike American Jewish writers, Hungarian Jews seldom used Jewish themes in fiction or poetry. However, they did write about urban life. The best interpretation of the new urban literature in the twenty-five years preceding the First World War is in Antal Szerb, Magyar Irodalom Történet (The History of Hungarian Literature). Budapest: Magvető Könyvkiadó, 1972, pp. 415-473. See also Zoltán Horváth, Die Jahrhundertwende in Ungarn: Geschichte der zweiten Reform Generation, 1896-1914. Luchterhand: Neuwied, 1966.

[51] Tibor Joó, <u>Magyar Nacionalizmus</u>. Budapest: Athenaeum Részvénytársaság, 1941, p. 290.

[52] For a description of traditional Jewish life in Eastern Europe, see Mark Zborovsky and Elizabeth Herzog, <u>Life is with People: The Jewish Little-Town of Eastern Europe</u>. New York: International Universities Press, Inc., 1952.

[53] Three hundred forty-six Jewish families were ennobled in Hungary in the beginning of the twentieth century for services rendered to the state. For the relationship between Hungarian Jewish scientists, industrialists and ennobled Jews, and an interesting interpretation concerning why so many internationally known scholars came from ennobled Hungarian Jewish families, see William O. McCagg, Jr., <u>Jewish Nobles and Geniuses in Modern Hungary</u>. New York: Columbia University Press, 1972.

[54] For the distribution of the Jews by selected fields of occupation see Végházi, "The Role of the Jews," pp. 73-81.
    The Wodianer, Hatvany-Deutsch, Kornfeld and Manfréd Weisz families were among the dozen or so wealthy industrialists who were instrumental in the development of capitalism in Hungary. They received baronetcies at the end of the nineteenth century. (The rest of the 346 ennobled families did not receive aristocratic titles.) Most of these families have been in Hungary at least a century preceding 1867. Some of the writers were sons of industrialists, e.g. Baron Lajos Hatvany. Most of the writers and journalists came also from long-assimilated families. And the grandfather of Béla Kun, leader of the Communist Revolution of 1919, was a patriot who fought in the War of Independence in 1849. For the origin of the most important ennobled Jewish families, see William O. McCagg, Jr., <u>Jewish Nobles and Geniuses in Modern Hungary</u>. New York: Columbia University Press, 1972. See also, Gyula Mérei, "Szekfű Gyula Történetszemléletének Birálatához" (About the Evaluation of Gyula Szekfű's Historical Views), <u>Századok</u>, XCIV (1960), p. 232. For the family background of Béla Kun, see Rudolf L. Tőkés, "Béla Kun: The Man and the Revolutionary," in Iván Völgyes ed., <u>Hungary in Revolution</u>, 1918-1919. Lincoln: The University of Nebraska Press, 1971, pp. 170-207.

CHAPTER VIII

NATIONALISM AND THE NATIONALITIES: HISTORIOGRAPHY AND THE REVISION OF THE TREATY OF TRIANON

Gyula Szekfü considered the achievement of the Compromise of 1867 and the establishment of the Austro-Hungarian Monarchy the zenith of Hungarian history.[1] But for the short-sighted liberalism of the Hungarian politicians and the obstructionist policies of the Party of Independence, Szekfü believed that the period between 1867 and 1914 could have been the basis of an age of national progress and stability. In one sense, the Dualist period was certainly a high-point of Hungarian history. The power of the Magyars over the non-Magyar nationalities in the Lands of the Crown of St. Stephen was greater and more secure than at any time since 1526. Had the Hungarians been able to achieve such a dominant and secure position a century earlier--before the age of nationalism--the history of Central Europe might have been profoundly and permanently affected. By the second half of the nineteenth century, however, a strongly developed nationalism among the Magyars, Germans, Slavs and Romanians brought about conflicts which could not be easily resolved even if the Hungarian policies were not as short-sighted and unaccommodating as they turned out to be.

It is an interesting commentary on Hungarian historiography that the problem of nationalities did not receive the attention of Hungarian historians until after World War One. This is all the more surprising because nationality conflicts were endemic since the 1830's and the Revolution of 1848 showed the isolation of the Magyars and the need for the co-operation and good will of the non-Magyar population of Hungary. The Nationality Law of 1868 was created in recognition of the importance of a peaceful relationship between the Magyars, Slavs and Romanians. However, this peaceful relationship was not achieved; nationality conflicts became ever more frequent and were carried on on several levels in Dualist Hungary. There were the actual conflicts which took place in non-Magyar populated areas: Slovakia, Transylvania, the Voivodina and Croatia-Slovenia; there were the tumultuous and, sometimes, violent parliamentary debates concerning the nationalities[2] and both the actual conflicts and the debates were endlessly related and often distorted in the press and chauvinistic literature. Very little of this found its way into the Hungarian history books.[3] On the whole, the non-Magyar peoples were ignored by Magyar historians.[4]

According to Hungarian statistics, the combined number of the non-Magyar people in Hungary made up 45.5 per cent of the country's population in the beginning of the twentieth century.[5] In addition to the Magyars, the people of Hungary included Germans, Croatians, Slavonians, Serbs, Romanians,

Slovaks and Ruthenians. The Jews comprised five per cent of the population; they were counted as Magyars, thereby allowing the Hungarians to claim absolute majority--54.5 per cent --in Hungary. With the exception of Croatia, which had a separate constitutional development, the non-Magyar peoples and the areas which they inhabited in compact masses, were considered integral parts of the Hungarian nation.

Szekfü disapproved of the nationality policies of the Dualist Era but, as we shall see, he did not consider them unduly oppressive. He certainly would not have agreed with those historians who held that the Compromise of 1867 was disastrous for the future of the Habsburg Empire and that the nationality policies of Hungary had a major share of responsibility for the dissolution of the Monarchy.[6]

After the Treaty of Trianon removed the nationality areas, an interest in the nationalities arose as a result of the Hungarian efforts for the revision of the borders of Hungary. The most important historical treatments of the non-Magyar nationalities were written by Gyula Szekfü. Magyar Szemle, the journal edited by Szekfü, became an important forum for the discussion of nationality problems.

In Három Nemzedék, written in 1919 before the finality of the Treaty of Trianon, Szekfü dealt with the nationalities only as a subject of controversy between the views of Széchenyi and Kossuth. After Trianon, Szekfü wrote several articles in which he discussed Hungarian nationality as a historical rather than an ethnic development.[7] In 1926, a Fontes publication of the Hungarian Historical Society appeared containing the documents pertaining to the history of Hungarian language laws of the administration from 1790 to 1848. Szekfű edited this volume and provided a 200-page introductory essay.[8]

The most important contribution to the history of nationalities came with the publication of Magyar Történet, a five-volume history of Hungary, written by Bálint Hóman and Gyula Szekfű.[9] The volumes of Magyar Történet were issued at intervals between 1929 and 1932; they are considered the finest achievements of the theory and application of Geistesgeschichte in Hungarian historiography.[10] In spite of its pro-Austrian, nagy-Magyar bias, Magyar Történet is perhaps still the best comprehensive account of Hungarian history from the earliest times to 1914.

There were two major themes in Magyar Történet. The first amounted to a revision of Hungarian history from the Labanc point of view. Because Szekfű considered the Compromise of 1867 the high-point of Hungarian history since 1526, he evaluated historical events, the character of statesmen, the outcome of wars and the wisdom of alliances in accordance with whether or not they hastened or retarded the day when Hungary could live, or could continue to live in harmony with the Habsburgs.[11]

The second major theme of Magyar Történet was the lasting significance which Szekfű assigned to the Turkish occupation of Hungary. "The source of all subsequent misfortunes was the Turkish conquest and nothing else," according to Szekfü.[12] He attributed the nationality conflicts of the nineteenth century and the dismemberment of Hungary following World War One to the demographic changes which took place in Hungary as a result of the 150 years of Turkish presence and its aftermath.

The effect of the Turkish occupation of Hungary received far more emphasis in <u>Magyar Történet</u> than in Szekfü's previous publications. In <u>Der Staat Ungarn</u> (1917), Szekfü stated that the destruction was the result of the war between the Austro-Hungarians and the Turks, especially during the War of Liberation in the seventeenth century. In <u>Magyar Történet</u> (1928), he claimed that by the middle of the sixteenth century the destruction was virtually complete. The Turks made a depopulated desert out of much of the area they occupied, not just the path of the armies. In the wake of the Turks, Southern Slavs entered Hungary in large numbers and, following the Turkish occupation, the depopulated areas and ruined cities were resettled by Germans and Slovaks. Szekfü also blamed the social and economic backwardness of Hungary on the Turks who, it was charged, had interrupted the normal development of the country, destroyed the cities and prevented the rise of new ones.[13]

Szekfü returned to the problem of nationalities in articles written in the 1930's and first published in the periodical Magyar Szemle. These articles were collected and, together with a long essay, "A Nemzetiségi Kérdés Rövid Története," (The Brief History of the Nationality Question) were published in book form under the title of Állam és Nemzet (State and Nation). This volume constituted the first serious treatment of the history of the non-Magyar nationalities in Hungary albeit from the Hungarian point of view. By the time these articles were published a subtle change in Szekfü's views was becoming apparent, but his writings on the problem of nationalities continued to express and justify Hungary's revisionist aspirations. This was not necessarily a conscious design on the part of Szekfü; most likely he sincerely believed, along with the overwhelming majority of his countrymen, that the Lands of the Crown of St. Stephen should rightly belong to Hungary. The idea of St. Stephen's state, together with the concept of the nation-state, made up the theory which provided the justification for revision of the Hungarian borders.[14]

Although the St. Stephen's State idea had changed over the centuries, it remained the basis of Hungarian constitutional law from the eleventh century to the end of World War Two. According to this concept, the Lands of the Crown of St. Stephen constituted a universal, Christian, supranational, centralized state under a king who ruled by divine right over the various nations of his realm, guiding his subjects over the sinful Civitas Terrena toward the

Civitas Dei. As a result of developing feudalism, by the thirteenth century this concept was altered to include the Hungarian Estates, and a decentralized rule emerged in the hands of the nobility. After the extinction of the House of Árpád (1309), during the rule of the Anjou kings the idea of the Holy Crown had developed as a symbol signifying the unity of the king, the state and the estates. This trinity of the components of the St. Stephen's State idea remained the same from the fourteenth century to 1848. During these centuries, the members of the Holy Crown, the Natio Hungarica, were the privileged class, the nobility. With the enactment of the March Laws of 1848, which included the abolishment of feudal privileges and the emancipation of the serfs, theoretically every citizen became a member of the state, possessing equal rights. This liberal theory remained a theory long after 1848, but it was the basis of the new Magyar nation-state idea adopted in the nineteenth century. The new liberal theory did not challenge the validity of the St. Stephen's State idea but coexisted with it. The nation-state was thought to be a Magyar nation-state which was extended to cover the supranational lands of the Crown of St. Stephen.

In 1867, when the makers of the Ausgleich still remembered the disastrous effects of the nationalistic excesses of the Revolution and the War of Independence in 1848-1849, an effort was made to work out a compromise between the cultural and administrative demands of the nationalities and the needs of the "unitary modern nation state." Thus the Nationality Law of 1868 began by stating that "all citizens of Hungary, by virtue of the constitutional Law, form one political nation, the indivisible unitary Hungarian nation, whose each individual citizen, regardless of nationality, shares membership of equal rights."[15] In spite of this preamble, the provisions of the Law insured the nationalities their own elementary and secondary schools, the development of their own ecclesiastic institutions, the use of the language of the native population in the local administration of the counties, districts and villages and the development of their national culture without curtailment.[16]

This law had never been enforced. It infuriated the Magyar superpatriots without satisfying the nationalities. By the 1870's subtle changes in the ideas concerning political equality of the nationalities with the Magyars began to appear. The Hungarian prime minister Kálmán Tisza (1830-1902) stated that "in every multinational state, by the nature of things one of the nationalities has to play a leading role, and its language becomes the language of the state . . ." This leading role is ensured not by law, but by the existing natural factors, such as their "number, level of culture, wealth and . . . past history."[17] A policy of systematic Magyarization ensued through education laws, language requirements in schools and the establishment of Magyar cultural organizations. Extension of central control to the nationality areas and gerrymandering of electoral districts prevented the small number of non-Magyars who possessed electoral rights to use them effectively. Conflicts between the Magyars and the embittered nationalities became more and more frequent.[18]

In <u>Magyar Történet</u> and in his essays in <u>Állam és Nemzet</u> Szekfü put a great deal of emphasis on the historical origin of the nationality problem, but discounted the seriousness of the conflicts of the Dualist period. His first article on the nationality question appeared in 1931, addressing itself to the duty of Hungarian historians to deal with the charge of prewar Magyar oppression of the nationalities of Hungary. Just as the German historians had been turning their attention to the <u>Kriegsschuldfrage</u>, Magyar historians should do research and provide documentary proof that the charge of oppression was false.[19] In a series of articles, all originally appearing in <u>Magyar Szemle</u>, Szekfü reviewed the history of the non-Magyar nationalities in Hungary. In "Kisebbségek a Középkorban" (Minorities in the Middle Ages), he established his thesis in the beginning of the essay:

> The Magyars are considered born oppressors, yet if there is a nation who by origin and development stands against oppression, if there is a people who is the example of the opposite (<u>szoborba kifaragható ellentéte</u>) of an oppressor, that is the Magyar! This the historian can easily demonstrate, and need not be embarrassed by the charge of national bias.[20]

Szekfü substantiated this view by reviewing the relationship of the Magyars and other peoples in their early history.

According to Szekfü, the Magyar treatment of the non-Magyars was based on the nomadic tradition and Christian charity. Nomadic peoples, when conquered or voluntarily joined another, more powerful group, were not integrated with the conquerors but remained within their own tribe, speaking their own language, learning just enough of the language of the conquerors to take military orders. This loose connection between nomadic peoples could be dissolved as rapidly as it was made. When the Magyars were conquered by Bolgars, or Turkic peoples, it meant only that the Magyar leaders had to follow the conqueror's orders. The people themselves were hardly involved. When the larger group settled somewhere temporarily or permanently, the diverse peoples that constituted it remained separate.[21]

When the Magyars settled in the Danube valley in the ninth century, there were Székelys, Pechenegs, Cumanians and other Turkic peoples with them and these were settled in groups in the peripheral areas. A slow, natural process of assimilation had taken place, but even centuries later when the above groups considered themselves Magyar, they kept their own traditions and characteristics. This kind of treatment of the minorities was what the Magyars had learned during their wanderings; they tended to conserve and defend their minorities instead of oppressing them.[22]

The Magyars did not immediately settle down in permanent communities. They were used to animal herding and fishing; they wandered around and mingled with the people they found in the area. There were about 500,000 Magyars, numerically superior to the Slavs they found in the Danubian basin, who did not live in densely populated areas. Hungarian linguists think that the Magyars brought with them a Finno-Ugric servant class who intermarried with the Slavs and all were in time assimilated to the Magyars. This is why there are so many words of Slav origin in the Magyar language, especially those pertaining to Christian religious usage, for the Slavs were already Christian when the Magyars arrived. But the assimilation was not coerced; it was a natural and gradual process and took place only where ever the Slav people lived in thinly inhabited areas of mixed population.[23]

By the year 1000, Hungary had become the medieval Christian Monarchy of St. Stephen, modeled on the Holy Roman Empire, where the king was the just ruler and defender of all his subjects: the diverse nationalities living within his realm. St. Stephen encouraged the settling of foreign individuals and groups as advantageous to the country. Foreigners would be helpful in his efforts to teach the people new skills and develop a settled agricultural Christian society out of a newly converted and still restless tribal nation. As he was a saintly man, Stephen also extended

Christian hospitality to strangers. St. Stephen's famous warning to his son: <u>unius linguae et unius moris regnum imbecille et fragile est</u>, was the basis of his policy and the earliest legacy of the Hungarian view of the non-Magyar peoples in their midst. It was a national advantage to have diverse peoples: the population could learn new, Western military skills and crafts from the foreign knights and artisans; it was also an opportunity to practice the Christian virtues.[24]

In the twelfth century it became customary to give privileges to foreigners which insured their rights to move freely, own a house or land, practice a trade and, if they so desired, to leave. The new-comers were Germans, Italians, French, Walloons and Ishmaelites (a Turkish group of people); they were artisans and traders settling in urban communities. Other Germans, Poles, Ruthenians and Vlachs were agricultural peoples who settled on the land or mountainous areas and they were permitted to wander with their herds. All were allowed to remain within their own group, with their own local administrative autonomy and they were served by their own priests. Special privileges went to groups providing military services. The rights and privileges of the non-Magyars depended on their role in society and paralleled those of the Magyars. There was the possibility for their leaders to become noblemen and for the group to maintain their language and customs. Thus, a group of Frenchmen who

arrived in the twelfth century from Liege and settled in
county Heves still spoke French in the fifteenth century,
constituting a small French island in the Magyar sea. Similarly, the Pechenegs, who came in with the Magyars, lived
together under their own leaders even in the fifteenth
century as an autonomous group while their brethren, who
remained outside of the borders of Hungary, had long been
extinct.[25]

Szekfü considered the Magyar treatment of minority
groups unique in Eastern Europe. North of the Carpathians
bloody struggles and "exterminating racial wars" were constant. First, the Germanic tribes annihilated the old Slav
Prussians, thereby removing the people that served as a
buffer between Germans and Poles who then faced each-other
with blind hatred. Further south a similar struggle took
place between Germans and Czechs and Czechs and Poles. To
stem the German expansion, Poland enacted language laws in
the thirteenth century and jobs for teachers and priests
depended on knowledge of the Polish language. "Compare
that with the Pax Hungarica of the Middle Ages!"[26]

Szekfü attributed the difference between Hungary and
Poland concerning the treatment of foreigners in their midst
to the lack of a feeling of inferiority on the part of the
Magyars. For the basis of the defensive language laws in
medieval Poland was fear. The Magyars had self-confidence;
they feared only God. They did not restrict the rights of

of nationalities. In the thirteenth century, sixteen different nationalities lived in peace in a system devised by the Hungarian genius.[27]

In the Middle Ages, economic and social changes caused a great deal of movement of the agricultural people in Hungary. Magyars moved from the central to the peripheral areas and mingled with Slovaks and Ruthenians who arrived from the North from the other side of the Carpathians; they mingled with Vlachs in the southeastern part of the country. The non-Magyar peoples came voluntarily or ahead of invaders such as the large group of Romanians before the Tatar invasion. Magyars welcomed foreigners especially after the destruction of the Tatars in 1241 and following the epidemic of Black Death in the middle of the fourteenth century; military and economic considerations dictated a policy of repopulation to provide manpower. The Germans in the Szepes (Tatra) area originated at this time as did the settlement of the Transylvanian Saxons.[28]

Little did the Magyar administration understand about the future consequences of the presence of non-Magyars. Most of their actions were the result of their traditional tolerance of alien peoples coupled with military and economic short-term necessities. Even the laws concerning the Jews and the Ishmaelites were religious rather than nationality laws. The Magyars did not have any nationality policies. "The Magyar kings walked among nationality factors as we do among the ultraviolet rays of the sun. These rays are present, they have a certain effect on us, but we are hardly aware of them"[29]

A change in the situation of the non-Magyars of Hungary came about at the end of the fifteenth century, not because a Magyar drive for power created an oppression, but because of the economic and social development in all of Central Europe removed the privileges of small groups and created a change: a vertical stratification of Hungarian society.

The removal of the autonomy of the non-Magyar peoples were closely associated with the political and economic changes which gave rise to the class of lesser nobles. Originally freemen and military *servientes*, they got their patents of nobility in the thirteenth century and rose to be a large and politically powerful landowning class. Aside from a small magnate class, the population of a few cities and this relatively numerous lesser nobility, the rest of the population sank to the status of the *jobbágy*. The leaders of the non-Magyar nationalities, formerly in charge of the administration of their own nationals, themselves became lesser nobles. They intermarried with their Magyar counterparts and, in time, became assimilated to them. On the other hand, the Slav and Romanian *jobbágy*, living in large groups among his own people, retained his national identity. Eventually, while the Magyars could be found in all social classes, the non-Magyar peoples were exclusively in the lowest class, that of the jobbágy or servant.[30]

As a result of the Turkish wars of the fifteenth century, together with a developing money economy and need for grain, there was a manpower shortage in Hungary that resulted in the restriction of the movement of the peasantry and the creation of legal serfdom in 1514. Thus, the formerly autonomous non-Magyar peoples became members of a strict feudal order which no longer provided any special rights to nationalities. Often on the same estates there were serfs of many nationalities who intermingled and became homogenous. Feudal estates provided a melting pot where the serfs became assimilated. This was not deliberate Magyarization but a gradual and natural process.[31]

As in Magyar Történet, in the essay, "The Brief History of the Nationality Question," the significant changes in the nationality problems of Hungary were attributed to the Turkish occupation following the Battle of Mohács in 1526. Here Szekfű went into great detail to describe how these demographic changes came about.

Szekfű estimated that approximately 85 per cent of the population of Hungary was Magyar in the beginning of the sixteenth century.[32] During the period between 1500 and 1711, two contradictory processes changed the make-up of the Hungarian population. The first was the direct destruction of the Hungarian military and the civilian population during the incessant Turkish wars followed by the wars of liberation. The Austrian mercenaries who were in charge of the latter did not distinguish between the Magyars and the Turks during the removal of the Turks from Hungary. The Wars of Liberation were followed by the <u>Kuruc</u> wars and the destruction went on until the Treaty of Szatmár brought peace to Hungary in 1711. "The hard truth was that those who fought in the wars were Magyars. Those who survived were the non-Magyar nationalities."[33]

The second factor that changed the ethnic make-up of Hungary was that the vacuum left by the destroyed or escaped population was filled by new-comers. In the south, the depopulated villages were filled by Serbs who followed in the wake of the Turks. Most of these Serbs were extremely poor, living in tents or cave-like underground shelters; a smaller, more prosperous group of Serbs sold cattle and served as middlemen between Turks and Hungarians. The latter moved into the larger cities and remained there after the Turkish occupation. They were a better educated and culturally advanced Serbians, living in prosperous colonies in the cities. In addition, after 1690, 200,000 Serbians came in with their own church organization under the leadership of the Patriarch of Peć. They were given privileges by Leopold I and they became tools of the Austrian government.[34] Unlike the groups of merchants in the cities, the Serbs who arrived in 1690 were in constant conflict with the Magyars.

At the same time, Croatians came in from Slavonia and penetrated the western border of Hungary all the way to Pozsony. They came either voluntarily or were brought in by Magyar or Croatian nobles who lost their lands in Slavonia or Central Hungary and moved to another of their estates in Transdanubia. The Croatian nobles of Transdanubia became Magyarized, but their jobbágy retained their national identity.[35]

Similarly, Vlachs came in and settled around the Temes area, and continued up north along the edge of the mountains in the wake of Turkish destruction. They came in as shepherds, then settled in depopulated villages. Those who came in from the Principalities of Wallachia and Moldavia found employment on the Transylvanian feudal estates where there was a shortage of farmhands. A constant stream of Romanians came through the Carpathians from the sixteenth to the eighteenth century. "As a result of Magyar losses in defense of the Fatherland and Christianity and nearly 200 years of massive and uninterrupted immigration, the majority of the population of Transylvania became Romanian."[36]

The growth of the Ruthenian (Ukrainian) population was the result of the Fifteen Year's War (1593-1606) and the Kuruc Wars. The Ruthenians found a situation in the Northeastern Highlands similar to that of the Serbs in the south: depopulated and weakened villages and a need of farmhands promoted the immigration of the Ruthenians from across the border.[37]

Even in these difficult times there was very little conflict between the nationalities. As in the Middle Ages, the Magyars continued to respect the spiritual needs of the non-Magyar nationalities. In the Highlands just north of the plains, where many of the Magyars settled after they escaped from their previous, Turk-occupied homes, there was a mixed population living in peace. Magyar, Slovak, or German, each had religious services in their own language. The gymnasium in Pozsony taught all three languages in addition to Latin. The princes of Transylvania provided Romanian schools also; they supported Romanian literature and established the first Romanian printing press. In the Highlands, the Magyar lords allowed the Hussite tradition of using Czech in church services and as a literary language.[38]

There was very little conflict between the Magyar, Slovak and Ruthenians serfs of the feudal estates. They were all loyal to their lords, following them in uprisings and wars.

Only the Germans of the cities acted in a way resembling modern minorities. They were better educated than the rest of the non-Magyars, affected by the Renaissance and humanism and conscious of their nationality. Many became Lutheran, sent their sons to Protestant universities in Germany, yet they called themselves Deutschungar and considered Hungary their fatherland.[39] What caused the conflict between them and the Magyars was that they had special privileges in the cities which they jealously guarded and that they excluded even the Magyar nobles who tried to move into their cities when they escaped from the Turks. This precipitated the first nationality conflicts which were in fact social and economic in nature. In some Transylvanian cities the Saxons managed to keep out the Magyars until Joseph II (1780-1790) ordered them to allow their residence.[40]

The population changes of the sixteenth and seventeenth centuries were extremely significant but they came about as a result of historical events, entirely unplanned. Not so in the eighteenth century. When peace finally came, the Austrian government became aware of the large-scale destruction of the country. This was the age of absolutism and the government in Vienna acted without regard for the interests of the rebellious Magyars. Since the country was liberated by the imperial army, they treated Hungary as their own newly acquired land.

Szekfü explained that the entire process of deliberate colonization by the Austrian government was not so much an anti-Magyar political act as an economic measure to restore Hungary after two centuries of destruction and decline. The action of the government rested on the mercantile philosophy that wealth was based on people who produce, consume and pay taxes; it prompted a comprehensive plan for the economic restoration of Hungary including the systematic recruitment

of German settlers from various parts of Germany. These
were settled on Magyar land, given tax exemption and agricultural equipment; occasionally the government provided
homes in newly built villages with a church and a school in
the center for the new settlers.[41] Unlike the earlier German settlers who came from among the better educated townspeople, the new settlers were simple folk, tillers of the
soil. They were not a homogenous group, but came from many
different German states and spoke different dialects. They
came in single families or small groups, eventually intermarrying and blending into one Swabian people. In time they
became assimilated Hungarians.[42]

The Magyar nobility also contributed to the increase
of the non-Magyar population. When they returned to their
former estates liberated from the Turks, they had a pressing
need for farmworkers to clear the land and bring it into
cultivation once again. Not having enough Magyar jobbágy
to go around, they imported foreign workers. The lords,
especially the Catholic landowners, were more interested in
the religion of their serfs than in their nationality.
"It would be ahistorical to blame them."[43]

The net result of the Turkish occupation and the
Austrian restoration was a radical change in the demography
of Hungary. In 1500, Szekfü claimed that 85 per cent of the
population of Hungary was Magyar. By the time the Turks
left, nearly two hundred years later, the ratio of the Magyars

declined to 45 per cent as a result of destruction and depopulation and the immigration of the Slavs and Romanians. In the century that followed, the settlement of Germans and the importation of Slav and Romanian jobbágy caused a further decline in the ratio of the Magyars: 41 per cent or three and a half million Magyars out of a total population of eight and a half million in the lands of the Crown of St. Stephen by the end of the eighteenth century.[44] It boded ill for the Magyars of the age of nationalism.

Szekfü thought that although Hungary was always a multi-national state the ratio of the Magyars in the Middle Ages was high enough so that, like other countries, it could have become a unitary nation-state in a natural process of assimilation. The Turkish occupation eliminated such a possibility, causing the demographic changes that made the Magyars a minority in their own land. The nationality question of Hungary was the result of circumstances beyond the control of Hungarians. There was no nationality policy of any kind until the 1840's; there were no sins of omission or commission against the nationalities.[45] That the non-Magyars were virtually all in the lowest economic class was not the result of systematic oppression; it was due to the fact that those non-Magyars who received nobility in the preceding centuries usually became Magyarized. "To rise in the social scale is a well-known agent of assimilation."[46]

As Szekfü pointed out, the medieval language laws against the Germans in Poland were enacted out of fear.

Similarly, the first conflicts of nationalism in Hungary were occasioned by the Hungarian language laws, which also rose out of Magyar apprehension in the face of the rising national consciousness of the non-Magyars in the nineteenth century. The age of liberalism was also the age of nationalism and the contradiction between the two ideas were not apparent to most of the nineteenth century Hungarians.

In Három Nemzedék, written in 1919, Szekfü argued that Magyar domination over the nationalities were justified on the basis of historical rights. He found it entirely understandable that nationalism prevailed over liberalism:

> Consider the circumstances. The liberal leaders were at a crossroads. The land was conquered by their ancestors who founded the Hungarian state and defended it with their blood against the Turks, Tatars and Germans; for centuries the culture of this land was Magyar . . . the state even in its Latin phase was Magyar . . . Magyar blood pulsed in all the members of Hungarian political organizations . . . should their descendants' task be the burden of carrying out the liberal principle, to interrupt the continuity of Hungarian history and take the country away from its own sons? If we have the least bit of understanding (méltányosság) and historical sense . . . we could not expect such sacrifices from this liberal generation.[47]

While critical of the Magyarization policy of the liberals, Szekfü explained that the Magyar liberals firmly believed that Magyar education and liberal ideas would turn the Slavs and Romanians into Magyars and solve the nationality problems once and for all. Their policy was an honest mistake and they were astonished to find the strong, adverse reaction on the part of the nationalities.[48]

In Szekfű's view, the nationality policies of Dualist Hungary not only did not benefit the Magyars but they encouraged and aided the nationalities. Slav and Romanian banks and manufacturing companies were created and much of their profits were used to further anti-Magyar political activity. The new Slovak, Serbian and Romanian intellectuals were more independent and economically better off than their Magyar counterparts; they were occupied in the more lucrative professional fields, not in government service like the Magyars. The Magyar state did not oppose the propaganda of the nationalities because their doctrinaire liberal principles were against the restriction of the rights of the people.[49]

In the first of a series of articles about the nationality question in Hungary, written in 1931 and appropriately entitled "Trianon Reviziója és a Történetirás" (Historiography and the Revision of Trianon), Szekfü did not claim that the Magyar policies were not oppressive but that they were no worse than similar policies in Western Europe. In the age of the nation-states--between the French Revolution and World War One in France and England, after 1848 in Hungary--equal rights of individual citizens took the place of the rights of communities and communal organizations. Individual rights superceded the rights of estates and precluded the rights of nationalities. Minority groups everywhere were at a disadvantage.[50]

Szekfü stated that the liberal nation-state everywhere based its laws on the culture of the majority and the members of the minority groups came under the jurisdiction of a strongly centralized, often oppressive state. The Frenchification of the Bretons, Provençals and Italians in France, the Prussification of the Alsatians and Poles in Germany, not to mention the inhumane oppression of the Irish by Great Britain, show that the rights of the nationalities were casualties of the system of the liberal nation-states. "We can refute the charge of oppressing our nationalities by comparison with the European situation in general."[51] The minorities of Hungary were in fact better off than those in Western Europe, Szekfü stated. The problems concerned only the question of language, they did not include social and economic matters as between the Germans and Poles and the Irish and British. The Hungarian administrations did not settle colonies of Magyars on the lands of the nationalities, they did not nationalize industries and banks and the Hungarian government even provided financial support to the Orthodox and Uniate churches. Nowhere in Europe were minorities better treated than in Hungary.[52]

In contrast to the view of nationality prevalent in Europe in the interwar period, Szekfü considered neither the racial nor the ethnic components of a people to be of deciding importance and considered nationality and nationhood a historic creation. Some of his articles dealing with the subject were prompted by an attempt to counter that lowly place that the new "scientific" racial literature assigned to the Magyars of Asiatic origin. Others clearly aimed to show that national self-determination, which was the basis of the territorial decisions of the Treaty of Trianon, did not provide a just and proper means to evaluate the nationality situation of Hungary.

Szekfü saw the modern Hungarian nationality not as a membership in a purely ethnic group but as part of a mixture of varied ethnic components. Just as the Celtic Bretons, Germanic Saxons and the Normans eventually formed a mixture which is the present day British, so, too, the Magyars of today are descendants of the original Finno-Ugric and Turkic people who in the course of a millenium acquired Germanic, Slav, Romanian and Jewish elements.[53] And there was enough intermarriage among the Magyar and non-Magyar peoples of Hungary over the centuries to justify the belief that a considerable number of the Slavs and Romanians of the Lands of St. Stephen were also products of a genetic mix which included Magyar elements. To speak of a Magyar "race" or even a Magyar nationality is merely to speak of the prevalent culture within the Hungarian state. All nations are historical creations and nationality is simply the sum total of those characteristics which makes the masses of individuals into a nation.

Szekfü was convinced that modern nationalism as a basis for the state could not be reconciled with the past and it would be dangerous for the future of Hungary.

> Germans, Frenchmen and Italians can accept a theory which restricts a state to contain but a single nationality. If we, the heirs of the ancient Magyar Kingdom here in the Danubian valley would adopt this point of view, it would be a testament to our decline; we would sell out our future if we gave up that historic Magyar theory of state which protected and allowed to live peacefully so many non-Magyar nationalities along with the Magyar.[54]

Like most Hungarians, Szekfü considered it the first priority of Hungary's foreign policy to achieve the revision of the Treaty of Trianon: the restoration of Hungary's territorial integrity.[55] While he firmly believed that the non-Magyars of Dualist Hungary were not really oppressed, or at least no more oppressed than minorities in other European countries, he differed from most of his countrymen in his view that the relationship between the Magyars and the nationalities, should they ever again be part of the Hungarian state, would have to be radically altered.

There were many Magyars within Hungary with German and Slav sounding names pointing to a non-Magyar ancestor decades, or perhaps centuries, earlier. Szekfü took issue with those who continued the advocation of Magyarization of names within Trianon-Hungary. Szekfü thought this wrong and unwise:

> If we want to be the leading nation in the Danubian basin ever again . . . we will want to have other nationalities join us and we will have to make people with foreign names and foreign nationality feel at home in our country. Magyarization is a proof of the Kismagyar view. If we resign ourselves to a country where there are no other nationalities but the Magyar . . . that is nothing but making the bitter fate of Trianon permanent.[56]

Most of all, Szekfü differed from the majority of his countrymen in his realistic assessment of the situation of the formerly Hungarian areas in the succession states. He understood that never again would the Slavs and Romanians acquiesce living in a state governed by a centralized Magyar administration. Like Kossuth in his exile and Count Mihály Károlyi (1875-1955) and Jászi during World War One, Szekfü came to the conclusion that the nationalities would have to be given administrative autonomy. He justified the change in his view by explaining that, before the war, the nationalities lacked experience; the only politically mature nationality capable of governing was the Magyar. With the experience gained in the succession states, the nationalities had grown to the maturity necessary for self-government. When the revision of the Treaty of Trianon restored the nationality areas to Hungary, the Magyars would only be primus inter pares.[57]

That the nationality problem masked an underlying socio-economic conflict in addition to the overt cultural one either went unrecognized or it was tacitly ignored by

Hungarian historians before 1945.[58] As Szekfű explained, those non-Magyars who received nobility became Magyarized, while the peasantry retained its Slav or Romanian identity. By the nineteenth century, the overwhelming majority of the non-Magyars of St. Stephen's State were at the bottom of the socio-economic scale and the driving forces behind the nationality struggle included demands for social and economic betterment as well as political rights. On the other hand, a contributing cause of the suppresion of the nationalities was the Magyar gentry's fear of losing their dominant position not only in the nationality areas but in the Magyar speaking areas as well. Since the gentry made its livelyhood by officialdom, the socio-economic factor was as important in their case as was the political. "Keeping the non-Magyar nationalities disenfranchised, as well as keeping the Hungarian peasants and workers off the voting rolls, seemed to be the only way to maintain the status quo and to secure the suppremacy of the nobility."[59] At the same time, a genuine fear that democratization would lead to the dominance of the nationalities over the Magyars was also present in an ethnic group which felt itself isolated and outnumbered. This fear was manipulated and used to frighten and to distract the dissatisfied masses of people. Thus "the democratic progress of Hungary was retarded greatly by the unsolved problem of integrating the other nationalities."

Neither Szekfű nor any other historian writing about the nationality question between the two world wars addressed themselves to the socio-economic side of the nationality conflicts. However, significant changes occurred in the thinking of a few intellectuals and politicians concerning the political rights of the nationalities. In the interest of the revision of the Trianon borders the nation-state idea was abandoned and the Lands of the Holy Crown of St. Stephen was to be revived as a union of federated, autonomous states. As former Prime Minister Bethlen explained in 1937:

> The realm of St. Stephen's State can be resurrected again; however, it will not be the unitary Magyar nation-state . . . using a unitary language . . . /it will be/ an arrangement of federalism and local privileges which will reduce the antagonism among the nationalities to a minimum. This new arrangement will restore the political, geographic and cultural-historical unity of the Danubian area within the Carpathian range although not the way our aging Magyar generation imagined it in their youth, . . . but the way St. Stephen established it centuries ago, giving each nationality its own rights, keeping them together and providing defense for all against the more powerful neighbors . . . respecting the national rights and needs of each nationality.[61]

Szekfü continued to believe in the idea of St. Stephen's State, both in the religious and the constitutional sense. In his view, Hungary was, and always meant to be, a multinational state; its population was the result of one-thousand years of turbulent history. Though not all Magyars, they were all Hungarians: children of the Lands of the Holy Crown of St. Stephen, possessing a similar genetic mixture, created by the same history. Szekfü's views were very much in tune with the revisionist theories voiced abroad by such Magyar spokesmen as Count István Bethlen.

FOOTNOTES

[1] Gyula Szekfü, Három Nemzedék és ami Utána Következik (Three Generations and What Comes After). Budapest: Királyi Magyar Egyetemi Nyomda, 1938, p. 198.

[2] Although 45.5 per cent of the population of Hungary belonged to a Slav or Romanian nationality, only 20 out of 413 members of the House of Representatives were non-Magyars. Zoltán Horváth, "The Rise of Nationalism and the Nationality Problem in Hungary in the Last Decade of Dualism," Acta Historica, IX (1963), p. 19.

[3] The most important primary reference materials pertaining to the nationality question of the Dualist period have been made available since 1952. They contain documents, parliamentary speeches, records of meetings, nationality demands and newspaper articles. Gábor G. Kemény, ed., Iratok a Magyar Nemzetiségi Kérdés Történetéhez, 4 vols. Budapest: Tankönyvkiadó, 1952-1968.
Three noteworthy monographs were published on the nationality question before 1925. Lajos Steier, A Tót Nemzetiségi Mozgalom Története (History of the Slovak Nationality Movement), Liptószentmiklós, 1912; Benedek Jancsó, A Román Irredentista Mozgalom Története (The History of the Romanian Irredentist Movement). Budapest, 1920 and József Bajza, A Magyar-Horvát Unió Felbomlása (The Dissolution of the Croatian-Magyar Union). Budapest, 1925. "Steier, Jancsó and Bajza provide a window through which we can view the enemy camp," said Szekfü in 1952. Bálint Hóman and Gyula Szekfü, Magyar Történet (Hungarian History). Budapest: Királyi Magyar Egyetemi Nyomda, V, p. 647.

[4] One reason may be that Hungarian history written before the First World War was, on the whole, the history of the nobility. Very little was written about the peasants, whether Magyars, Slavs or Romanians, and almost all the non-Magyar population belonged to the peasantry.

[5] Hóman-Szekfü, Magyar Történet, V, p. 684.

[6] Hans Kohn stated that in the Compromise of 1867 the aspirations of the still loyal Czechs, Slovaks, Croats, Serbs and Romanians were sacrificed because the Magyar ruling class became dominant not only in Hungary but throughout

Austria-Hungary. "The Compromise was a blow not only to federalism but to equality and democracy." Hans Kohn, "The Viability of the Habsburg Monarchy," Slavic Review, XXII (1963), p. 38.

[7] Gyula Szekfű, "A Faji Kérdés és a Magyarság" (The Racial Question and the Magyars) and "Fajbiológia vagy Történeti Egység" (Racial Biology or Historical Unity), in Történetpolitikai Tanulmányok (Historical-Political Studies). Budapest: Magyar Irodalmi Társaság, 1924.

[8] Gyula Szekfű, Iratok a Magyar Államnyelv Kérdésének Történetéhez (Documents Pertaining to the History of the Question of the Magyar Language of the State). Budapest: A Magyar Történelmi Társulat Kiadása, 1926.

[9] Bálint Hóman, who wrote the first two volumes, was a university professor of medieval history at the time of the writing of Magyar Történet. He became a minister of culture in the 1930's. For his role in Hungarian politics during the Second World War he was tried and condemned to life imprisonment in 1946 as a Nazi collaborator. He died in prison in 1953. Eugene Lévai, "The War Crime Trials Relating to Hungary," Hungarian Jewish Studies, II (1969), p. 275.

[10] László Németh, one of the major novelists and playwrights of twentieth-century Hungary, called Magyar Történet one of the most important and lasting cultural achievements of the interwar period. László Németh, Gyula Szekfű, Budapest: Bólyai Akadémia, 1940, p. 64.

[11] One feature of the Labanc point of view in Hungarian history was that it minimized the historical importance of Transylvania; it viewed the Princes of Transylvania more as feudal lords reigning jealously over their demesne than trying to preserve an independent Magyar state. Szekfű saw the suzerainty of the Turks over Transylvania as a humiliating historical episode and the willingness of the Princes to make alliances with the Ottoman Porte against the Habsburgs was a proof of their lack of scruples. The historical mission of the Magyar nation was to serve as a bulwark against the barbarian East, and this concept could not be reconciled with the cooperation with the Turks. Hungary could perform this mission only as long as it remained part of the West under the Habsburg kings. Hóman-Szekfű, Magyar Történet, III, pp. 101-168.

[12] Ibid., III, p. 499.

[13] Much of the interpretation of the results of the Turkish occupation is contrary to those of some other historians. Until the decline of the Ottoman power and the sale of the offices of the administration and tax collection, the Magyar peasants were no more--and possibly less--oppressed than under Magyar rule. Németh, Szekfü, p. 81. See also Erik Molnár, et al. eds., Magyarország Története. Budapest: Gondolat Kiadó, 1967, I, pp. 182-196.

It can also be argued that the social and economic backwardness of Hungary was due to factors which predated the Turkish occupation. It was during the two centuries preceding Mohács that the political and economic path of Hungary veered from that of the West. While the rising bourgeoisie allied itself with the rulers against the nobility in Western Europe, the foreign kings in Hungary gave increasing privileges to the nobility in order to gain the throne. Thus, feudalism in Hungary became stronger at the time when it was breaking up in the West. Irene R. Epstein, "The Hungarian Peasant Revolution of 1514." Unpublished.

[14] Tibor Joó, Magyar Nacionalizmus. Budapest: Athaneaum Részvénytársaság, 1941, contains a cogent description of the St. Stephen's State idea. See also Szekfü's essay, "A Szentistváni Állam" (St. Stephen's State) in Állam és Nemzet (State and Nation). Budapest: A Magyar Szemle Társaság, 1942, which was originally written for a Catholic publication and it puts the emphasis on the moral and religious aspects of the Holy Crown.

[15] Kemény, Iratok, I, p. 125.

[16] Ibid., pp. 125-129.

[17] Cited in Zoltán I. Tóth, "A Nemzetiségi Kérdés a Dualizmus Korában" (The Nationality Question in the Age of Dualism, Századok, XCI (1956), p. 380.

[18] For the nationality conflicts in Dualist Hungary, see the volumes of Kemény's Iratok. See also Zoltán Horváth, "The Rise of Nationalism and the Nationality conflicts in Hungary," Acta Historica, IX (1963), pp. 1-38.

[19] Gyula Szekfü, "Trianon Reviziója és a Történetirás" (The Revision of Trianon and Historiography), in Állam és Nemzet, p. 181.

[20]Gyula Szekfű, "Kisebbségek a Középkorban" (Minorities in the Middle Ages), Ibid., p. 42.

[21]Ibid., p. 45.

[22]Ibid., p. 46.

[23]Gyula Szekfű, "A Nemzetiségi Kérdés Rövid Története" (The Short History of the Nationality Question), Ibid., pp. 96-98.

[24]Szekfű, "Kisebbségek a Középkorban" (Minorities in the Middle Ages), Állam és Nemzet, pp. 46-67.

[25]Ibid., pp. 50-51.

[26]Ibid., p. 52.

[27]Szekfű, "Népek egymás közt a Középkorban" (Ethnic relationships in the Middle Ages), Állam és Nemzet, p. 82.

[28]Szekfű, "A Nemzetiségi Kérdés Rövid Története" (The Short History of the Nationality Question), Állam és Nemzet, p. 100.

[29]Ibid., p. 110.

[30]Ibid., pp. 106-107. See also István Szabó, Tanulmányok a Magyar Parasztság Történetéből (Studies in the History of Hungarian Peasantry), Budapest, 1948 and Gyula Szekfű, Serviensek és Familiárisok, Budapest, 1912.

[31]Szekfű, "Nemzetiségi Kérdés," Állam és Nemzet, p. 107.

[32]Ibid., p. 109.

[33]Ibid., p. 115.

[34]Ibid., p. 120. The number of Serbs who entered Hungary in 1690 are given as 200,000 in Hungarian history books. Jászi cites 40,000 families, while Stavrianos puts the total number as "some thirty thousand." Oscar Jászi, The Dissolution of the Monarchy. Chicago: The University of Chicago Press, 1961, p. 403. L. S. Stavrianos, The Balkans Since 1453. New York: Rinehardt and Co., Inc., 1958, p. 234.

[35] Ibid. The Zrinyi family provide the best examples of the Magyarized Croatian noblemen. Their members included one of the most famous military heroes of the sixteenth century and one of the earliest Hungarian poets who wrote in the Magyar (rather than Latin) language.

[36] Ibid., p. 122. Szekfü did not explain what defending Christianity had to do with the Transylvanian nobles who welcomed Romanian farmhands while living in peace under Turkish protection. In fact, the only war and distruction in Transylvania occurred in the fighting between the imperial army and the Magyars or between opposing Magyar camps: the Kuruc and the Labanc.

[37] Ibid., p. 122.

[38] Ibid., p. 125.

[39] Ibid., p. 126.

[40] Ibid., p. 127.

[41] Ibid., p. 143. A village of German origin still differs from the long street-like Magyar village because it was planned and built on a German model for the settlers of the eighteenth century.

[42] Ibid.

[43] Ibid., p. 134.

[44] Ibid., p. 145. László Németh takes issue with Szekfü on the decline of the ratio of Magyars: no more than a ten per cent decline was due to the Turkish occupation in his view. More important were the anti-Magyar policies of Austria, the German settlements and Kuruc wars. The proportion of the Magyars to the rest of the population in 1500 was lower than 85 per cent and at the end of the eighteenth century it was not 41 per cent but about 35 per cent, according to Nemeth. In his view--the Kuruc view of Magyar history --the chief enemies of the Magyars were the Austrians. László Németh, Gyula Szekfü. Budapest, 1940, pp. 80-81.

[45] Szekfü, "Nemzetiségi Kérdés," Állam és Nemzet, p. 150.

⁴⁶Ibid., p. 98. A similar view less elegantly expressed was behind the Magyarizing policy of closing the Slovak gymnazia at the end of the nineteenth century: "The secondary school is like a big engine which takes in hundreds of Slovak youths at one end who come out at the other end as Magyars." Kemény, Iratok, I, p. 674.

⁴⁷Szekfü, Három Nemzedék, pp. 110-111.

⁴⁸Ibid., p. 121.

⁴⁹Ibid., p. 123. Some years later, however, Szekfü wrote that the non-Magyars took advantage of the almost unlimited freedom of the press, seizing upon and exaggerating the smallest misunderstandings, or mistaken policies. When they went too far in expressing anti-Magyar sentiments, the punishment was "merely a prison sentence" where they were decently treated. Untalented publicists and politicians gained an advantage in increased prestige for having been in prison, and the nationalities gained the sympathy and support of European public opinion. Szekfü, "Nemzetiségi Kérdés," in Állam és Nemzet, p. 167.

⁵⁰Szekfü, "Trianon Reviziója," Ibid., p. 186.

⁵¹Ibid., p. 187.

⁵²Ibid.

⁵³Szekfü, "A Faji Kérdés," Történetpolitikai Tanulmányok, p. 73.

⁵⁴Szekfü, "Népiség, Nemzet, Állam" (Ethnicity, Nation, State), Állam és Nemzet, p. 210.

⁵⁵Szekfü, Három Nemzedék és ami Utána Következik, p. 390. This was written in 1933, in an addition entitled "Trianon Óta" (Since Trianon), included in the third edition of Három Nemzedék. The new edition assumed a slightly changed title: Three Generations and What Comes After.

⁵⁶Ibid., p. 398.

⁵⁷Ibid., p. 393. Szekfü's ideas on the relationship between Magyars and nationalities differed from the pre-World War One nationalists in that he wanted Magyar dominance to be

on the basis of genuine moral superiority rather than on political basis. Lajos Gogolák, "Nemzetpolitika" (National politics), Magyar Szemle, XLIV (1943), p. 247.

[58] Oscar Jászi and the Bourgeois Radicals recognized the connection between the socio-economic factors and the nationality conflicts, but their opinions and proposals for reforms were not taken seriously by either the politicians or the historians.

[59] Joseph Held, "The Heritage of the Past: Hungary Before World War I," in Iván Völgyes, ed., Hungary in Revolutions, 1918-19. Lincoln: The University of Nebraska Press, 1971, p. 7.

[60] Ibid.

[61] Count István Bethlen, "Szent István Napján" (On St. Stephen's Day) Pesti Napló, August 20, 1937. Cited in Lóránt Tilkovszky, Revizió és Nemzetiségpolitika Magyarországon (Revision and Nationality Policies in Hungary). Budapest: Akadémiai Kiadó, 1967, pp. 324-325.

PART THREE

THE REALIST SZEKFŰ: 1933-1955

FROM ST. STEPHEN'S STATE TO THE
HUNGARIAN PEOPLE'S REPUBLIC

CHAPTER IX

THE FIRST DOUBTS: AFTER THREE GENERATIONS

In 1933, Gyula Szekfü was at the height of his career. The fifty year old historian was a professor of modern Hungarian history at the University of Budapest, editor of the establishmentarian Magyar Szemle (Hungarian Review), a highly respected influential author and intellectual leader and a friend and associate of Count István Bethlen, the former prime minister of Hungary. To his contemporaries he must have appeared as the pillar of Hungarian establishment. Yet by the early 1930's, Szekfü perceived that the edifice of the Hungarian state needed more than support; there was a necessity for parts of it to be torn down and rebuilt.[1] The "Christian National State" of the 1920's was not equipped to cope with the economic and social problems of the 1930's and the "Christian National Society," so closely associated with Szekfü's Három Nemzedék (Three Generations), was particularly vulnerable to Nazi German influences. This was especially true when, after ten years of the relatively stable Bethlen regime, followed by the short-lived government of Count Gyula Károlyi (1871-1947), a new breed of political leaders, personified by Gyula Gömbös (1886-1936), achieved power. For Bethlen and Károlyi were traditional conservatives with the respect of their class for constitutional liberty, devoted, at least, to the form of parliamentarianism. Gömbös, on the other hand, was the representative of the pro-Nazi elements of the Hungarian military who despised the liberal traditions and appointed army officers to important government posts. He also introduced politics into the army. Henceforth, the Hungarian government and Hungarian society moved steadily to the Right of the political spectrum.[2]

By 1933, Szekfü realized that the Christian National slogans he helped formulate achieved the opposite effect intended and there was little likelihood that the discredited liberalism would give way to an age of Széchenyiesque conservative reform. Szekfü prepared a long addition to Három Nemzedék, due to be published in its third edition in 1934. In this section, entitled "Trianon Óta" (Since Trianon), he assessed the previous decade, sorted out the problems and suggested some solutions.

Szekfü called the period since the end of World War One the age of neo-Baroque. The decade of the 1920's seemed to him to be characterized by the slavish copying of the form of the eighteenth century in architecture, in behavior, and in mode of thinking. Reaction to the Revolutions of 1918-1919 manifested itself in turning away from the interests, needs and problems of the ordinary people to the concerns of the gentlemanly lifestyle.[3] Szekfü attributed this to the continuing influence of the gentry who retained their prestige even when they lost their wealth and much of their traditions.

One of the changes in the society of postwar Hungary occurred as a result of a greatly enlarged class of gentry. The "gentlemanly" (úri) class was no longer a closed estate consisting of the untitled nobility. Any middle-class (non-Jewish) Hungarian could, and often did, affect the airs of the gentry. This class increased both in absolute number and in proportion of the population for yet another reason. The gentry and pseudo-gentry who held the state and county offices in the non-Magyar areas of prewar Hungary lost their jobs in the succession states and elected to move to Trianon Hungary. The greatly enlarged civil service had difficulty accommodating them and their younger members often waited for years to get a job. In such a society the youth could not successfully challenge their elders; they were willing to adjust to the ways of the older generation, because getting a job depended on their relationship with older members of their families or friends.[4] For this reason, the characteristic of the neo-Baroque society was its extreme respect for authority (tekintélytisztelet). In the eighteenth century Age of Baroque the principle of authority was associated with religious and political leadership and power. Landowners had jurisdiction over large areas and population; lords and bishops built cities, established and maintained public works, such as hospitals and schools and supported artists. Neither the power nor the willingness for such acts could be found in the twentieth century even among the wealthiest aristocrats. And the pseudo-gentry lacked the tradition of public service. The authority of the neo-Baroque was based on form not on substance.[5]

In Trianon Hungary, civil servants on all levels and anyone possessing a political or cultural role in society was automatically looked upon as a person of prestige. This resulted in a complicated system of authority. The average person had difficulty knowing the many titles and modes of address, therefore, he tended to pay exaggerated respect. As a result, there was little open criticism for fear of saying or doing anything which would put obstacles in the path of social or economic success. It resulted in a willingness to conform, a voluntary curtailment of intellectual independence. Even humor and irony were rarely found in the literature of the 1920's.[6]

Szekfü may have been an overly severe critic. He certainly disregarded the thriving cultural life of the decade. The conformity of the "gentroid youth" waiting for job openings in officialdom and the servility of the petite bourgeoisie was one aspect of life in the 1920's. But it coexisted with an intellectual brilliance manifested by such writers and poets as Mihály Babits (1883-1941), Zsigmond Móritz (1879-1942) and, at the end of the decade, Attila

József (1905-1937), to mention only the most important of
them. Móricz, possibly the finest novelist in the history of
Hungarian literature, published a novel in each year of the
1920's. Béla Bartók (1881-1945) and Zoltán Kodály (1882-
1967) were at the height of their achievement as composers
and musical critics. The fine arts also flourished. Even in
architecture, while the neo-Baroque was the reigning style in
public buildings, the influences of the Bauhaus style of functionalism could also be found in the designs and furnishings
of the private homes of the rich.[7]

Yet Szekfü captured the tone and the essential mood
of the period between the signing of the Treaty of Trianon
in 1920 and the beginning of the Gömbös regime in 1932. His
term of neo-Baroque was an apt one. For this society was
based on class and authority which was not rooted in real
wealth and power. The servility which it engendered was accompanied by resentment instead of respect. Knowing one's
place did not result in a feeling of community with one's
fellows because there was just enough upward mobility to
make it possible to renounce one's lowly origins. The servility toward those above one's status was balanced by the contempt and abuse of those below.[8] The order and stability,
even a measure of well-being of the Bethlen years, was an
overlay covering a great deal of frustration, uncertainty
and a multitude of unsolved social and economic problems.
In "Trianon Óta," Szekfü removed the neo-Baroque veil from

the ailing body social and politic and examined the underlying problems.

The most important economic and social problems concerned the system of land ownership and the peasantry and the question of capitalism and the Jews.

In understanding the problem of the agrarian people Szekfü was indebted to a new breed of young Hungarian men of letters, generally referred to as Populist writers or Village Explorers. The Populist movement was both a political and a literary movement concentrating on the condition of the peasantry and advocating land reforms. Among the Populist writers there were poets, novelists, sociologists and agronomists. Politically they ranged from crypto-Communist to crypto-Fascist, the majority of them advocating a "third way" with a nationalistic, Populist flavor. The characteristic literary manifestation of this movement was the essay based on first-hand exploration of the wretched rural conditions and on careful, accurate and scholarly research into every aspect of the life of the peasantry.[9] Szekfü gave many of these young writers a forum by publishing their articles in <u>Magyar Szemle</u>. Thus, he helped disseminate their ideas and familiarize a large and influential segment of the intellectuals of Hungary with the plight of the people.[10] And Szekfü had drawn upon these articles in his discussion of the rural problem in "Trianon Óta."

With characteristic thoroughness Szekfü presented ample statistics to show that, in spite of the counterrevolutionary rhetoric and the promise of land reform, the actual change in the ownership of the land was negligible. Protection of the peasantry was one of the neo-Baroque slogans without much substance. The number of dwarf-holders (owners of five <u>holds</u> or less) increased slightly, so that the owners of such areas now cultivated ten per cent of the land instead of the previous 9.1 per cent; at the same time, the area cultivated by landowners owning more than a thousand <u>holds</u>, while decreasing somewhat in proportion, actually increased. In an agricultural country with a total population of less than eight million, a million and a half of the peasantry owned no land at all, and another million possessed too little land to support their families. Together with the several hundred thousand estate servants who lost their jobs as a result of the agrarian crisis and the limited land reform, there were nearly three million unemployed or severely underemployed people living in extreme poverty, lacking adequate food, fuel and housing.[11] "In 1830," Szekfü wrote, "István Széchenyi was agitated over the fate and 'human dignity' of the <u>jobbágy</u> . . . their human dignity is as imperiled today as it was a hundred years ago."[12]

In contrast with the aristocrats, who had intermarried for centuries with people of foreign blood, and the middle class, who had done the same for the past one hundred years, the poverty stricken peasantry was almost entirely of pure Magyar extraction. Therefore, Szekfű viewed the protection of the peasants as the protection of the future: the very survival of the Hungarian people.

> To save the agricultural working class, to raise them to human dignity is perhaps our only great national task . . . . If we succeed . . . we can become once again a vital, healthy, brave and independent nation. We shall possess a self-sufficient material and spiritual armor once we have this broad layer of support for our national life.[13]

Szekfű speculated on specific measures to provide relief for the hardship of the peasants. The logical alternative of absorbing the agricultural surplus population in industry was impractical because industrial development itself was affected by the depression. Therefore, he suggested that the limited social security developed during the Bethlen regime should be extended to cover the peasantry. He thought it shameful that an agrarian country enacted a law of social insurance but excluded the agrarian population from its coverage.[14]

Szekfű used the articles of the Populist writers to disprove the claim made by the opponents of land reform that large landholdings were more efficient both in quantity and quality of production and that dividing the land would result in an economic disaster. Statistics showed the opposite to be true.[15] Szekfű considered land reform to be imperative and urgent. He argued with passion: "Nothing could be more important in the life of the nation than the existence of the people themselves . . . . For the good of the entire nation . . . it is our duty to provide work for the unemployed . . ."[16] The historian referred to Pope Pius XI who recognized the right of the state to control and limit property and invoked the emphasis of the Church on the social responsibilities of the owners of wealth. The state even had a moral right (<u>vallásban gyökerező etika</u>) to nationalize privately owned wealth when private ownership imperiled the common weal, according to Szekfü.[17] By 1933, Szekfü was clearly convinced that only a thoroughgoing land reform would solve the dire social and economic problems of the nation.

Solving the problems of the peasantry by reforming the landholding system was of the first priority in bringing about a desired social and economic change. This was the most important new idea in Szekfü's writing in the beginning of the third phase of his career. When he turned to the "Jewish problem," he expressed no significant change of his previously held views.

According to Szekfü, the role of the Jews in Hungarian economic and intellectual life continued to occupy a large part in Hungary's postwar problems. Circumstances had changed, some of the old problems had given way to new ones, but the possibility of a new solution had also appeared on the horizon. In reviewing the situation, Szekfü saw two interrelated problems. One was the "alien" Budapest culture which developed in the quarter of a century preceding World War I. In 1933, he noted with satisfaction that the influence of the Jews was checked. After the war and the revolutions, Socialism was discredited and its influence was limited to the Trade Unions. Radical democracy as a threat to the political order was eliminated and its reappearance was prevented by the evil campaign Oscar Jászi continued to wage in exile, publishing his anti-Hungarian books and articles abroad.[18]

But while the new Christian spirit succeeded in reducing Jewish intellectual influence, its success was limited. Szinházi Élet (Life in the Theatre) was still the most popular periodical; theatre, night life and other types of popular culture still reflected Jewish taste. For the new Christian spirit was a political orientation rather than a moral and religious one, and the new slogans, besides expressing anti-Semitism, did not offer anything to take the place of the Budapest culture. Szekfű blamed the surviving spirit of the "third generation" for this turn of events. Frightened by the revolutions, these previously liberal members of the upper class changed direction and became anti-liberal. The Christian slogans and anti-Semitism became a political method rather than an honest reappraisal leading to a spiritual change. Thus, the big-city Jewish culture continued, albeit in a somewhat subdued form and coexisted with the neo-Baroque.[19]

The other, and perhaps more important Jewish problem, was the continuing economic role of the Jews. The law of the <u>Numerus Clausus</u> put a quota on the Jews allowed to study at Hungarian universities and prevented the Jewish intelligentsia from choosing a career which required a university education. Civil service, teaching (except in Jewish schools) and the military were closed to them. "Our Jews did not take advantage of the vent provided by Zionism," Szekfü lamented.[20] Those who in previous decades would have entered intellectual fields, now turned to capitalism also.

Because of political and cultural factors, it seemed that in the middle class, all the people on fixed incomes, working as state or local officers, were Christians and the people in business, or employed by business, were Jews. This situation worked well during the Bethlen years when there was a certain amount of prosperity among all the people of Hungary. When the world crisis came, all were affected but, according to Szekfü, people on fixed income suffered more economic hardship than those in business.[21]

Szekfü explained the re-occurrence of overt anti-Semitism by the relative economic disadvantages of those on fixed income compared to the Jews during the depression. The frustration of unemployed, non-Jewish, intellectuals and the extreme poverty of the rural agrarian masses, together with the reduced circumstances of the civil servants, explained the rising success of racialist rhetoric in reviving anti-Semitism. Szekfű noted that many people were receptive to such proposals as the creation of Storm Troops because they were told that the jobs taken away from the Jews in the Third Reich were given to Stormtroopers.[22]

But even disregarding the effect of the depression, the fact that capitalism in Hungary was entirely in Jewish hands was just as dangerous as that of the ownership of forty per cent of the land by two thousand people:

> Like the latifundia, the capitalistic enterprises and means of production are among those national assets of the country which in private hands under certain circumstances become too large and powerful and constitute a danger for the public interest.[23]

Szekfű believed that the age of capitalism was passing. He saw the world-wide economic dislocations as the first stage in the transformation of capitalism and, therefore, did not expect that the depression would be temporary. He apparently saw the rising anti-Jewish measures of Nazi Germany as closely related to the demise of capitalism:

> The Hitler movement is powered by a single but enormous motor: antisemitism; but behind it is an economic phenomenon: the breaking up of capitalism.[23]

Szekfű expected that capitalism everywhere would give way to another form of economy within a few decades. In the meantime, he thought it was in the interest of the Jews themselves that Magyars should take part in every facet of capitalism.

But if large numbers of Jews gave up their jobs in business in order to accommodate Magyars, the law of <u>Numerus Clausus</u> prevented them from attending universities and entering professions, and they could not obtain jobs as officials, what would the unemployed Jews do to make a living? Szekfü suggested a solution: The Jews of Hungary should become Zionists and emigrate to Palestine.

> Since the war . . . Jews discovered their own national feeling . . . they are no longer required to sacrifice their inherited personality and assimilate in the western "Galuth." The pioneers of Zionism from everywhere are flooding to the Jewish land, which has its own language, its science, university, libraries, economic and human potentials . . . . There are possibilities for the Jews of Hungary in Zionism and, until the resettlement, they could be organized into a minority group . . . .
>
> If the Jews would adopt this logical point of view, the Jewish culture of Budapest would be much less significant . . . and the relationship between the Magyars and the truly Magyarized Jews who would elect to remain in the Christian country could be a peaceful one.[35]

However, the Hungarian Jews did not share Szekfü's enthusiasm for Zionism. For nearly a hundred years they were counted as Magyars; an overwhelming majority of them knew no other language but Hungarian and thought of themselves not as a national but as a religious group. The Jews considered the discriminations against them the manifestation of a a religious rather than a racial antipathy. This was the first time that a Hungarian of intellectual stature called upon them to organize themselves as an ethnic minority. The juxtaposition of Magyar and Jew as opposites seemed strange to them, although they readily understood the conflict between Christian and Jew.[26]

In addition to the unsolved domestic problems, Szekfü also discussed the changes and problems in Hungary's international relations. Less than a year after Hitler came to power in Germany, Szekfü saw clearly that Hungary faced a new international danger. He watched the developments in Germany with interest, but until 1933, had not expressed any definite opinion about National Socialism. Szekfü's changed view of Hungary's relationship to Germany was revealed from what he did not say. For example, the phrase of "Christian-German cultural community" did not appear in the new section of Három Nemzedék. Nor did Szekfü approve of political ideas based on racial purity. He did not oppose natural and unforced assimilation, except for the Jews whom he considered incapable of total assimilation into another nationality.[27] He was uneasy also about the anti-religious nature of National Socialism; he saw the movement as the "dethroning of Christian ethics." He had reservations about a totalitarian political system, nevertheless, he examined it from a position of neutrality.

> The new nationalism . . . substitutes dictatorship for liberal democracy, but it is only a one-man rule to the outside world, within the country it is based on collective forces. These forces rise out of the party structure which in turn have a democratic origin . . . . Without the approval of a wide segment of the population . . . neither the Italian nor the German dictatorship . . . could remain in power . . . . The new nationalism can be considered the first attempt of the realization /of the French revolutionary concept/ of equality. It is immaterial that this realization of equality is done by an impersonal, involuntary and brutally oppressive method; nevertheless, the interest of the masses of the people is paramount.[28]

Szekfű explained that, in the National Socialist states, the idea of equality was further developed into the collectivity of the nation. Individual will was considered archaic and evil; its place was taken by the concept of Volkgemeinschaft. Everyone belonged to this community and only those who were unwilling to subordinate themselves to the collectivity were excluded.[29]

But Szekfű also noted that a society based on force and lacking humanistic and moral ideals presented a danger for the international community. He viewed a totalitarian state based on a Machiavellian raison d'état and self-interest as far more dangerous than the old dynastic absolute states or parliamentary liberal governments based on similar principles. For the totalitarian state had the total support --voluntary or forced--of its people. In such a state the individuals were like parts of a machine, carrying out the functions of the national collectivity.[30]

With a prophetic accuracy and with his legendary pessimism, Szekfű looked to a bleak future:

> We know that the principle of the European balance of power caused a great deal of bloodshed since the sixteenth century, but without it the three centuries would have been <u>bellum omnium contra omnes</u>; like highway robbers of old, the armed nations would have slain the unarmed, the strong would have overpowered the weak. It was due to the balance of power, maintained by the likes of the Holy Alliance and the Triple Alliance . . . that nations of varying size and power could exist side by side in Europe. Such a power-grouping which would shelter the small nations today seems neither permanent nor effective. If the alliance of the "victors" continues to disintegrate, the naked self interest of the totalitarian states will be the integrating principle of the new Europe . . . the big fish will devour the small ones.[31]

Just in case this theoretical discussion of the new danger from a previously unforeseen source was not clear enough, Szekfű became more specific:

> If Austria and perhaps Czechoslovakia melt into the sea of the German nation in accordance with the <u>Reichsidee</u> of Hitler, our situation would be the same as if nineteenth-century Russia succeeded in occupying Galicia, Bukovina and the Romanian Principalities and, as an immediate neighbor, interfered in our domestic affairs by manipulating our Slav nationalities. The difference is that Hungary was large and strong then, and behind it was the support of a powerful Monarchy, while today we are a small nation supported by no one.[32]

Yet if Szekfű saw the problem clearly, the solution he offered was pitifully inadequate. Once again he warned against the danger of the <u>kismagyar</u> way, the emphasis of

the purely Magyar, the aping of the Volk ideas of Germany.
He offered instead the nagymagyar idea which would provide
all people, of whatever origin, the rights of citizenship.
He considered the first priority of national purpose the
working toward the revision of Trianon through international
forums so that Hungary might become a larger, more populous
and, presumably, stronger state. He called for far reaching
reforms concerning landholding and advocated secret ballot-
ing in rural areas as well as in the cities. He saw the
significance of the secret ballot not as a more effective
manifestation of a democratic will but as a means of educating and politicizing the masses of people.[33] He considered
raising the level of education of all segments of society
and securing the rights and well-being of all citizens as the
only hope of strengthening the national consciousness and
thus making the population of Hungary less susceptible to the
ideas emanating from Nazi Germany.

By 1935, Szekfü's opposition to Nazi ideas crystallized.
In that year, he edited a new volume of Széchenyi's writings
and, in the introduction, he wrote about the significance of
Széchenyi for post-Trianon Hungary and the lessons of
Széchenyi's ideas applicable to the 1930's. He invoked the
teachings of Széchenyi to reiterate that, in the light of
the danger from Germany, extreme caution should be used in
the treatment of minorities. The only sizable minority left
in Hungary after World War I was the German one; there was
good reason for Szekfü's concern.

The significance of Széchenyi's life and ideas still seemed to Szekfü to be more in the spiritual rather than the political sphere although he saw the two as interrelated. Széchenyi opposed efforts to achieve independence from Austria, because he understood that a small nation needed the support of a larger one and that independence in itself was not the highest good for the nation. Széchenyi saw his own country as one small segment of humanity. The country should do everything in its power to benefit its own population, but the life of the nation should be in harmony with the interest of humanity and find favor in the eyes of God.

> Széchenyi stood on the ground of a Christian democracy and he respected human individualism. Etatism, totalitarianism, the usurpation of the function of the individual by the state, the oppression of the individual under the pretext of the interest of the community, in reality by the arbitrary will of the rulers, would have elicited violent opposition from him.[34]

By 1935, the author of <u>Der Staat Ungarn</u> which less than twenty years previously emphasized that Hungary was part of the Christian-German cultural community, saw Germany as the foremost danger not only to Hungary's political independence but also to its national spirit. For if Szekfü eliminated the "German" from the Christian German culture, he emphatically retained the Christian which was the anchor of his life no less than it was that of Széchenyi. Szekfü's objection to Nazi Germany was due to the anti-Christian and inhumane aspects of National Socialism rather than the political and economic changes in the structure of the state and the society. Domestically and in international relations, Szekfü considered Nazi Germany immoral. For Hungary, the danger emanating from the Third Reich was twofold. First, the anti-Christian, inhumane ideology might subvert the Hungarian nation, and, second, German expansion constituted a political danger to the future integrity of Hungary.

It was to make Hungary less susceptible to Nazi ideology and to bring about an economically and politically stronger nation capable of withstanding the dangers posed by Germany that Szekfü moved from the Right of the political spectrum to a position that was, by the middle of the 1930's, to the Left of center. Henceforth, a recurrent phrase in his writing was one which can be translated as "consciousness raising" (öntudatositás).[35] It was in the face of the danger of Nazi propaganda that Szekfü advocated a heightened awareness of Hungarian national consciousness. He considered a knowledge of Hungarian history and Hungarian traditions the prerequisite for intelligent participation in the political process. By politicizing a wider segment of the Hungarian population-- specifically the peasantry and the working class--Szekfü thought that new, uncorrupted political talent would arise, eventually taking over the leadership of Hungary. He also thought that a heightened national consciousness might serve as an agent of resistence against German ideology.

Szekfü was not alone in the alarm over the acceptance of Nazi propaganda by a sizable faction of the non-Jewish middle class. The term "intellectual national defense" (<u>szellemi honvédelem</u>) came to be used by a group of intellectuals made up of writers, journalists and historians. The literary periodical <u>Szép Szó</u> (Beautiful Word) was the forum of the leftist, anti-Fascist intellectuals, among them the more radical members of the Village Explorers.[36] The newspaper <u>Magyar Nemzet</u> (Hungarian Nation) was established by the historian-journalist Sándor Pethö (1885-1940) and became the organ of those dedicated to the maintenance of Hungarian intellectual and political independence in opposition to Nazi ideology and German political encroachment.[37] Pethö himself and a number of contributors to the <u>Magyar Nemzet</u> traveled the same ideological road from traditional conservatism to a belief in the need for reform which characterized Szekfü's path in the 1930's. Some of the writers who had regularly contributed to Szekfü's <u>Magyar Szemle</u> were associated with the <u>Magyar Nemzet</u> also. Beginning in 1940, Szekfü himself wrote a regular column for this paper and also contributed to the Catholic journal, <u>Korunk Szava</u> (The Voice of our Age), an organ of young, progressive Catholics who were dissatisfied with the more conservative traditional Catholic journals.[38]

In 1936, Szekfü and a number of friends and associates --among them such luminaries as the poet Mihály Babits and the composer Zoltán Kodály--joined in planning a book devoted to the enlightenment of the readers about Hungarian intellectual traditions. "We had an uneasy feeling about the future," said Szekfü in the introduction, "and we thought that this book may serve as a guide to those Hungarians who, in the flood of intellectual currents and the chaos of propaganda, no longer know what is authentically Magyar. We planned this book to serve as a norm and save them from mistakes, illusions . . ."[39] The book was called Mi a Magyar? (What is Magyar?), a collection of essays forming a part of the "intellectual national defense" by providing a realistic portrayal of Hungarian traditions in literature, art, language and history. Szekfü edited the book and contributed the chapter entitled "Hungarian Character in our History."[40] To the careful reader this essay is the key to the understanding of Szekfü's subsequent career.

In writing about national character as was manifested in Hungarian history, Szekfü made it clear that he did not believe in any innate biologically or racially determined traits. He saw the special national character of a people as a result of sharing a culture and undergoing identical environmental and historical influences. Such a group of people in the course of time would acquire similarities which would distinguish them from other groups.[41] This national character was not a permanent one; it was continually affected by new influences if these influences were maintained continuously for a lengthy period. The national character could also be modified by sudden, drastic historical changes. The change from nomadic wandering to settled agricultural life, the adoption of Christianity and the ensuing social and political transformation, lost wars resulting in a lengthy occupation and assimilation of groups of people whose national character differed from the Magyar constituted factors which continually and subtly changed the character of the people. Nevertheless, some of the early characteristics survived over the centuries although they might have been manifested in a narrow segment of the population or have been blurred to a fading tradition.

Szekfü cited the opinion of the Byzantine Emperor, Leo the Wise (866-911), about the Hungarians: they loved freedom, excelled in military virtues but they were treacherous and could not be trusted.[42] This was the way the Hungarians were seen by others. Szekfü turned to Bálint Hóman, the medievalist, to present the Hungarian point of view. What seemed to outsiders as untrustworthiness in the eyes of the Hungarians appeared as a positive trait: the Hungarian was a man of shrewd politics. Hungary was an essentially political nation in two senses. First, there was a universal participation in the political process in the early part of Hungarian history, and, second, they manifested a healthy suspiciousness, caution and realistic politics when dealing with others.[43]

What Leo the Wise termed treachery and Hóman called shrewd politics and suspicion of outsiders was the result of the Hungarian nation being a late-comer to the European scene where they were an island in an alien sea surrounded by Slavs and Germans. In times of crisis there was always a strain of melancholy arising from the fear for the survival of the Magyar people. But this was not a morbid trait of pessimism but a realistic, clear appraisal of being alone and friendless in the world. This realism as well as an ability to adapt to new circumstances in times of danger was another characteristic of the Magyars in the Middle Ages.[44]

The cultural and political equality of the early centuries gradually gave way to a break-up first into classes and then into closed estates. The increased burdens and deprivation of rights of the peasantry culminated in the institution of legal serfdom by 1514. By the beginning of the sixteenth century nineteen out of every twenty people were outside of the framework of the constitution. Henceforth, the jobbágy (serf) status was practically a closed caste; the development of any sense of responsibility or initiative was destroyed by hopelessness. The spirit of self-government was bound to disappear. The love of freedom and political sense became irrelevant concepts the peasant no longer understood. This hopeless state affected his sense of pride and human dignity. The jobbágy became lazy and irresponsible since he had only duties and burdens and no privileges.[45]

But the realistic political sense of the nobility had undergone a decline also after the Battle of Mohács. Both the Labanc and the Kuruc substituted illusions for realism. The Labanc deluded themselves into believing that Hungary's constitutional rights were intact and the Hungarian state institutions continued to function even though they carried out the orders which came from Vienna. The Kuruc, on the other hand, searched for an independence which was impossible to attain, deluding themselves by elevating the goal for an illusory freedom to a national purpose. In the process, each of these groups lost its sense of political responsibility.[46]

There were, however, men in all ages who retained their sense of realism. Szekfü illustrated what he meant by realism by reviewing the career of three men of "great political talent," who faced practically insurmountable problems and used the traditional politics in a new and more effective way, "giving their time, their honor, sacrificing their fate with a passion which previously burnt only in St. Stephen who destroyed even some of his relatives for the sake of Hungary."[47]

The first of these men was György Fráter, also known as Martinuzzi (1482-1551), a monk of Croatian origin in the service of János Zápolya (1487-1540) who was elected King of Hungary by the anti-Habsburg faction of the Magyar nobility in 1526. György Fráter was neither a conspirator nor an opportunist; he was a sincere man. Yet he followed two contradictory political courses, both with sincere conviction, risking his own life both times. He used "a political method which is useful and necessary in times of danger for a Hungarian statesman."[48] As a supporter of Zápolya who was allied with the Turks against the Habsburgs, György Fráter believed that the future of Hungary depended on the defense of the House of Zápolya and the maintenance of Transylvania independent of Austria. György Fráter was instrumental in allowing the Fall of Buda to the Turks in 1541. At the time, he sincerely believed in the righteousness of his action. When the brutality of the Sultan made him realize that his previous politics were wrong, he became the supporter of the Emperor Ferdinand I (1526-1564). As soon as he recognized his mistake, the monk put aside his previous politics without the slightest hesitation and followed the new course. A few months after the occupation of Buda by the Turks, György Fráter swore allegiance to the Habsburg House and spent the rest of his life trying to unify the two parts of the country under the Habsburg king. At all times he tried to do the best for his country, changing his allegiance when he felt it was in Hungary's best interest.[49]

While the monk György Fráter turned from East to West, the other two statesmen Szekfü used to illustrate Hungarian political realism started out supporting the Habsburgs and later looked to the East and turned against their former ally. Stephen Báthory (1533-1586) as Prince of Transylvania was a faithful supporter of the Habsburg House until he was elected to be King of Poland in 1575. As the ruler of Poland, he perceived the possibility of making Hungary independent of both the Habsburgs and the Turks by the combined military forces of Poland and Transylvania. He never realized his goal because the problems of Poland prevented him from carrying out his plans, but his was also a case of changing sides: in the sincere belief that it was in the interest of Hungary's future, he changed from supporting the House of Habsburgs to become their adversary.[50]

Finally, Szekfű reviewed the political career of another Transylvanian Prince, István Bocskay (1557-1606), who also supported the Habsburgs during the first phase of his career. When he saw that Austria was not willing to wage an energetic war against the Turks and, especially, when he realized that the German "help" amounted to a reign of terror by the Habsburg Army stationed in Transylvania, he changed his life-long political views and prepared the uprising against the Habsburg House. "He was not bitter or repentant; just as his nomadic ancestors on horseback were not overcome by emotion when they lost their way in the pathless Russian steppes . . . and had to turn back."[51] He neither loved nor hated the Germans or the Turks, but coldly and calmly viewed the instruments and methods of their power. Bocskay became the ally of the Turks as a means to save Hungary; it was a realistic, unsentimental, purely political act worthy of Machiavelli's Il Principe. The difference was that the Machiavellian politicians of Hungary neither had the Machiavellian contempt for humanity nor did they carry the amorality of their politics into their private lives.[52]

According to Szekfü, the basis of this ability to utilize any realistic political means in the interest of Hungary was an uncanny objectivity on the part of the best Hungarian statesmen. This objectivity was the other side of the apathy with which the Hungarians--beginning with the nomadic ancestors on horseback--regarded outsiders. The Hungarians loved and hated only their own kind. When they had to associate with others, they were only interested in whether or not the others would be helpful or harmful to the Magyars. "How could an attack be forestalled, perhaps even turned to an advantage?" Hungarian politics amounted to the answer to this basic question. This lack of sentimentality was often viewed as treachery or untrustworthiness by others; the Magyars saw it as a matter of survival. Hungarian Realpolitik was based on sad experiences and the knowledge that "the nation is alone in the world and it has neither friends nor enemies for any other reason except to serve political purposes."[53]

The three men who had to change their political course in the interest of Hungary's future lived during times of upheaval. In the sixteenth and seventeenth centuries Hungary was a battlefield between East and West; that fact alone was responsible for the choices that had to be made and the drastic changes that were sometimes necessary. After the end of the seventeenth century and the removal of the Turks, the choice of Hungarian politicians was limited to accommodation with the Habsburgs or defiance. Szekfű indicated, as he did in his previous writing, that those who could evaluate the interest of Hungary most dispassionately, always tried to find a modus vivendi with Austria. The wisest Hungarians never championed lost causes. Sándor Károlyi (1668-1743), who signed the Treaty of Szatmár in 1711, turning from Kuruc to Labanc, "soberly weighed the realistic possibilities . . . as a man of ancient Magyar wisdom."[54] Széchenyi, too, acted in the old tradition when he wanted to achieve reforms which were attainable rather than demanding independence which was impossible to obtain. The realistic policies of Ferenc Deák (1803-1876) and Count Gyula Andrássy (1823-1890) achieved political advantages with the Compromise of 1867 which could have been a firm basis for a healthy society unlike that which went down in catastrophe in 1918. But by then the ancient political talent for realistic political action was no longer manifested in the Hungarian political scene. The decline of the nobility and the continued disenfranchisement of the peasantry resulted in a political vacuum. Realistic policies gave way to illusions; policies were based on sentiments rather than on reason.[55]

Szekfű saw the reappearance of the ancient political virtues as the only hope for the future of Hungary. Those included the political participation of all people and the reinstatement of cautious, realistic politics.

> Until the poor people who are not responsible for the shortcomings of the last decades and who are not members of our present ruling class can again act in accordance with our historical tradition, we, the intellectuals, have to fulfill this responsibility.[56]

With the hindsight given us by the knowledge of subsequent events, Mi a Magyar? a title in the form of a question, gives the answer to the most obvious problem of analysis of Szekfű's career. Why did the conservative nationalist Szekfű who in 1923 envisioned a government by an elite which would think for the people, abandon his former beliefs and turn into an anti-German pro-Soviet champion of the people? Given the illustration of the "best politicians" of Hungarian history, one has to conclude that Szekfű considered abandoning one erroneous political view and turning to another, more useful to the interest of the country as a political act in the best Hungarian tradition. It is also obvious that, in the absence of an effective political leadership, he thought that the intellectuals had to lead the way. Like Leo the Wise, an outsider may see Szekfű's definition of "what is Hungarian" in unflattering terms: the Hungarian is an opportunist or a Machiavellian; to Szekfű, he was a patriot for whom ideology was secondary to the survival of Hungary as a nation.

It may not have been apparent to contemporary readers of *Mi* *a* *Magyar*? but by 1939, the devoutly Catholic Szekfű was obviously reconciled to the possibility of an alliance with Soviet Russia against Germany just as in the past the Christian leaders of Transylvania were willing to ally themselves with the Turkish "non-believers" against the Habsburgs. In this light Szekfű's actions and writings after 1939 become understandable.

FOOTNOTES

[1] Zoltán Szabó, "Naplójegyzetek: A Historikus Halálhírére Emlékek Elevenednek" (Diary notes: The News of the Death of the Historian Evoke Memories), Látóhatár (Horizon), VI (1956), p. 17.

[2] For Hungarian politics in the 1930's, see C. A. Macartney, October Fifteenth: A History of Modern Hungary 1929-1945, II vols. Edinburgh: The University Press, 1957. For the Marxist interpretation, Erik Molnár et al., Magyarország Története (The History of Hungary). Budapest: Gondolat Könyvkiadó, 1967, II, pp. 400-479.

[3] Gyula Szekfü, Három Nemzedék és ami Utána Következik (Three Generations and What Comes After). Budapest: Királyi Magyar Egyetemi Nyomda, 1940, p. 413. The above reference is to the sixth edition of Három Nemzedék, unchanged since the fourth edition was published with a slightly altered title in 1934.

[4] Ibid., p. 415.

[5] Ibid., p. 416.

[6] Ibid., pp. 418-420.

[7] For Hungarian literature of the interwar period, see Miklos Béládi and György Bodnár, A Magyar Irodalom Története 1905-tól Napjainkig (The History of Hungarian Literature from 1905 to Our Own Day). Budapest: Gondolat, 1967, pp. 285-722. For Hungarian art, see Anna Zádor, ed., Magyar Müvészet 1900-1945 (Hungarian Art 1900-1945). Budapest: Gondolat, 1958.

[8] A Hungarian slang expression for such a person was one characterized by a "bicycler's mentality:" bent over towards those above, treading on those on the bottom.

[9] Béládi, Magyar Irodalom, pp. 435-436. A selection of Hungarian Populist literature in English translation is available in Ilona Duczynska and Karl Polányi, The Plough and the Pen: Writings from Hungary 1930-1956. London: Peter Owen, 1963.

[10] The relationship between the conservative scholar and the young radical writers was one of mutual respect and sympathy. Szekfü's support of the Populist demand for land reform and his willingness to publish the articles of the Populist writers in the Magyar Szemle created the paradox that the journal established by Count István Bethlen advocated the reform of the system created by the Bethlen regime. Szabó, "Naplójegyzetek," Látóhatár, p. 18.

[11] Szekfü, Három Nemzedék, pp. 424-426. 1 hold = 1.066 acre.

[12] Ibid., p. 427.

[13] Ibid.

[14] Ibid., p. 428.

[15] Each hold of land was shown to produce fifty per cent more when cultivated by an owner of a small farm; it also provided employment for 66 per cent more people. More food and more employment was the justification for land reform. Mátyás Matolcsy, A Mezőgazdasági Munkanélküliség Magyarországon (Agricultural Unemployment in Hungary), 1933, p. 25, cited in Szekfü, Három Nemzedék, p. 431.

[16] Ibid., p. 432.

[17] Ibid., p. 433.

[18] Ibid., p. 441. Szekfü referred to Oscar Jászi's Revolution and Counter-revolution in Hungary. Westminister: P. S. King and Son, Ltd., 1924, and The Dissolution of the Austro-Hungarian Monarchy. Chicago: The University of Chicago Press, 1929.

[19] Szekfü, Három Nemzedék, p. 444.

[20] Ibid., p. 445.

[21] In contrast with his agricultural argument, Szekfü did not present detailed statistics to support the thesis that people on fixed income suffered more economic hardship during the depression than those who were self-employed or employed by business and industry. The opposite may have

been true. People on fixed income did not lose their jobs, although their pay was reduced. Business was immediately affected; their employees were more likely to lose their positions. Furthermore, the majority of the Jews also lived on a reduced, fixed income. The fact that they were employed by capitalistic enterprises rather than by the state meant only that their jobs were less secure than those of civil servants. This can be seen from statistics Szekfű did supply. Between 1929 and 1933, 650 industrial enterprises went out of business and the value of the total industrial production was reduced from nearly three billion pengő to less than two billion. Elemér Simonits, Jr., "Gazdasági Szemle" (Economic Review), cited in Szekfű, Három Nemzedék, p. 447.

Perhaps the reason that Szekfű failed to provide statistics about the economic situation of the Jews was that statistics would have disproved his statement that all the Jews were associated with capitalism. The proportion of the Jews in business and the professions did exceed their proportion in the general population but--except for the civil service and the army--they could be found in every occupation, including agriculture and factory labor. 45.1% of the Jews were owners or employees of business and industry. For statistics on the distribution of the Jews according to occupation in postwar Hungary, see István Véghazi, "The role of the Jewry in the Economic Life of Hungary," Hungarian Jewish Studies, II, pp. 71-82.

[22] Szekfű, Három Nemzedék, p. 448.

[23] Ibid., p. 449.

[24] Ibid., p. 448.

[25] Ibid., p. 450.

[26] A poem by Miklós Radnóti (1909-1944), written less than a year before he was shot to death during a forced march, serves to illustrate the feeling of the great majority of Hungarian Jews:

> I don't know what this land means to others,
> this little country circled by fire, place
> of my birth, world of my childhood, rocking
> in the distance.
> I grew out of her like the fragile branch
> of a tree, and I hope my body will sink
> down in her.
> Here, I'm at home . . . .

Miklós Radnóti, Clouded Sky. Translated from the Hungarian by Steven Polgar, Stephen Berg and S. J. Marks. New York: Harper and Row, 1972, p. 73.

[27] Gyula Szekfű, Történetpolitikai Tanulmányok (Historical-Political Studies). Budapest: Magyar Irodalmi Társaság, 1924, p. 65.

[28] Szekfű, Három Nemzedék, pp. 475-476.

[29] Ibid., p. 476.

[30] Ibid., p. 477.

[31] Ibid., p. 478.

[32] Ibid., p. 479.

[33] Ibid., p. 493.

[34] Gyula Szekfű, ed., A Mai Széchenyi (Széchenyi Today). Budapest: Révai Kiadás, 1935, pp. 27-28.

[35] Other similarities between Szekfű's vocabulary and current American usage include "generation gap" and "changes in lifestyle." Szekfű, Három Nemzedék, p. 480 and passim.

[36] Szép Szó, the name of an anti-Fascist periodical, literally translated means "beautiful word," but as an idiomatic Hungarian phrase it means "persuasion." E. g. to convince someone with "szép szó" and avoid conflict. Szép Szó was banned in 1939.

[37] János Johancsik, "A Magyar Nemzet Szellemi Honvédelme és az Antifasiszta Függetlenségi Mozgalom, 1938-39" (The Intellectual National Defense of the Magyar Nemzet and the anti-Fascist Independence Movement), Századok (Centuries), CIV (1970), p. 98.

[38] Ibid.

[39] Gyula Szekfű, ed., Mi a Magyar? (What is Magyar?). Budapest: A Magyar Szemle Társaság, 1939, p. 7.

[40] According to contemporary critics, Szekfü's contribution was the most significant part of the book. Aladár Schöpflin, "Mi a Magyar," <u>Nyugat</u> (West), XXXIII (1940), p. 77.

[41] Szekfü, <u>Mi a Magyar</u>, p. 490.

[42] <u>Ibid</u>., p. 494.

[43] <u>Ibid</u>.

[44] <u>Ibid</u>., p. 501.

[45] <u>Ibid</u>., pp. 545-546.

[46] <u>Ibid</u>., pp. 541-543.

[47] <u>Ibid</u>., p. 520.

[48] Szekfü saw no contridiction in finding a Hungarian character trait in a man of Croatian origin. It only proved "the well-known law of assimilation: large alien masses of people cannot be assimiated . . . , an individual, however, could become just as good a Magyar as a man of Magyar blood." <u>Ibid</u>.

[49] <u>Ibid</u>., pp. 520-521.

[50] <u>Ibid</u>., pp. 522-523.

[51] <u>Ibid</u>., p. 527.

[52] <u>Ibid</u>., p. 528-529.

[53] <u>Ibid</u>., p. 530.

[54] <u>Ibid</u>., p. 543.

[55] <u>Ibid</u>., pp. 553-555.

[56] <u>Ibid</u>., p. 556.

CHAPTER X

"SOMEWHERE WE LOST OUR WAY:"
SZEKFÜ AND THE POPULAR FRONT

Until the late 1930's, whenever Szekfü wrote about the poor, disenfranchised masses of people, he meant the peasantry. Henceforth, a new object of concern began to appear in Szekfü's writing. The historian turned his attention to the industrial workers and the urban poor:

> . . . the modern industrial worker is a strong and conscious member of the nation . . . and could be looked upon as a link between intellectuals and the lower classes, between city and village. The Magyar industrial worker grew out of the Magyar soil, he has Magyar roots.[1]

Szekfü was now willing to cooperate not only with Populist writers but also with Social Democrats, Trade Union officials and crypto-Communists in the Popular Front activities with the ostensible purpose of resisting Nazi German encroachment and promoting social and economic reforms.

As in other countries, the Popular Front in Hungary arose on the initiative of the Communist Party (an illegal organization in Hungary) as a result of a decision of the Seventh Congress of the Comintern in 1935 in Moscow. The purpose of the Popular Front was to create a unified opposition against Fascism, to defend democratic rights and to promote resistance movements in those countries which were threatened by Germany, according to Marxist historians.[2] The members of the Communist Party were not to promote Communism; they were to emphasize the need for unity among the anti-German and the democratic elements for a common purpose. The goal was to unite the industrial proletariat, the peasantry, the petite bourgeoisie of the cities and the progressive intellectuals into a Popular Front which would promote social and economic reforms as well as anti-German resistance. But the disparate elements which the crypto-Communists wanted to enroll had little in common and modest success came only after the <u>Anschluss</u> of Austria in 1938 made the threat of German encroachment more imminent.[3] Even then, the majority of the non-Communist anti-German groups or individuals looked to the West--England and the United States--for support rather than to Russia.

The Popular Front activity became more successful in 1939 when emphasis was put on advocating a radical land reform and the group thereby attained the support of the National Peasant Party, a segment of the Smallholders and many of the Populist writers. After the outbreak of the Second World War, and, especially, after 1941, intellectuals, such as those supporting the "Intellectual National Defense," began to participate in the Popular Front.[4] The majority of those who supported the Popular Front were unaware that it was directed by Communists. "Had the war ended differently, the role played in the movement by the Communists . . . would doubtless never have been revealed at all, and it would have gone down to history as simply another chapter in Hungary's national resistance to Germany."[5]

With the exception of a few demonstrations, the Popular Front, or Independence Front as it later became known, had little more than a literary manifestation. Szekfü was one of those intellectuals whose journalistic writings reflected the ideas of the Popular Front. He had been in favor of land reform since 1933, and his concern about the industrial workers began to be expressed in the newspaper Magyar Nemzet (Hungarian Nation) beginning in 1939.[6] More significant was Szekfü's participation in the Christmas issue of Népszava (Voice of the People), a daily newspaper of the Social Democratic Party. This Christmas issue was planned by the Popular Front and it carried articles by Social Democrats, Communists, Populists and two formerly conservatives intellectuals, one of whom was Gyula Szekfü.[7]

A historian of the Popular Front movement of Hungary considered the Christmas issue of the Népszava a milestone in the history of the movement. It was devoted to the expression of the ideas about cooperation of all people who believed in democratic reform, national independence and liberty.[8] There was not much more than general platitudes and patriotic sentiments expressed in these articles; rather its significance lay in the fact that such a team of writers could be assembed for the Népszava. The paper created a sensation. Right wing groups were appalled and demanded some kind of action against the newspaper. On the other hand, letters to the editor poured in from those who approved. It was even noted and applauded by the British Broadcasting Company as an indication to the West that there was an effective starting point in Hungary for anti-German resistance.[9]

Within months, as a result of this first successful public cooperation of the disparate elements of the Popular Front, the idea was advanced to create an organization which would be the legal arm of the Popular Front. This informal cooperation of groups with common aims gave birth to the Historical Memorial Committee. The avowed purpose of the Committee was to prepare for the centennial celebration of the Revolution of 1848 and the War of Independence of 1849 and to collect and exhibit documents and artifacts pertaining to those events. Plans for the exhibition of these artifacts, coupled with a series of lectures, would involve interested people across the country and serve to focus on Hungary's traditional struggle for independence. Such an organization was acceptable to a larger segment of the population and attracted writers and intellectuals who would not have participated when the Popular Front was concentrated around the Népszava. The Historical Memorial Committee continued to be directed by the Communists.[10]

The only successful effort of the Historical Memorial Committee was the organization of a commemorative ceremony on March 15, 1942, the anniversary of the Revolution of 1848. In organizing the ceremony emphasis was put on the figure of Sándor Petőfi (1823-1849), the nineteenth century poet whose name was practically synonymous with the Hungarian Revolution. An article appearing in the Magyar Nemzet pointed out that Petőfi was "a revolutionary yet a good patriot."[11] A lapel pin was issued featuring a profile of Petőfi. A book of essays entitled Petőfi Útján (On the Path of Petőfi) was published, written by progressive intellectuals and journalists. Szekfü contributed to this volume and wrote about the role of the industrial and agrarian workers in the struggle for independence. The theme of being a patriot while working for change was echoed by Szekfü also;

> The industrial and agrarian workers will be the followers of national tradition in the struggle for independence, tracing the footsteps of the great Hungarians who rose up in revolution against the social system of their day without turning against the nation or denying its heroic past struggles for independence.[12]

The message was, obviously, that one could be a revolutionary and still be a patriot and that one can oppose the policies of the Government without being a traitor. The difficulty of convincing the average Hungarian could be compared to an attempt to convince the American "silent majority" in November, 1969, to view the Washington demonstration as a patriotic act.

Szekfű's participation in the Popular Front was an active and continuous one but it was restricted to a literary function. He attended no demonstrations. The historian was not a man of the people, but an old-fashioned, courtly gentleman who did not feel comfortable in large crowds. He did not attend the commemorative ceremony on March 15, 1942 because he knew that it would not be a simple wreath-laying ceremony at the statue of Petőfi but a well organized, large demonstration, and there were rumors that a counter-demonstration was prepared by the Arrow Cross Party, the National Socialist Party in Hungary.

There was relative freedom of written expression in Hungary even during the war and the sentiments expressed in the Popular Front literature were not censured. Nevertheless, anti-government action, such as a peace demonstration--which is what the March 15 action turned out to be--would not be tolerated. The estimated 8 to 10,000 people, assembled on Petőfi Square around the statue of the poet, were attacked by the police wielding rubber truncheons, who arrested several hundred people and dispersed the rest.[13] Almost all those apprehended were soon released as a result of the intervention of the Social Democratic Party. The government took no action against the Popular Front or the Social Democratic Party against requested assurances for future good behavior.[14] As a result, the Social Democratic Party, which had a respectable and relatively conservative leadership and had a measure of cooperation with the government since the early years of the Horthy-regime, became inactive in the Popular Front activities. The activities of the Communist Party became disrupted a few weeks later when approximately five hundred Communists (about eighty per cent of the trained cadre) were arrested in a series of raids.[15]

The material that came into the hands of the government during these raids revealed, not only to the government but also to the members of the Popular Front, that the Popular Front and the Historical Memorial Committee were Communist led organizations. Many anti-Fascist Hungarians declined to cooperate with the Popular Front thereafter. Since the Communist Party was crippled and the Social Democrats were inactive, the Popular Front, for all practical purposes, disintegrated. In the months that followed, the bourgeois democratic <u>Magyar Nemzet</u> continued to carry on a kind of civilized literary resistance, expressing sentiments for independence, economic reform and democratization. These articles were written by the "progressive intellectuals" on the Historical Memorial Committee such as Gyula Szekfű.[16] Until November 8, 1942, Szekfű was one of the few people writing about the aims of the Independence Front. On that day, the Allied Armies landed on the coast of Africa, reviving the hope of the Anglophiles in the government and among the people. There were a great many Hungarians, in and out of government--among them the Prime Minister Miklós

Kállay (b. 1887) himself--who were against both the Nazis and the Communists. They expected that the war would end with an Allied victory and the "Anglosaxons" would have a predominant voice in the peace settlements. The Allied presence in North Africa gave rise to speculation of a Mediterranean or Balkan landing in the near future and the physical presence of the Western Allies at the end of a lost war seemed far more desirable to most Hungarians than occupation by the Red Army.[17]

As a result of the changed attitude of the government the Popular Front suddenly became revitalized. All but the right wing newspapers carried articles about the need for unity between workers, peasants and intellectuals. The Népszava came out with another weighty Christmas issue containing articles by bourgeois intellectuals as well as by Socialists. Szekfű was again among the contributors.[18]

During the Second World War Szekfű continued to teach history at the University of Budapest, but his writing was limited to journalistic articles. He contributed regularly to the daily Magyar Nemzet and the monthly Magyar Szemle discussing current issues in a historical context or expressing a currently applicable opinion under the guise of interpretations of past events. In the winter of 1943-1944 Szekfű wrote a series of articles entitled "Valahol Utat Vesztettünk" (Somewhere We Lost Our Way). In these articles the historian returned to the period preceding the

Revolution of 1848 in order to trace the history and development of Hungarian liberal democratic theory and to point out where the practice had turned away from the original ideas. He did this through the examination of the activities of a small group of people who advocated a middle course between Széchenyi and Kossuth in the 1840's.

The Reform Era of Hungarian history, the period between 1825 and 1848, had been usually treated as a conflict between the followers of Széchenyi who concentrated on social and economic reform and the adherents of Kossuth, who emphasized constitutional reforms and independence from Austria. Little had been written about the ideas of a third group, the Centralists; their role was not significant, although some of their members became important political and intellectual figures in Dualist Hungary.

The Centralist Party consisted of young, well-educated and well travelled noblemen who were familiar with the workings of West-European political systems. They introduced the concepts of "parliamentarianism" and "responsible government" into the Hungarian political rhetoric. The main difference between them and Kossuth's Liberals was the conviction of the Centralists that the provincial system of administration was inconsistent with liberal reforms, while Kossuth and his followers were devoted to the provincial system because it was the stronghold of Hungarian independence. The goal of the Centralists was the transformation of the feudal state into a democratic system by removing the privileges of the nobility. They envisioned a state with a centralized body of lawmakers elected by the population. Franchise would depend on education rather than wealth. The civil rights of the people would be protected by laws and the provincial system would be replaced by a centralized administration.[19]

In the series of articles entitled "Somewhere We Lost Our Way," Szekfü examined the Centralist program in detail. His analysis showed that the Centralists were interested in the limitation of the power of the state and that their ideas of the government worked from the bottom up. The political power of the nobility would have been replaced by a system of free, self-governing communities and elected representatives in provincial and state governments. The Centralists believed that healthy, free communities could weather political and historical adversity much better than a society dependent on the state for all the functions of the community.[20]

The Centralists put special emphasis on a franchise based on education, believing that enactment of educational policies would enable an ever larger segment of the population to vote. Corrupt election practices would be eliminated by reforms that would bring about economic security for the agrarian people and, thus, their vote could not be bought or unduly influenced.[21]

Some of the ideas of the Centralists found their way into the post-1867 system, at least in form, if not in substance. But the political power of the aristocracy and the lesser nobles were not eliminated and the democratic institutions never developed. Szekfű pointed out that the liberalism of Hungary developed the right of the state, not those of the people; etatism was a more apt name for it.[22] Hungarian liberalism lacked a real concern for human rights. But then, in Szekfű's view, liberalism failed everywhere, not just in Hungary.

> The liberalism of the nineteenth century, which could not prevent 1914 and the subsequent horrible events, cannot be resurrected because it had, long ago, lost its humane and moral values. We must be careful that these values . . . human rights and love for our fellow man should survive the present destruction so that they may serve . . . as a new basis of our existence.[23]

Thus ended Gyula Szekfű's last published writing before the end of World War II. After the war, these articles formed the first part of his new book, Forradalom Után (After the Revolution). In the introduction, Szekfű pointed out the meaning of these articles:

> Some phases of development which brought great progress to the nations of Western Europe were missing or found only in rudimentary form in Hungary . . . Western-style democracy is one of them: in spite of long and laborious attempts, these concepts could not take root in our society . . .[24]

The political institutions which could not be achieved in a hundred years were lost forever, no longer attainable.[25]

At the end of the war, just as he did at an earlier phase of his career, Szekfü saw "Western-style democracy" as an alien system which could not take roots in Hungarian society. It was also obvious to the historian that the remnant of St. Stephen's State would never again be a monarchy. By that time Szekfü came to believe that the postwar Hungarian state would have to be closely associated with Soviet Russia. How he came to this conclusion was revealed in an article written in 1955, just before his death. "Az Értelmiségiek Átállása a Felszabadulás Idején" (The Conversion of the Intellectuals at the Time of the Liberation) gives an insight into Szekfü's own views.

Szekfü explained that, in 1945, Communists constituted only a small segment of the intellectuals. Those with strongly anti-Communist views or those whose collaboration with the Nazis made them fearful of Russian retaliation escaped to the West before Budapest fell to the Red Army. The majority of the intellectuals who remained at home soon joined in the rebuilding of the devastated country.[26] They worked together with Communists, workers and peasants. Political principles had very little to do with their willingness to participate; cooperation with them was a culmination of a complicated system of transformation which began several years earlier.

Those who were among the first to undertake the task of rebuilding were "inwardly prepared" by their opposition --even if passive opposition--to the ruling class and the character of the Horthy regime. After 1941, these people lived in an internal emigration.[27] Their opposition was due to a combination of foreign and domestic developments.

By 1941, it became obvious, especially to those who could read foreign newspapers, that Germany faced the greatest powers of the world. Against the alliance of the West, including the United Stated, with the Soviet Union, Germany had no chance to win. Those who saw the situation clearly understood that the war "would lead to a new historical disaster for all those who would tie their boats to the fantastic pirate-ship of Hitlerism."[28]

But the thought of a German victory was just as likely to affect a well-informed, thoughtful Hungarian. For Hungary a victory of Hitler would mean no less a disaster. If Nazi ideology prevailed in Europe, the small non-German nations on the borders of Germany would be considered inferior states; they would be compelled to perform as beasts of burden in agrarian societies supplying the German masters. Those who understood this were "predestined" to look with favor on the Red Army which rid Hungary of the Germans. They were not likely to oppose the new order.[29]

There were many of these intellectuals but they were not organized into a political group. There were politicians among them. István Bethlen himself opposed all the Hungarian administrations after Gömbös but did not want to play the role of an opponent of the Horthy regime openly.[30] The basis of the pro-Hitler forces resided with the army. Horthy's incompetence and apathy enabled the general staff to become more and more powerful, yet Horthy was amazed to find that his generals defied him when he was ready to ask the Allies for an armistice.[31]

Szekfü stated that there were many intellectuals who opposed the German alliance of Hungary on domestic grounds. The pro-Nazi administrations following Bethlen failed to carry out any radical reform. The agrarian structure of Hungary remained unchanged despite the fact that, by the early 1930's, a great many intellectuals favored a redistribution of the land. The Populist writers and Village Explorers were in the forefront of this movement, and these ideas were shared by a great many people. Even the Catholic youth were concerned about the large landholding of the Church and almost the entire new generation of intellectuals were dissatisfied with the agrarian situation. They demanded land reform to bring about the elimination of the political power of the aristocratic landholders and thereby enable the "three million beggars" to live in human dignity.[32] There were more of these "silent land reformers" who opposed the government than those whose opposition was based on grounds of foreign developments.

Still another aspect in gaining the allegiance of the intellectuals, according to Szekfü, was the elimination of capitalism, which did not happen immediately but could be foreseen. Capitalism was not popular in Hungary; it was never looked upon with favor by the professional people. The majority of the intellectuals were officials, not really familiar with the workings of capitalism; they opposed the relationship between capitalists and workers on humanistic grounds. "Simply stated they sided with the poor people against the rich."[33] This unexpressed silent consensus resulted in a wide support of the policies of the new government which immediately began to limit capitalism. The situation was viewed with apathy even by those who did not support the anti-capitalist policy of the government.

Finally, there were many apolitical intellectuals who participated in the new political system for economic reasons, or perhaps because, after the dislocations, destruction and degradation in the last few months of the war, they were eager to embark on a new beginning.[34]

Thus, in Szekfü's view, the Hungarian intellectuals were ready to support the postwar regime because they were dissatisfied with both the foreign and the domestic policies of the Hungarian pro-Nazi administrations. They were afraid of a German victory as well as a German defeat, they wanted radical economic and political reforms at home and they were not in favor of a capitalistic economic system. These reasons coincided with Szekfű's own views. Szekfű apparently never abandoned the theory of the decisive importance of foreign policy over domestic developments. However sincerely he may have believed for the need for reform, and however distasteful he may have found capitalism, the major reason for his about face from West to East was that he considered the alliance with Hitler's Germany a bankrupt foreign policy. He saw that, from the Hungarian point of view, a German victory would have been just as disastrous as a German defeat.

Szekfű was almost certainly aware from the beginning that the Popular Front and the Historical Memorial Committee were Communist controlled organizations. He collaborated with them willingly. He saw, early on, the inevitability of Allied victory and he understood the significance of geopolitical realities. Unlike the majority of non-Communist anti-German Hungarians, Szekfű did not entertain any hope that, with the aid of the "Anglosaxons," Hungary would be able to emerge after the war as a "Western-style" liberal democracy. As a student of European history, Gyula Szekfű understood that the Western European nations had little to gain from championing the interest of Hungary. As a Hungarian historian, Szekfű saw clearly that, in Hungary's choice between East and West, the West always meant Germany alone. In his view, anti-German Hungarians had no other choice but to turn toward Russia. Szekfű's writings and behavior during the war years bear out this supposition.

On March 19, 1944, the Germans occupied Hungary. As a known opponent of the Nazi regime, Gyula Szekfű had to flee for his safety.[36] Characteristically, he found asylum with the Church. Of all his previous beliefs, an unwavering, strong religious faith was all that remained to him.

FOOTNOTES

[1] Szellemi Honvédelem Naptára (Calendar of Intellectual National Defense), 1940, pp. 95-96. Cited in János Johancsik, "A Magyar Nemzet Szellemi Honvédelme és az Antifasiszta Függetlenségi Mozgalom" (The Intellectual National Defense of the Magyar Nemzet and the Anti-Fascist Independence Movement), Századok, CIV (1970), p. 116.

[2] Gyula Kállai, A Magyar Függetlenségi Mozgalom 1936-1945 (The Hungarian Independence Movement 1936-1945). Budapest: Kossuth Könyvkiadó, 1965, p. 18; Erik Molnár et al., Magyarország Története (The History of Hungary). Budapest: Gondolat Könyvkiadó, 1967, II, pp. 416-419.

[3] Molnár, Magyarország, II, p. 419.

[4] Johancsik, "Szellemi Honvédelme," Századok, CIV, p. 114.

[5] C. A. Macartney, October Fifteenth: The History of Modern Hungary 1929-1945. Edinburgh: The University of Edinburgh Press, 1957, II, p. 47.

[6] Johancsik, "Szellemi Honvédelme," Századok, CIV, p. 117.

[7] The other non-Communist writer was Endre Bajcsy-Zsilinszky (1886-1944), a colorful politician who traveled an ideological road even more extreme than that of Szekfű. Bajcsy-Zsilinszky was among the extreme nationalist "race-defenders" in 1920, active in the White Terror. By 1930, he was a member of the Opposition in the House of Representatives. As a member of the Smallholders Party, he supported the Populists and became active in the Popular Front. On March 19, 1944, when the Germans occupied Hungary, Bajcsy-Zsilinszky was arrested by the Gestapo. He resisted arrest and wounded two of his captors, himself being wounded in the melee; he had the distinction of being the only civilian casualty in Hungary on the day of the German occupation. Eventually, he was condemned to death and executed on Christmas day, 1944. For a biography of Bajcsy Zsilinszky, see László Dernői Kocsis, Bajcsy-Zsilinszky. Budapest: Kossuth Könyvkiadó, 1966.

[8] Kállai, Függetlenségi Mozgalom, p. 115.

[9] Macartney, October Fifteenth, II, p. 79.

[10] Kállai, Függetlenségi Mozgalom, pp. 127-129.

[11] Magyar Nemzet, February 15, 1942. The article was written by the Populist writer Imre Kovács (b. 1913), leader of the Peasant Party and active participant in the Popular Front. Macartney, October Fifteenth, II, p. 79.

[12] Cited in Kállai, Függetlenségi Mozgalom, p. 128.

[13] Ibid., p. 132.

[14] Macartney, October Fifteenth, II, p. 129.

[15] Ibid. Among those arrested were the two leaders of the Communist Party, Ferenc Rózsa (1906-1942) and Zoltán Schönherz (1905-1942). Rózsa died in prison as a result of mistreatment two months later. Schönherz was tried and condemned to death. Szekfü and Bajcsy-Zsilinszky testified in behalf of Schönherz at his trial; they "did everything within their power to try to save him," without success. Kállai, Függetlenségi Mozgalom, p. 149.

[16] Macartney, October Fifteenth, II, p. 107.

[17] Gyula Juhász, Magyarország Külpolitikája, 1939-1945 (Hungary's Foreign Policy, 1939-1945). Budapest: Kossuth Könyvkiadó, 1969, p. 259.
    For a non-Marxist Hungarian point of view of the foreign policy of the Kállay Administration, see István Kertész, Diplomacy in a Whirlpool: Hungary between Nazi Germany and Soviet Russia. Notre Dame, Indiana: University of Notre Dame Press, 1953, pp. 57-58.

[18] Macartney, October Fifteenth, II, p. 129.

[19] Bálint Hóman and Gyula Szekfü, Magyar Történet (Hungarian History). Budapest: Királyi Magyar Egyetemi Nyomda, V, pp. 325-327; Molnár, Magyarország, II, pp. 472-474.
    The best-known figures among the Centralists were the statesman Baron József Eötvös (1811-1871), the historian László Szalay (1813-1864) and the novelist and politician Baron Zsigmond Kemény (1814-1875).

[20] Gyula Szekfű, Forradalom Után (After the Revolution). Budapest: Cserépfalvi, 1947, p. 28.

[21] Ibid., p. 35.

[22] Ibid., p. 39.

[23] Ibid., p. 40.

[24] Ibid., p. 8.

[25] Ibid.

[26] Gyula Szekfű, "Az Értelmiségiek Átállása a Felszabadulás Idején" (The Conversion of the Intellectuals at the Time of the Liberation), Csillag (Star), IX (1955), 1634. The above is an inexact translation of the Hungarian title. The word "értelmiségi" means a larger segment of the population than "intellectual" connotes. It includes everyone who used his mind rather than doing physical labor to make a living. It means office workers as well as scholars. The word "átállás" here means political support for the new regime with or without ideological conviction. The intellectuals who formerly opposed the Communists came to support them.

[27] April, 1941 is considered a turning point in Hungarian politics. Up till then, the Hungarian government gave only a limited cooperation to Germany in order to achieve a revision of the borders in Transylvania. On April 3, 1941, Hitler demanded full military participation in an attack on Yugoslavia just three months after a pact of eternal friendship was signed between Hungary and Yugoslavia. The Hungarian general staff whole-heartedly supported the German plans, made all preparations for the attack and confronted the government with a fait accompli. When Prime Minister Count Pál Teleki found the government was powerless to stop the army, he committed suicide on the eve of the attack. By the end of 1941, Hungary officially entered the war against the Allies.

For Teleki's policy of keeping "two irons in the fire," i.e., provide a limited cooperation to Germany, while staying out of the war and leaving the door open toward the Allies, see Gyula Juhász, A Teleki Kormány Külpolitikája, 1939-1941 (The Foreign Policy of the Teleki Administration, 1939-1941). Budapest: Akadémiai Könyvkiadó, 1964.

[28] Szekfű, "Az Értelmiségiek Átállása," Csillag, IX, p. 1635.

[29] Ibid.

[30] It has been said that the group around the Magyar Nemzet promoting Intellectual National Defense, "derived its money from Baron Móric Kornfeld, its protection from Count Bethlen and its intellectual prestige from Professor Szekfű." Macartney, October Fifteenth, I, p. 380.

[31] Ibid. For the events of October 15, 1944, when Horthy unsuccessfully tried to achieve an armistice with the Allies, see Macartney, October Fifteenth, II, pp. 391-443.

[32] The phrase, "three million beggars" came from one the first Populist books published in Hungary: György Oláh, Három Millió Koldus (Three Million Beggars), Miskolc, 1928.

[33] Szekfű, "Az Értelmiségiek Átállása," Csillag, IX, p. 1638.

[34] Ibid.

[35] "Anglosaxons" was a shorthand phrase for the Western Allies, meaning the English and the Americans.

[36] Szekfű's name was mentioned in a German diplomatic report from Budapest in connection with the secret diplomatic efforts to extricate Hungary from the German grasp. According to a report of the Forschungsamt dated July 30, 1943, ". . . the Hungarian Democratic parties are revived. The historian Szekfű (he is close to Count Bethlen) serves as an intermediary between the government and the labor unions." György Ránki et al., eds., A Wilhelmstrasse és Magyarország: Német Diplomáciai Iratok Magyarországról, 1933-1944 (Wilhelmstrasse and Hungary: German Diplomatic Documents about Hungary, 1933-1944). Budapest: Kossuth Könyvkiadó, p. 737.

CHAPTER XI

VOLTE-FACE: FROM WEST TO EAST

On April 4, 1945, after a four-month siege of Budapest, the Red Army entered the devastated city. The Hungarian capital had suffered a great deal of destruction; many of its buildings were ruined and its transportation system was totally destroyed. Every bridge across the Danube between Buda and Pest had been blown up by the retreating Germans and "their pillars, with dangling ribs and chains, looked like the carcasses of ice-age monsters."[1] The people emerged from their cellars and returned from their hiding places seeking to resume a normal life under exceedingly difficult circumstances.

Gyula Szekfü was among those who returned after spending the year of the German occupation at the Monastery of Pannonhalma. He found his house in the Buda hills damaged but habitable; only his library was totally ruined. The historian resumed his teaching shortly after the war ended; lack of public transportation made it necessary for him to walk for several hours each day between his home and the university. Once a former student, traveling on a motorcycle, noticed the tall, slightly bent, 62 year old professor walking briskly toward the city and offered him a ride in the rickety side car of the vehicle. "What do you think of the times we live in?" the student asked the professor when they reached the university. "It is like the Age of Zápolya," answered the historian.[2] The Turkish parallel was never far from Szekfü's mind.

While a great many of the former non-Communist members of the Popular Front who initially supported the postwar regime became disenchanted and, eventually, left the country for Western Europe or the United States, Gyula Szekfü's support for the Communist regime never wavered during the ten years between 1945 and the time of his death. Furthermore, the historian who had never before held any political office served as Hungary's first ambassador to the Soviet Union from 1945 to 1948. In 1953, he became a member of the House of Representatives and, in the last year of his life, he served on the Presidium of the People's Republic of Hungary.[3]

Friends and contemporaries recall Szekfü at the end of the war as a profoundly disillusioned, embittered man who retained only his religious faith. According to Zoltán Szabó, a former colleague of Szekfü on the <u>Magyar Nemzet</u> and a fellow Popular Front supporter who left the country in 1949, Szekfü was the "victim of a conflict of the proportions of a Greek tragedy."[4] Szabó was one of the few people who knew that Szekfü was asked to be ambassador because the Russian Chairman of the Allied Control Commission specified that the ambassador should not be a Communist, a Jew or a politician. The Hungarian authorities were told that someone like Gyula Szekfű would be welcome.[5] Presumably, they reasoned that such a man would contradict the thesis that Russia imposed its will on Hungary through the Hungarian Communist Party. For any other Hungarian, accepting the ambassadorship would not have required a compromise of principles, for this was a time preceding the onset of the Cold War and Hungary's contact with England and the United States was carried on through Russian mediation.[6] But Szekfű was called to be the Hungarian representative in a country which held his friend and mentor Count István Bethlen in captivity. It was like being the ambassador at the Porte in another age, "compelling him to oppose everything he previously worked and stood for."[7] Szekfű undertook the task even though he knew that he would be looked upon as a opportunist. But the strain took its toll. Just before leaving for Moscow, at a celebration of the anniversary of the October Revolution of Russia, Szekfű made a commemorative speech referring to Lenin as the "greatest figure in the history of the world."[8] Concluding his talk, he went backstage and collapsed.[9] Szabó compared the last ten years of Szekfű's life in Communist Hungary as full of doubts and suffering as the years Széchenyi spent in an insane asylum in Döbling.[10]

This romanticized view of Szekfű, elicited by the news of the death of the historian, was not borne out by the examination of the book written by Szekfű in Moscow. The paradoxical turns in Szekfű's life were hardly akin to the fate of the hero in a classical tragedy. The historian was characterized by the exact opposite of the inflexibility of principles which causes the downfall of a tragic hero: he had an ability to accommodate himself to new circumstances. It was a complex mixture of ordinary human frailty coupled with a measure of moral strength which enabled him to side with what must have appeared to him as life instead of death, survival instead of extinction both for himself and for the Hungarian state. Years before 1945, Szekfű must have decided that, for Hungary, it was to be "better Red than dead."

If Szabó were right and Szekfű's life was that of a tragic hero who was broken by the necessity of denying everything he believed in for a lifetime, there is no evidence of it in the subsequent writing of the historian. But there is evidence of the opposite: that he was so deeply convinced of the necessity of changing his political course that a feeling of moral righteousness may have accompanied his actions. Szekfű thought that the wisest Hungarians never championed lost causes. His admiration for those men who tried to find a modus vivendi with a former enemy in the interest of the future of Hungary rather than cling to old principles and unattainable goals, and his postwar book, Forradalom Után (After the Revolution), contradict Szabó's hypothesis. Profound irony characterized Szekfű's career, but there was no evidence of tragedy.

Gyula Szekfű remained in Moscow until September, 1948, when ill health forced him to resign from his post as ambassador to Russia and return to Hungary. Forradalom Után was written in Moscow; it included several essays which were published together with the series of Magyar Nemzet articles written in the winter of 1943-1944. After the Second World War, Szekfű's historical scholarship was limited to a contribution to the two-volume Kossuth Emlékkönyv (Kossuth Memorial Volume), commemorating the one-hundred and fiftieth anniversary of the birth of Lajos Kossuth, in 1952.[11] His third and final postwar publication, the previously mentioned "The Conversion of the Intellectuals at the Time of Liberation," appeared in a journal which also carried his obituary.

Forradalom Után is the most important of Szekfű's postwar publications. In it Szekfű evaluated the period preceding the Second World War and passed harsh judgments on the Hungarian administrations which followed that of Count István Bethlen. Szekfű did not provide a documented, systematic examination of events, rather he wrote an account of those years as an eyewitness and participant of history. The book also contained essays on the first two years of the postwar regime of Hungary and, on the basis of his experiences in Moscow, Szekfű included a discussion about the "new, great neighbor," the Soviet Union. The title of the book, "After the Revolution," is significant. One must assume that Szekfű used the title of a well-known pamphlet written in 1850 by one of the Centralists, Baron Zsigmond Kemény, on the basis of careful thought. Perhaps he wanted to provoke a historical comparison. Therefore, before examining Szekfű's book, a brief review of the career of Baron Zsigmond Kemény and an examination of the work which supplied the title for Szekfű are necessary.

Baron Zsigmond Kemény (1814-1875) was an impoverished Transylvanian nobleman active in the politics of the Hungarian Vormärz. Kemény was in favor of reforms, but his emphasis was on administrative, social and economic rather than constitutional changes. He was a member of the Centralist Party before the Revolution of 1848, although he was politically more conservative than the rest of the Centralists. In 1849, Kemény joined the Peace Party which tried to work out accommodations between the Magyars and the government of Vienna without losing the rights achieved by the Revolution of 1848. Zsigmond Kemény was also one of the important nineteenth-century novelists and editor of the newspaper Pesti Napló (Pest Journal) from 1855 to 1869.[12]

Szekfű discussed the ideas of Kemény in connection with the Centralists in "Valahol Utat Vesztettünk" (Somewhere We Lost Our Way), the series of articles which constituted the first part of the book bearing the title barrowed from Kemény. Szekfü emphasized that Kemény had not agreed with all the views of the Centralists. Kemény had strong reservations about liberal institutions and considered corrupt electioneering inherent in the representative system.[13]

Kemény was never in favor of independence from Austria. The experience of the Revolution and the defeat of the War of Independence made him more conservative. His reservation about democracy and radicalism now turned into opposition to those concepts. In <u>Forradalom Után</u> (After the Revolution) written in 1850, Kemény appeared conservative and authoritarian. Szekfü quoted extensively from Kemény's pamphlet in his post-World War I book, <u>Három Nemzedék</u> (Three Generations), in support of his thesis that Kossuth and the Liberals were wrong and radicalism, revolution and democracy were alien to the Magyar nation.[14]

According to Marxist scholars, Kemény's <u>Forradalom Után</u> served a double purpose. On the one hand, he attempted to convince his countrymen that they must give up their dream of independence and adjust themselves to the new circumstances: living under the absolutism that followed the defeat of the War of Independence. On the other hand, he attempted to convince the Bach Administration that the Hungarians were basically anti-revolutionary and anti-republican and the Hungarian national character was passive, reserved and cautious. Kemény's thesis "resembled a legal argument in an attempt to assure the absolutist politicians that such basically peaceful . . . people deserve to be treated with tolerance."[15] Or, as another literary historian put it, "he obsequiously kow-towed to the bloody-handed Haynau . . . to save the Hungarian nation . . ."[16] A few years later, Kemény became instrumental in developing a passive resistance against Austria and he participated in the planning of the Compromise.[17]

There is no indication that Szekfü interpreted Kemény's pamphlet to be other than it purported to be: an affirmation that Széchenyi was right and Kossuth was wrong and that Hungary should not have attempted to become independent from Austria because it needed the protection of a large power.[18] It is more likely that Szekfü used the title because, like Kemény in 1850, he lacked faith in liberal parliamentarianism and he saw the need for being under the protection of a great power. There were other parallels as well. In 1945, as in 1850, the affirmed need for protection was directed toward the country which recently crushed Hungary. In 1945, as in 1850, there was a possibility of future accommodation for a more advantageous relationship with that great power and a hope for a renewed life of the nation. Finally, Szekfü may have used the title "After the Revolution" because, even in the absence of a revolution in the literal sense of the word, the drastic changes in Hungary at the end of the Second World War were truly revolutionary.

Just as Három Nemzedék examined the period before the First World War and blamed the liberal leadership for the disaster of Trianon, Forradalom Után similarly reviewed the thirteen year period before 1945 to show just how the new catastrophe came about. But while Három Nemzedék was merely an expression of political and intellectual disapproval of policies which Szekfű considered harmful, Forradalom Után expressed a moral revulsion of "the most shameful period in Hungarian history."[19]

"Never was there a political leadership as incapable of governing as ours from the beginning of the 1930's . . ."[20] Beginning with Gyula Gömbös, no Hungarian leader acted on the basis of reality, in accordance with the needs of the Hungarian state and Hungarian society; instead, they followed their emotions. Fear, hatred or sympathy governed their actions instead of common sense and realism.[21] They refused to believe to the very end that Hitler's Third Reich would be defeated; they believed blindly in a German victory based on the new "miracle weapons," followed by a conflict between the "Anglo-Saxons" and the Soviet Union and, ultimately, an alliance between Churchill and Hitler. Even those like Miklós Kállay (Prime Minister 1942-1944), who did see the coming German defeat and did want to break with the German alliance, would negotiate only with the Western Allies and refused to take into consideration that "the world's most powerful army" was nearing the borders of Hungary. Kállay would surrender only to the English or the Americans.[22]

Domestically, what Szekfü described seemed like a "trickle-down theory" of political and moral decay. As the intellectual and moral quality of the leadership and the army continued to decline, an ever increasing segment of the Hungarian society became infected by the misguided political ideology and inhumane and immoral behavior toward their fellow men. Thus, the lack of realistic policies on the part of the government was reflected in the lack of an effective anti-Nazi resistance movement, and the inhumane policies of the administration were echoed by the inhumanity of many and the apathy of most of the people toward the plight of their neighbors.

Szekfü showed that the moral decline of the ordinary Hungarian was the direct result of the behavior of the leadership. Respect for civil law and property declined when, as a result of the Jewish Laws,[23] government officials and army officers acquired "confiscated" property, bought land "for a pittance" (potom áron) from Jews "with their backs against the wall" (sarokba szoritott zsidóktól), or acquired a sinecure in a Jewish enterprise. The latter amounted to a tolerance tax enabling the owner to continue operating his business. These examples coming from above created a feverish rush by a great many people looking for Jewish property "for sale" which they bought for next to nothing, or for "positions" in Jewish enterprises amounting to extortion of an unearned income.[24]

These legal robberies (papirosoktól megengedett kifosztás) became more and more widespread and resulted in a total disregard of law and property. The lesson was not lost on the peasantry and was often voiced in the villages: "What the gentlemen (urak) can do with the Jewish land, sooner or later the peasantry would do with the big estates."[25] Szekfü saw a direct line leading from the "free contracts" exploiting the helplessness of the Jews to the criminal depravity of the Arrow Cross men in later years.[26]

The moral disease went hand in hand with the intellectual decline in the leadership beginning with Gyula Gömbös. He was the one who connected Hungarian politics with friendliness toward Nazi Germany and with anti-Semitism. Since then, the press and the government propaganda attributed every book or article voicing criticism of Hungarian politics or Hungarian society as the work of the Jews, not to be believed, probably designed at a secret meeting of the "wise men of Zion." High officials in the government and in the army believed in this.[27]

The corruption of Hungarian youth was attempted with some success by the army through the paramilitary Levente organization. Pro-German and anti-Semitic views were inculcated in the young men who were encouraged to spy and report on each other. The Levente instructors were not successful in high schools and universities where the students were sophisticated enough to be amused by the ignorant, mannered instructors. But the village youth and the children of the urban poor were greatly influenced by them. Many of the future members of the Arrow Cross first became interested in pro-Nazi politics in the <u>Levente</u> organization and practiced the brutality and inhumane behavior which they learned there.[28]

In the beginning of his administration, Gömbös voiced some Populist sentiments, but they remained slogans. The real problems of the country went unsolved. Land reform was never seriously considered; Hungary went down to defeat at the end of the Second World War as a land of latifundia. By then, instead of land reform, a complete reorganization of the land system, a land distribution, was necessary.[29]

The unrealistic, shortsighted and harmful policies were nowhere more apparent than in the nationality question. This was all the more unfortunate because in the late 1930's there was reason to believe that the great powers realized the injustice of the Treaty of Trianon and there was hope that, through normal international channels, those borders would eventually be revised.[30] But this possibility disappeared with the Vienna Decisions in 1938 and in 1940, when the Hungarians were willing to accept through Hitler's aggression what could have been returned through peaceful international means.[31] Of course, after years of revisionist propaganda, to refuse the "gift" would not have been possible without precipitating public outrage. The real mistakes were committed by the Hungarian attitude toward those Slavs and Romanians who once again became the citizens of Hungary. The emphasis was on the geographic integrity of the country: its mountains, rivers and the old historic places. The people were secondary. "We looked at the land and not at the people who tilled its soil."[32]

The administration of the areas newly restored by the Vienna Decisions began by the appointment of representatives to the Hungarian Lower House, thus disallowing them even the appearance of a true representation. The local administrations were taken out of the hands of the local people and officials from Trianon Hungary, unable to speak the language of the people, took over. In the Dualist Era, the Magyars in the provincial administration, even if they did not speak the language of the non-Magyar people, were local lesser nobles; in spite of their mistakes they were heirs to a long tradition of public service. The ruling class of the 1930's came from a different segment of the population. They alienated even the Magyar people in the newly restored areas. "For decades we demanded more democratic rights [for the Magyar minorities] in the succession states and then we sent them opponents of democracy."[33] All the evils of the Hungarian state and Hungarian society: corruption, discrimination, limitation of freedom and Jewish Laws, were extended to the recovered areas.

>The Allmighty had put us to a test when part
>of the nationality areas were returned to us . . . .
>We failed the test shamefully . . . . Therefore,
>all revisionist effort and propaganda must be abandon-
>ed once and for all. We have lost the moral basis of
>our demand . . . . At the decisive time we proved
>ourselves incapable and unwilling to do justice to
>the nationalities; we have broken with the century
>long Magyar practices which enabled the Magyars to
>live together peacefully with the non-Magyars.[34]

Szekfű explained that the concept of St. Stephen's State implied that the non-Magyar nationalities of Hungary should have the degree of self-government to which their political development and educational condition entitled them at a given era. Noting that the non-Magyar peoples of the formerly Hungarian areas lived in their independent states and became experienced in self-government, the revisionist plans of István Bethlen proposed a federalized system of autonomous nationality areas in the event that they would be restored to Hungary. However, in 1938, autonomy for the Slavs and Romanians was not even considered. The spirit of Hitler besmirched the name of St. Stephen, just as the leadership of Hungary cheapened the concepts of Christianity and nation. "The traditional Magyar values disintegrated, rotted away in their hands."[35]

The wartime Hungarian leadership maintained the unified Hungarian state system toward the restored non-Magyar areas. At the same time, they willingly injured Magyar sovereignty when they allowed the German claim for the allegiance of the Magyar citizens classified as <u>Volkdeutsch</u>

and when they handed over citizens of Jewish origin to the Germans. In both cases, Hungary abandoned its own citizens in the interest of a foreign state. Aside from the moral considerations, this was an admission that Hungary was incapable of fulfilling the most elementary task of an organized state: to protect the life and security of its citizens against an alien power.[36]

Even before the German occupation, the state and the society sank to such a low moral level that the possibility of ever recovering a moral integrity no longer existed. The society consisted of a small layer of exploiters, a larger layer of the exploited and the great masses of people who were apathetic toward everything except their own interests. The exploiters' opportunity to profit at the expense of others surpassed that of any capitalistic society; the exploited had no support or defense whatsoever. Such a society could not be united. A bourgeois system resting on compromise between conflicting class interests could not be restored. Reform and evolution became empty phrases, no longer meaningful or applicable. Disorder, chaos, cruelty and moral decay characterized Hungary at the end of the war.[37]

> The state disintegrated, the decayed society
> fell apart . . . .
> A long historical line came to an end,
> ingloriously, shamefully . . .
> in a grotesque, bloody tragicomedy.
> There remained one way out: Revolution.[38]

This portrayal of Hungarian society before and during the Second World War was interesting also for what it did not include. In 1920, Három Nemzedék accounted for the events at the end of World War I by examining the life and times of three generations; Szekfű included nearly one hundred years of political history, as well as the social, economic and intellectual developments of every segment of Hungarian society. In assigning the blame in 1945, it suited Szekfű's purposes to examine only the period after 1932, and to deal primarily with one segment of the Hungarian society.

It was true that the pro-Nazi, "gentroid" leadership was intellectually and morally inferior to the previous aristocrat-dominated administrations which possessed a tradition of "noblesse oblige." Nevertheless, many of the mistakes of the Horthy regime originated in the 1920's when an opportunity to modernize and democratize the state was missed. The "long historical line" really came to an end in 1918, not in 1945. The years between 1920 and 1945 were an incongruous, artificial extension of the past which no longer existed. The Kingdom of St. Stephen died on the battlefields of World War I but the Hungarians, with the intensity of a profound religious faith persisted in believing in its future resurrection.[39]

"Beginning with Gyula Gömbös, no Hungarian statesman acted on the basis of facts," said Szekfű. But neither did the traditional Magyar statesmen, Bethlen and Teleki, realize that the old, trusted institutions of political power, based on an antiquated land system had become anachronistic and inadequate to deal with the problems of a small, weak Central-European state which was unsupported by a large power for the first time in four hundred years. The political, economic and social institutions had to be changed before Hungary could become a viable state. It was during Count István Bethlen's ten-year administration, especially during the peaceful and relatively prosperous years before 1929, when the land reforms could have been achieved. Instead of modernization and reform, the 'twenties were years of political and cultural reaction, in which no small intellectual role was played by Szekfü himself. Strangely, while Szekfü felt responsibility for policies he actively opposed and acts committed when he himself was a fugitive, he never acknowledge any responsibility for the reactionary intellectual influence he exerted in the 1920's. Of the inept leadership of the interwar period, he exempted his friend, Bethlen, of any blame. If he mentioned him at all, it was with praise.

The historian connected the anti-Semitic propaganda and the Jewish Laws with the final brutalities which occured in the last year of the war. Yet he apparently failed to perceive a "direct line" between the anti-liberalism and anti-Semitism of his own writings in the 1920's and the belief of that segment of Hungarians who looked for salvation in National Socialism complete with the elimination of the Jewish problem.

Szekfü also failed to point out that much that happened in Hungary was caused or accelerated by events which the Hungarian leadership could not control. The most capable statesmen of high moral integrity could not have escaped the effect of German expansion and the Second World War. Opposing Hitler would have saved the country's honor but not its fate; Hungary would have been occupied early in the war and, at the end, the country would have been a battlefield between the Germans and the Russians just the same.

These, of course, are moot points. Yet it is impossible not to conclude that Szekfü's portrayal of Hungarian society and Hungarian leadership served a purpose: he needed villains for the justification of the "revolution." Villains were not hard to find; there were an abundance of them and they had an opportunity to do a great deal of harm. But there were others, some in the government and the Church, who tried to do the best they could during difficult times. In addition to the men like Gömbös and some of his successors who were blinded by their devotion to Germany, there were also among the leadership traditional lesser nobles and others who may have been biased, misguided but not inherently evil. One example was Miklós Kállay, a man of lesser noble origin and mediocre intellect who as prime minister, cooperated with Germany when he had to, and resisted Hitler's demands when he could.[40] Another prime minister, Count Pál Teleki, committed suicide in 1941 rather than participate in the attack on Yugoslavia. And many of the intellectuals who tacitly supported the pro-German leadership held views similar to those of Szekfü in the 1920's, but they lacked the historian's insight and flexibility; they remained frozen in the position Szekfü prescribed in Három Nemzedék.

Among the ordinary people, the great majority were neither saints nor sinners, but ordinary fallible human beings, living in hardship and fear. In such a society many of the niceties that come naturally in normal times tend to fall away. Szekfü did not exaggerate the corruption and inhuman behavior he described, but by presenting it as the only kind of behavior, the sole manifestation of Hungarian morality, he was giving us a distorted picture of Hungary before the German occupation in 1944.

Szekfü's description of Hungary before the end of the war served to show that the state and the society had to be completely rebuilt. In the following essay, "A Forradalom Elindul," (The Revolution Begins), Szekfü analyzed the political events and the changes in the political system during the first two years of the postwar regime.

According to Szekfü, after ridding Hungary of the Germans, the Russian occupying force aided the Hungarians in their endeavor to rebuild the country. Soviet Russia initiated the organization of a Western-style democratic government, instead of insisting on a government on the Soviet model. Russia wanted Hungary to avoid a civil war which would have been inevitable before a "dictatorship of the proletariat" could assume power in such a socially and economically backward country. This "proved that /Russian/ political superiority equalled their military brilliance."[41]

Szekfü explained that the European treatment of the Soviet Union in the interwar years created a feeling of suspicion in the Russians toward people outside of their borders. The Second World War convinced the Russians of the necessity of preventing any possibility of an enemy attack on the entire length of their Western border. Therefore, at the end of the war, they helped each of their neighbors in setting up a democratic parliamentary form of government in order to avoid civil war and create friendly relationships with the bloc of states from the Baltic Sea to Bulgaria. At the same time, this friendly relationship enabled the Soviet Union to use its influence and to ensure that the previously anti-Bolshevik segments of power would be eliminated. Therefore, in each of these countries, the aristocrats, capitalists, reactionary intellectuals and the Church had to be made politically harmless. Only in this way could the Soviet Union be certain that the Western type of democracy which they helped establish would not allow the existence of a reactionary opposition and would, in fact, serve as a basis of an Eastern type of democracy.[42] Incredibly, what Szekfű seemed to be saying was that Russia helped Hungary (and its neighbors) in setting up a Parliamentary Democracy, in order to eliminate the power of all segments of society which would favor such a governmental system.

The Russian purpose of political and economic reorganization of its small neighbors coincided with the need of Hungary to find a new basis for its society and substitute a new social class to take over the leadership from the politically bankrupt traditional ruling class. The purposes of both the new Hungarian leaders and the Soviet occupiers were incompatible with the original plans for democratic rights as designed by the Centralists of a hundred years ago. Nor could the English and the American governments serve as models.[43]

According to Szekfű, rights of liberty had to be sharply curtailed, because freedom of the press and assembly would have become weapons in the hands of the anti-Bolshevik and reactionary people, posing a serious threat to the stability of the new regime. Similarly, the extreme left groups had to be prevented from advocating the immediate achievement of the dictatorship of the proletariat. The lack of personal freedom was not a principle with the new regime; they could be restored later, when they no longer posed a political danger. However, there were changes of permanent nature and

these changes in the governmental system would not only make
it impossible to revive the prewar regime but would also
create a democratic society of the Eastern type, differing
from the Western liberal systems. Both the Hungarians domestic needs and those of the U.S.S.R. required these changes.
Hungary needed domestic stability to rebuild the country
laying in ruins and Russia wanted a government which was sympathetic toward the Russian system. Therefore, the previously powerful classes had to be made permanently powerless.[44]

Through the distribution of the land the source of
the political power of the aristocracy and the Church would
be eliminated. Szekfü showed sympathetic concern toward the
Church and regretted that many sincere ecclesiastic people
and worthwhile charitable organizations had fallen on hard
times, nevertheless, he found justification for the treatment
of the Church by the new regime. Szekfü took pains to show
that his devotion to Catholic principles and Christian ethics
remained unchanged and he hoped that by getting rid of the
feudal burden (kölönc) of the large estates the material and
political aspects of the Church would give way to a true
Catholic spiritual awakening.[45]

The political rights of the middle class also had to
be curtailed. After the war, the standard of living of the
professional people, civil servants, white collar workers and
capitalists was severely reduced; many may have felt that
they were better off under the old regime. Therefore, steps

had to be taken to prevent the middle class from organizing an opposition to the government. The temporarily rescinded civil rights were designed to deal with this problem. Fortunately, the old habit of obedience to government authority helped lessen the danger of opposition.[46]

Once the aristocracy, the Church and the middle class, became politically harmless, the power would remain with the industrial workers and the peasantry. The latter was in need of education, but the urban working class could effectively lead the nation. The problem was that the need to abolish the political power of the great majority of the people had to be reconciled with the existence of a general franchise. The first election brought in an overwhelming majority for the Smallholders which had the support not only of the peasants but also of the non-Communist middle class.[47] The government consisted of a coalition between the majority Smallholders and the minority Social Democrats and Communists. Szekfű noted that, in all parliamentary conflicts, the majority party gave in to the working class minority. They were compelled to do this, he explained, because the constituents of the Smallholders were unorganized and dispersed over the entire country and in a conflict they would have been no match for the industrial workers who were concentrated in the capital and in the few large cities. The Trade Unions and the Industrial Committees effectively controlled the political power of the country. It was understandable that the non-working class parties continually had to give in to the minority in the matter of civil rights, private property and other bourgeois concerns.[48]

Szekfü accorded high praise to the Communist Party for its wisdom and experience. The lessons of 1919 were not lost on them. They did not talk about nationalization of the land, avoided religious conflicts and tried to win over the bourgeoisie. They had the task of guarding against the opposition of those who preferred the pre-war regime or wanted a liberal democracy. It was obvious that the Hungarian reactionaries would turn to the Western democracies because they knew that England and the United States would "give asylum to all failed /political/ orientation because of their liberal principles."[49] Therefore the Communists organized the police in the very beginning and used it in the struggle against the reactionary opposition. The aim was the preparation of an economic and social system consistent with an "Eastern style democracy."[50]

As Szekfü saw it, the tragedy of the middle class consisted in its failure to understand that their role in society had been radically altered. Even after the distribution of the land and the increasing importance of the industrial workers, they did not perceive that Hungary was becoming a radically new and different society. The formerly persecuted or anti-Nazi elements of the middle class were amazed to find that more was required of them than a clean record and a clear conscience. They were misled by the democratic rhetoric of the new regime and did not notice that a revolutionary change was taking place in Hungarian society. They believed that the deviations from the Western-style democratic practice was a temporary disorder due to the dislocations in the aftermath of the war. The old wartime illusion, the hope of the coming conflict between the West and Russia, again became widespread among the middle class.[51]

Szekfű recounted the events which precluded such a development. He cited the diplomatic arrangements at the Conferences of Yalta and Potsdam, the military history of the war and the reasons for General George Marshall's decision not to follow Winston Churchill's plan for invading the Balkans. He thought that when the Americans established the first beachhead in Normandy, the fate of Central Europe was sealed; the Conferences at Yalta and Potsdam only made the arrangements official.[52] A Russian presided over the Allied Control Commission in the countries occupied by the Red Army and all signs indicated that the Russians had a free hand to impose arrangements on Hungary and on the other neighbors of Russia. After Roosevelt's death and the subsequent dropping of the atom bomb a certain animosity became apparent between the West and Russia. Speculation in the American press in the use of the atom bomb as a general panacea gave the discontented Hungarian middle class a hope as unrealistic as the belief of the pro-Nazi elements during the war that Hitler's new weapons would reverse the fortunes of Germany.[53] Eventually a great many anti-Nazis who enthusiastically greeted the Red Army and supported the new regime in the beginning became disillusioned and went into exile. They made a mistake in judgment when they failed to cooperate with the Communists: an unattainable Western-style liberal parliamentary system of government and an economy based on capitalism were more important to them than joining the working class in the rebuilding the country.[54]

Szekfű's continued active support for the repressive Communist regime throughout the Stalinist years was based on a knowledge of the diplomatic events and an insight into realistic politics. He also had an uncanny ability to adjust to new circumstances. In addition, he had the experience of living in Russia for two and a half years and there he found a society which had many aspects which he favored. The essence of his account of Soviet Russian society was reminiscent of a statement once made by Lincoln Steffens: "I have been to the future and it works."[55]

Whether Szekfű sincerely believed in the superiority and the virtues of the Communist leadership and the humanitarianism and wisdom of Stalin is not possible to determine. With the exception of Széchenyi, Szekfű had never written as admiringly of any historical figure as he did of Stalin.

> Everyone knows /Stalin's/ long and bitter struggle for the freedom of the people . . . he put the Soviet economy on its feet . . . . He created the Red Army . . . the Army and the people

> trust him and follow him faithfully . . . . The numerous pictures of Stalin seen everywhere . . . are the expression of the sincere feelings of the Russian people, rather than a new kind of Russian icon. The Soviet people love Stalin for they know that he lives and works in a simple style, in virtual seclusion for the betterment of the people . . . .[56]

Szekfü did not speak Russian and throughout his two and a half years in Russia he may have seen only that which the Russian authorities allowed him to see. In his essay on Russia, he did not discuss the political or economic theories of Communism, nor did he claim to write a learned and systematic treatise. He wrote about his own experiences and referred to the "Red Dean," Hewlett Johnson's highly favorable book on Soviet Russia.[57] While his assessment on how the Soviet political system worked in practice seems naive, he did make some observations about the Russian people and Russian society which are worth reviewing.

Szekfü noted, with approval, that the planned Communist economy--which he thought morally superior to one based on the profit motive--was more suitable to provide security and a slow steady improvement in the standard of living for the masses of people than a free market economy.

> One does not have to be an adherent of Marxism to know, one can learn that from some of the Papal Encyclicals also, that the poor and the weak have to be protected and not allowed to become victims of the inhumanities of the economic forces.[58]

The right to economic security did not mean that the standard of living was the same for all segments of society. Party functionaries, academicians, artists and scientists were compensated according to the importance of their work; their standard of living was much higher than that of the workers. But there was an equality of opportunity for education for all and higher education was free. All this proved to Szekfü that the Soviet system was a humane system with a conern for every human being. Its devotion to the welfare of society seemed to him not unlike the Christian virtue of <u>Charitas</u>.[59]

The lack of sophistication of the Russian people also appealed to the essentially puritanical Szekfü. He noted that the Russians were peaceful, good natured, orderly; their sense of humor lacked the know-it-all cynicism and maliciousness (<u>rosszmájuság</u>) one could find among the people of Budapest. The erotic literature of a modern metropolis was unknown in Moscow; it would not be tolerated, perhaps it would not even be understood. The sensationalism of the press was also missing. Szekfü thought that families spent more time together in Russia. He observed family groups in parks, restaurants, and libraries, the men carrying the smallest child, the women leading the older ones by the hand. The people read the Russian classics, not escapist literature; crime novels and pornography were unknown in Russia.[60] In short, Szekfü came to the conclusion that the Soviet society was morally superior to the Hungarian.

Szekfű was especially interested and pleased to find that the religious faith of the Russian people survived the Revolution and religious organizations, churches and monastaries continued to function. He explained that the members of the Communist Party were atheists, "a Christian world view is alien to them, but perhaps it will not always remain so."[61] The Orthodox Church as a pillar of the <u>ancien régime</u> was abolished by the Revolution, but after a while it became apparent that religion itself was not necessarily an enemy of the state. The 1936 Constitution restored the freedom of religion and reestablished religious life. Szekfű recounted his experiences at religious services: on Sundays the churches were overflowing and the Midnight Mass on Easter Sunday was attended by so many people that services had to be held in front of the Church for those who were unable to get inside.[62]

Szekfű understood that the Russian Church would enjoy freedom only as long as it did not oppose the state. He was convinced that the Church could support a Communist state without sacrificing any of its dogmatic or ethical principles. He saw the interest of the Church and the state as identical: both were dedicated to the welfare of the people.

Still another reassuring factor to Szekfű was his discovery that the Russian Revolution did not abolish the prewar culture and the Soviet regime consciously promoted historical traditions. Frequent comparisons between the

Second World War and the Napoleonic Wars served this purpose. Historical novels and plays acquainted the people with the great figures of their history. The historian found that museums, historical memorials and royal residences were carefully preserved. "The Russian Communist culture succeeded in assimilating the spiritual aspects of the Czarist, capitalist and feudal stages of Russian history."[63]

Last but not least, the historian of the Lands of the Holy Crown of St. Stephen noted that the multinational Soviet state was governed by the most liberal nationality law. The non-Russian nationalities freely cultivated their own national culture with the support and encouragement of the state. All the nationalities were united by Soviet patriotism.[64]

The most important part of Forradalom Után dealt with Hungary's relationship to Russia and the new, and--most likely--permanent situation of Central Eastern Europe. Here Szekfü's insight was keen and his argument convincing. It also provided a final glimpse into the reasons for the historian's peculiar willingness, even enthusiasm, to support a political system which he had opposed most of his life.

The U.S.S.R. and its two-hundred million people became the immediate neighbors of the small and insignificant Hungary.[65] In the aftermath of the war, Hungary was not completely sovereign in her own state; the government functioned in the shadow of the Red Army. The country incurred tremendous obligations to the Soviet Union and the Soviet demands on Hungary had the support of the Western Allies. These were the basic facts Hungarians had to consider when contemplating the future of Hungary.

Even after the eventual removal of the Russian occupying forces, Hungary must remember that Poland, Czechoslovakia and Yugoslavia were allied with Russia and this alliance was infinitely more powerful than the old "Little Entente." Therefore, all previous theories and practices of foreign policy which did not take into account the Soviet Union's presence on Hungary's borders became irrelevant. Hungary was one in that bloc of nations between Finland and Bulgaria which included victorious as well as defeated countries. Victory or defeat became much less important in the post war life of these nations than the fact that all came under the political and economic influence of Russia. The combined effect of the result of the war and the geographical realities brought about this situation. Along with the other small countries adjoining the Western borders of Russia, Hungary was part of Eastern Europe:

> Up till now we believed that /our forefathers/ brought us to the West, forever separating us from . . . Eastern peoples . . . . Eurasia had overtaken us . . .[66]

In 1947, Szekfü was ready to shed many of his old convictions.

> We can no longer continue to dream about serving as a bridge between East and West, not only because the East had spread westward beyond our longitude,

> but also because we constitute only a small, modest part of that seam that goes from north to south separating the two parts of Europe.

And he added bitterly:

> We can throw the "bridge" among the useless junk on the junkpile, there to rest forever together with the many other senseless, grandiose, unrealistic phrases of our political past.[67]

Szekfű saw no alternative to "sincere acceptance" of the situation and to the creation of a policy to gain the confidence of Russia. "Only then can we ensure Hungary's peaceful development under the new and, in my opinion, permanent circumstances."[68] Being permanently in the Russian sphere of interest was acceptable to Szekfű because he was convinced that the people of Hungary could remain Magyar and Christian in spite of Russian political and economic influence. He clearly addressed those Hungarians who opposed the new system on religious grounds. There were many among them who put their hope in the atomic bomb--possessed then only by the United States--and the coming war of the "Anglo-Saxons" against Russia. Szekfű knew better and tried to convince his Catholic brethren of the necessity of reconciling themselves to the new situation. He emphatically assured his Christian readers that accepting the new system did not mean that they had to abandon their religion. The Roman Catholic Church did not require its adherents to be

Monarchists, nor was there any special relationship between capitalism and the Church. Szekfü noted that Pope Pius XII spoke frequently urging peace; the Church was not advocating war against the Communists. It was sinful to presume that the Pope was pleased about the development of atomic weaponry.[69]

Szekfü also believed that Hungary's cooperation with Soviet Russia would not be inconsistent with cultivation of Magyar values and Magyar traditions. After a few years of selective use of those aspects of the Hungarian culture which fit in with the Communist propaganda, Szekfü expected that Hungarian culture with all its historic traditions would thrive once again. And it would be available to all, not just to the privileged classes.[70]

In the final analysis, Szekfü was devoted only to his nation and to his Church. The economic and the political form of the state and the nationality of the larger power providing security had not concerned him as long as the existence of Hungary as a Magyar nation was assured. He must have sincerely believed that the new system would bring about an economic and social improvement in the condition of the people. He was also convinced that the survival of the Church was not dependent on ownership of large landed estates and that the separation of Church and State would not eliminate the religious life of the nation. For these reasons, the historian Gyula Szekfü, a Christian Magyar citizen of

St. Stephen's State, had been transformed into an active and willing participant of the People's Democracy of Hungary.

FOOTNOTES

[1]Paul Ignotus, Hungary. New York: Praeger Publishers, 1972, p. 191.

[2]Szekfű referred to a time of great upheaval, immediately after the Battle of Mohács in 1526. Zoltán Szabó, "Naplójegyzetek: A Histórikus Halálhirére Emlékek Elevenednek" (Diary notes: The News of the Death of the Historian Revives Memories), Látóhatár (Horizon), VII (1956), pp. 19-20.

[3]Gyula Kállai, A Magyar Függetlenségi Mozgalom (The Hungarian Independence Movement). Budapest: Kossuth Könyvkiadó, 1965, p. 323.

[4]Szabó, "Naplójegyzetek," Látóhatár, p. 20.

[5]Ibid.

[6]For the workings of the Allied Control Commission and the Soviet High Command during the Russian occupation of Hungary, see Stephen D. Kertész, Diplomacy in a Whirlpool: Hungary between Nazi Germany and Soviet Russia. Notre Dame: The University of Notre Dame Press, 1953, pp. 101-107.

[7]Szabó, "Naplójegyzetek," Látóhatár, p. 20.

[8]László Bóka, Válogatott Tanulmányok (Selected Studies), Budapest: Magvető, 1966, p. 1057.

[9]Szabó, "Naplójegyzetek," Látóhatár, p. 20.

[10]Ibid. The Marxist writer Gyula Ortutay also drew a parallel between the final years of Széchenyi and those of Szekfű and arrived at a different conclusion. In an article commemorating the one hundredth anniversary of Széchenyi's death, Ortutay stated that after 1856, when Széchenyi recovered from his mental illness but remained in Döbling living in solitude, he reevaluated his previously held views and

> his examination justified neither the monarchist view of his peers, nor his own doubts and vacillations, nor the previously so deeply revered and feared Habsburg Monarchy--but Kossuth's policy . . . . /Széchenyi/ turned against /his/ own former ideas and political conceptions.

In the same article, Ortutay discussed Szekfü's view of Széchenyi and stated that it was not a true portrayal of Széchenyi but one which substantiated Szekfü's own historical and political ideas and moral principles. Ortutay then added:

> It is all the more stirring to see how Szekfü
> . . . turned against the whole of his outlook on
> history, including his image of Széchenyi . . . .
> After the liberation, Szekfü was one of the few
> people who owned up to his mistakes . . .

Gyula Ortutay, "The Living Széchenyi," The New Hungarian Quarterly, I (1960), p. 47 and p. 39.

[11] Gyula Szekfü, "Az Öreg Kossuth, 1867-1894) (The Old Kossuth), Emlékkönyv Kossuth Lajos Születésének Százötvenedik Évfordulójára (Memorial Volume for the Onehundredfiftieth Anniversary of the Birth of Lajos Kossuth). Budapest: Magyar Történelmi Társulat, Akadémiai Kiadó, 1952, II, pp. 341-433.

[12] For the historical views of Zsigmond Kemény as manifested in his journalistic work and his historical novels, see István Sötér, Nemzet és Haladás (Nation and Progress). Budapest: Akadémiai Kiadó, 1963, pp. 445-572.

[13] Gyula Szekfü, Forradalom Után (After the Revolution). Budapest: Cserépfalvi, 1947, p. 32.

[14] Gyula Szekfü, Három Nemzedék (Three Generations). Budapest: Királyi Magyar Egyetemi Nyomda, 1940, pp. 180-181.

[15] István Sötér, "Szerb Antal Magyar Irodalomtörténete," an Introduction in Antal Szerb, Magyar Irodalomtörténet (History of Hungarian Literature). Budapest: Magvető Könyvkiadó, 1972, p. 13.

[16] Tibor Klaniczay et al., History of Hungarian Literature. Budapest: Corvina Press, 1964, p. 153. Baron Julius Haynau (1786-1853) was the Commander of the Austrian forces which defeated the Hungarian Army in the War of Independence in 1849. He was the military dictator of Hungary until July, 1850.

[17]Sötér, Nemzet és Haladás, p. 447.

[18]Szekfü, Három Nemzedék, p. 181.

[19]Szekfü, Forradalom Után, p. 71.

[20]Ibid., p. 52.

[21]Ibid., p. 51.

[22]Ibid., p. 53.

[23]For the Jewish Laws of 1938 and 1939, see Erik Molnár, ed., Magyarország Története (History of Hungary). Budapest: Gondolat Könyvkiadó, 1967, II, pp. 422-424, 446-447.

[24]Szekfü, Forradalom Után, pp. 57-58.

[25]Ibid., p. 59.

[26]Ibid.

[27]Ibid., pp. 60-61.

[28]Ibid., p. 62.

[29]Ibid., p. 65.

[30]Szekfü cited "a book by C. A. Macartney" (presumably Hungary and her Successors, London: Oxford University Press, 1937) as being influential in creating a better understanding in the West about the injustice of the Trianon borders. Szekfü, Forradalom Után, p. 66.

[31]After the Munich Agreement in September 1938 enabled Germany to annex the Sudetenland, the German-sponsored negotiations between the Hungarian Government and the Czechoslovak representatives resulted in the First Vienna Decision in November 1938. An area of 12,400 square km with a population of 1,100,000 were returned to Hungary. Six months later, with German and Polish support, Hungary obtained Ruthenia.

In August 1940, the Second Vienna Decision--made by the representatives of the German and Italian Governments-- revised the boundary between Hungary and Romania. Forty-three square kilometers of the Transylvanian area with two and a half million inhabitants were returned to Hungary. The area of the Bácska was occupied by the Hungarians after the participation of the Hungarian Army in the German attack on Yugoslavia in April, 1941. Gyula Juhász, Magyarország Külpolitikája, 1919-1945 (Hungary's Foreign Policy, 1919-1945), Budapest: Kossuth Könyvkiadó, 1969, pp. 177-197, 219-233.

[32] Szekfü, Forradalom Után, p. 67.

[33] Ibid., p. 68.

[34] Ibid., p. 69.

[35] Ibid., p. 70.

[36] Ibid., p. 71.

[37] Ibid., p. 73-74.

[38] Ibid., p. 75.

[39] A prayer recited in all elementary and secondary schools in the beginning and end of each school day (a practice similar to the recital of the Pledge of Allegiance in the United States) serves as an illustration:

>I believe in one God,
>I believe in one Fatherland,
>I believe in eternal, divine justice,
>I believe in the resurrection of Hungary.
>   Amen.

[40] For Kállay's foreign policy, see Juhász, Magyarország Külpolitikája, pp. 256-306. See also Béla Vágó, "Germany and the Jewish Policy of the Kállay Government," Hungarian Jewish Studies, II (1969), pp. 183-210.

[41] Szekfü, Forradalom Után, p. 83.

[42] Ibid., p. 88.

[43] Ibid., p. 90.

[44] Ibid., pp. 90-92.

[45] Ibid., pp. 101-103.

[46] Ibid., p. 104.

[47] The first election in the Fall of 1945 resulted in 57% of the vote for the Smallholder Party. The Social Democrats and the Communists received 17% each, and 7% of the vote was cast for the National Peasants. For a detailed analysis of the election see Sándor Balogh, "Az 1945 November 4-i Nemzetgyűlési Választások Magyarországon" (The November 4, 1945 Elections to the National Assembly in Hungary), Századok, CIV (1970), pp. 869-936, 1192-1239.

[48] Szekfű, Forradalom Után, p. 110.

[49] Ibid., p. 112.

[50] Ibid., p. 113.

[51] Ibid., pp. 165-166.

[52] Ibid., pp. 166-167.

[53] Ibid., p. 169.

[54] Ibid., p. 171.

[55] Lincoln Steffens, Autobiography. New York: Harcourt Brace and Co., 1958, p. 799.

[56] Szekfű, Forradalom Után, p. 156.

[57] Hewlett Johnson, The Soviet Power. New York: International Publishers, 1940.

[58] Szekfű, Forradalom Után, p. 142.

[59] Ibid., p. 145.

[60] Ibid., pp. 149-150.

[61] Ibid., p. 135.

[62] Ibid., p. 152.

[63] Ibid., p. 155.

[64] Ibid., p. 156.

[65] Hungary became the immediate neighbor of the Soviet Union for the first time in centuries when Ruthenia became part of the U.S.S.R. at the end of World War II.

[66] Ibid., p. 121.

[67] Ibid., p. 122.

[68] Ibid.

[69] Ibid., p. 206.

[70] Ibid., p. 207.

CONCLUSION:

CONTINUITY AND CHANGE IN SZEKFÜ'S IDEAS

The first important book written by Gyula Szekfü in 1913 contained a scathing attack on the historian Kálmán Thaly for subordinating his historical interpretation to his political views. It is not the least of the multiple ironies of Szekfü's career that his own books and articles reveal a similar close connection between the political events in Hungary and his own historical scholarship. Indeed, because of the drastic changes in Hungarian politics during Szekfü's long career, his is perhaps the best example of this single most important characteristic of Hungarian historiography.[1] This is true in spite of the fact that Szekfü's historical works were based on impeccable scholarship and no one challenged the facts on which he based his interpretations. His case was an illustration of Macaulay's statement: "A history in which every particular incident may be true, may, on the whole, be false."[2]

In the course of a half-century, Szekfü's political views had seemingly undergone drastic changes. Examining his writings, one could reasonably come to the conclusion that these changes were deliberate and purposeful rather than the results of a gradual transformation of belief. After his initial, Dualist, phase, Szekfü's political ideas and historical writings contained the paradox of sincerity even in the absence of conviction. The sincerity of doing or expressing what he considered to be in the best interest of Hungary was overriding his antipathy or lack of personal belief.

There were many who felt that the changes in Szekfű's views were manifestations of political opportunism. One expatriate Hungarian writer wrote that Szekfű "combined metaphysical idealism with a pragmatic belief in success and the established power and saw not only necessity but also virtue in siding with authority . . . . His point of view was in a way unchanged; simply the established power to be relied on was now the Soviet Union . . . ."[3] This view is contradicted by the fact that Szekfű did not side with the pro-Nazi authority from the mid 1930's to the end of the Second World War even though opposition to the government could have affected his career and, after the German occupation, posed a danger to his life. Furthermore, when we consider that, in spite of the changes, there was a great deal of continuity in Szekfű's political ideas--especially striking was the similarity between his views expressed in the early 1920's and those written in 1947--the change of personal opportunism has to be discarded.

To Szekfű, throughout his lifetime, the most detested political theory was liberalism. In two articles, written in 1922 and published in <u>Keresztény Politika</u> (Christian Politics),

Szekfü discussed what he saw as alternatives to a liberal, parliamentary form of government. He showed that in countries where Christian Socialists as well as Social Democratic parties opposed liberalism, the liberal parties were on the decline by the turn of the century and, after the First World War, their importance was slight. Thus, the Center Party in Germany and the Christian Socialists in Austria not only successfully opposed liberalism but also served as alternatives to Social Democracy. Szekfü thought that liberalism ignored the needs of the rural population and the urban workers; the Christian Center parties, on the other hand, represented the interests of the lower classes who could not successfully compete in a system dominated by the liberal free market. "A system of free competition turned out to benefit the powerful, rather than serving as a means for those of merit to achieve success."[4]

In the 1920's, Szekfü saw the answer to the postwar problems of Hungary in a system which he called a "Christian National Estate State." He described this system as one which would be based on Christian principles. Instead of the cruelty of _laissez faire_ liberalism which condoned the principle of the survival of the fittest, the Christian state would not abandon the poor and the weak but would provide welfare measures for them.[5] Szekfü believed that the parliamentary form of government should be abolished because under that system the government was at the mercy of the mechanical and impersonal workings of party machinery and party politics. Instead, he envisioned a Christian National system devoted to the welfare of the people, its governing body free of the issues of party politics and its leadership entrusted to men who were "members of the intellectual and moral elite of the state and conscious representatives of the nation."[6] Every member of the society would possess a basic economic security and the chance for education. Thus, the difference between the rich and the poor would lessen. The fruits of the labor of an individual would be rewarded according to the importance of his work. To Szekfü, the essence of the Christian National politics was to ensure and maintain spiritual and national values. "In the case of tragic conflict between the state and the nation, the Christian National policy would favor whichever represented a higher moral value."[7]

In the beginning of the interwar period almost everyone in the "Kingdom of Hungary" believed in the eventual revision of the Trianon borders. Szekfü was no exception. But the historian understood that the semi-feudal social and economic structure of the state would have to be changed if Hungary were to be a viable multi-national state once again. He thought that a benevolent, authoritarian Christian National state could be an alternative to liberalism or Social Democracy. However, by the middle of the 1930's, Szekfü realized that the Christian Socialists of the German speaking countries had either ceased to function or that they were powerless to prevent the spread of Fascism. This might have been the reason behind Szekfü's changed attitude toward Social Democracy.

Szekfü had an ingrained respect for authority. He took the biblical injunction literally, and was willing to "render unto Caesar the things which are Caesar's; and unto God the things that are God's." He had no quarrel with a disciplined, closely regulated, authoritarian state. Significantly, when he wrote his enthusiastic report about Russia in 1947, he emphasized those traits in the Soviet system which he considered essential in his description of the Christian National Estate state twenty-five years previously. He claimed to find in the Soviet Union a concern for the welfare of all the people on the part of the Soviet State and this to him seemed to resemble the Christian concept of <u>Charitas</u>. He found a maintenance of religious and national values side by side with the Marxist principles and he noted that the work of the Russian people was rewarded according to the importance of their functions. Thus, Szekfü was able to support the Communist regime without changing his previous convictions.

Nor was there a change in Szekfü's view throughout his career that the interest of the state came before domestic considerations. The influence of the ideas of Leopold von Ranke was manifested in Szekfü's political thought at the end of his career no less than in the beginning. It has been said that Ranke's view that "the state . . . is obliged to organize all its internal resources for the purpose of self-preservation," was a revolt against Western ideas "which in time grew into Germanophilism."[8] Szekfü's views expressed in 1939, in <u>Mi a Magyar</u>? in which he extolled Machiavellian politics in the interest of the survival of the Hungarian state and emphasized the maintenance of the Magyar national and religious values, clearly show that the German intellectual influences he acquired in the very beginning of his career continued to be among his intellectual baggage to the end of his life.

Similarly, Szekfü continued to believe that the stability of the state took precedent over the rights of the people. In 1920, he justified the corruption of the Dualist government by stating that the Tisza administration was compelled to oppose the extension of the franchise and use economic political pressures in order to return a parliamentary majority for the Dualist Party; this was in the national interest. Similarly, in 1947, he explained that the civil rights of the people had to be curtailed because they endangered the stability of the new regime.

There was no change in Szekfü's life-long suspicion and distrust of capitalism and modernity. His violent dislike of Oscar Jászi and the Bourgeois Radicals was due more to the ideas they advocated than to their Jewish origin or even to their proposals of nationality reforms. "They attacked the nation from the outside with their free-mason-like world view from the self-satisfied heights of Spencerian sociology."[9] Indeed, Szekfü's anti-Semitism, like that of some of the German conservative nationalists, was not so much an expression of religious or racial antipathy but a rejection of liberalism and Western ideas; Jews, he felt, were responsible for popularizing those ideas in Hungary.[10]

One of the seemingly most profound changes in Szekfü's attitude was that his early belief in Hungary's place as part of the Christian-German cultural community gave way to a feeling of the necessity, or perhaps the inevitability, of being closely associated with Russia. Yet even this apparent volte-face masked an underlying continuity: throughout his career Szekfü stressed the need for Hungary to be closely associated with another, more powerful, state.

The fact is that it was not difficult for Szekfü to turn from his belief in an authoritarian conservative nationalist state to the support of an authoritarian Communist regime because it was a purely political change which did not require him to change his historical outlook. The real change for Szekfü would have been if he had espoused the ideas of a liberal, parliamentary democratic system at the end of his life. He rejected "Western-style democracy" in 1945, no less than he did in 1920, as a form of government and as a social system which was incompatible with Hungary's traditions.

In 1913, writing about Rákóczi's years in exile, Szekfü stated that the life of every exile was futile and that reconciliation and adjustment to new circumstances was more important than clinging to old principles. The senselessness of championing a lost cause was the other side of the Machiavellian politics in which the interest of the state was paramount: it had nothing to do with ideology.[11]

Szekfü once said that the Hungarian Machiavellian politicians had neither possessed the Machiavellian contempt for humanity, nor carried the amorality of their politics into their private lives.[12] This was certainly true of Szekfü. Although many people disliked and attacked his political views, no suggestion of personal wrongdoing, or even unkindness, was ever made about Szekfü. On the contrary, even in the early 1920's, just after he charged Jews and Socialists with the responsibility for the national disaster in Három Nemzedék, Szekfü was said to have aided at least one Jewish Socialist emigrant.[13] His anti-Semitic views notwithstanding, in 1940, he delivered a eulogy at the memorial service for the historian Henrik Marczali, in defiance of the official attitude of the Hungarian Historical Society which neglected and reviled the venerable old scholar in his infirmity. Szekfü professed to be proud to call himself a pupil of Marczali.[14] And it certainly took personal courage for him to testify in behalf of the Communist leader Zoltán Schönherz at his trial in the summer of 1942.

Underneath a continuous external move from the Right to the Left of the political spectrum, Szekfű's views on history and politics were constant. Yet he always remained suspicious of ideological certainties. His strong religious belief notwithstanding, Szekfű retained a basic skepticism of eternal verities and a fundamental pessimism concerning the future. He once said that

> what we call 'truth' contains an objective core but on the whole it is a subjective, relative concept, age-bound or dependent on circumstances or people; therefore, one should not elevate too many truths into dogma because the subjective elements surrounding the kernel of objectivity create a resistance which tends to overpower or eliminate the objective core of the concept. On the other hand, a concept which is completely true cannot be defined without subjective elements because it is devastating; it eliminates all hope.[15]

Szekfű was something of an enigma. He was a devout Catholic who often quoted Nietzsche and whose favorite author was Anatole France. He disliked the cynicism and the malicious humor of the "Budapest culture," yet he himself was called "the most cynical man I have ever known."[16] He was extremely polite and considerate, yet "fantastically sarcastic," puritanical and opinionated, yet possessed of an ironic, self-deprecating humor. He was a man who--whether he backed the aristocratic Bethlen or the communist Rákosi --championed the welfare of the people. A man who justified the curtailment of civil rights in the interest of the state, yet always believed in Christian consideration for his fellow man.

Early in his career, Szekfű stated that historical writing was created on the twin foundations of politics and psychology.[17] The inconsistencies in the historian's character and the motivation behind his purposes fell in the realm of psychology, outside of the scope of this study. But his purposes were clearly revealed in his published books and articles and they were intimately connected with the political events of his time. In the history of Hungarian historiography Gyula Szekfű's place will be a significant one. He was a scholar of merit and a writer of eloquence perhaps unequaled in Hungarian historiography to this day. And more than any other writer's, his historical and journalistic writings were accurate reflections of the half-century of political and intellectual changes which took place in Hungary during his lifetime.

FOOTNOTES

[1] It is interesting to note that Marxist historians think that it is the historical scholarship of Western Europe and the United States which is dominated by politics. In an article which originally appeared in Voprosi Istorii and was reprinted in the Hungarian journal Századok, M. A. Barg discussed "bourgeois historiography" of the West and found it to be in a "state of profound crisis." He quoted the Swiss historian, H. Lüthy: "Never was a science so deeply and persistently dependent on political purposes as history." M. A. Barg, "A Módszer Problémája a Mai Polgári Történetirásban." (The Problem of Method in Today's Bourgeois Historical Writing) Századok, CVII (1973), p. 721.

[2] Thomas Babington Macauley in "History." Cited in Fritz Stern, The Varieties of History. Cleveland, Ohio: The World Publishing Co., 1965, p. 84.

[3] Paul Ignotus, Hungary. New York: Praeger Publishers, 1972, p. 170.

[4] Gyula Szekfü, "A Liberális Pártalakulás Társadalmi Alapjai," (The Social Bases of the Formation of a Liberal Party), in Történetpolitikai Tanulmányok, (Historical-Political Studies). Budapest: Magyar Irodalmi Társaság, 1924, p. 50.

[5] Gyula Szekfü, "Állam és Nemzetfenntartás," (The Maintenance of State and Nation) in Történetpolitikai Tanulmányok, p. 32.

[6] Ibid., p. 33.

[7] Ibid., p. 35.

[8] Theodor H. von Laue stated that this German revolt against the West resulted in a chain reaction: " . . . Wherever the standards of the most advanced Western nations clashed with local traditions, a similar ideological revolt was the logical consequence of local nationalism . . . ." Cited in Hans Kohn, The Mind of Germany: The Education of a Nation. New York: Harper and Row, 1965, p. 264.

⁹Bálint Hóman and Gyula Szekfü, Magyar Történet (Hungarian History). Budapest: Királyi Magyar Egyetemi Nyomda, 1938, V, p. 597.

¹⁰cf. Kohn, The Mind of Germany, p. 276.

¹¹Szekfü once half-jokingly stated that "a politician can not have any convictions, although he may find it necessary to profess this or that under certain circumstances. Even a scholar can seldom afford /to have convictions/ unless he is an astronomer or paleographer." László Bóka, Válogatott Tanulmányok (Selected Studies). Budapest: Magvető, 1966, p. 1055.

¹²Gyula Szekfü, Mi a Magyar? (What is Hungarian?). Budapest: Magyar Szemle Társaság, 1939, p. 529.

¹³Bóka, Tanulmányok, p. 1056.

¹⁴Emma Léderer, "Marczali Henrik helye a Magyar Polgári Történettudományban," (Henrik Marczali's place in the Hungarian Bourgeois Historical Sciences), Századok, XCVI (1962), 467.

¹⁵Bóka, Tanulmányok, p. 1056.

¹⁶Ibid., p. 1054.

¹⁷Gyula Szekfü, "Az Osztrák Központi Kormányszerve Történetének Irodalma" (The Literature of the History of the Austrian Central Government Organizations), Történeti Szemle, I (1912), p. 185.

BIBLIOGRAPHICAL ESSAY

The present examination of Gyula Szekfű's historical and political views and their connection with twentieth century Hungarian history focused on the gradual shift in the historian's political orientation and on the political and intellectual influence his historical and journalistic writings exercised on his contemporaries. Szekfű's political purposes were achieved through his books and articles and, therefore, the published works of Gyula Szekfű served as primary sources for this dissertation. Special emphasis has been put on those of his works which reveal more clearly the connection between Szekfű's views and the changes in Hungarian politics. For the purposes of this study archival material was of lesser importance.

Unpublished material on Gyula Szekfű can be found in two archives. His correspondence, lecture notes and material pertaining to his role as professor of modern Hungarian history are kept at the Egyetemi Könyvtár, Eötvös Lóránd Tudományegyetem (University Library, Eötvös Lóránd University) in Budapest. Other material pertaining to Szekfű's historical scholarship is housed in the Magyar Tudományos Akadémia Kézirattár (Manuscripts of the Hungarian Academy of Sciences) also in Budapest. The latter includes unfinished manuscripts, collections of sources, contemporary newspaper clippings pertaining to the controversy about the publication of A Száműzött Rákóczi and reviews of Szekfű's early books. There appears to be little if any archival material relevant to Szekfű's career in the decade preceding the end of the Second World War. This may be due to the fact that Szekfű burnt many of his personal papers in March 1944, when the German occupation of Hungary compelled him to go into hiding.[1]

Although Szekfű had been an extremely prolific letter-writer, none of his correspondence is published. A diligent quest for material on Szekfű may require the examination of the correspondence of those of his friends and associates whose legacy is also in the public domain. For instance, the material pertaining to the historian Dávid Angyal (1857-1943), also at the Archives at the Academy of Sciences in Budapest, lists 303 letters written to Angyal by Gyula Szekfű.[2]

No all-inclusive bibliography of Szekfű's works has been published up till now. Because he had contributed his journalistic articles to a wide variety of periodicals, a vigorous attempt to trace them notwithstanding, the list of his works provided in pp. 343-351 is probably incomplete.

As yet no biography has been written of Gyula Szekfű nor has there appeared any comprehensive evaluation of Szekfű's oeuvre. However, certain aspects of his scholarship have been discussed in books and articles during his life time and in the nearly twenty years since his death. During the interwar period, two brief books with diametrically opposed opinions of Szekfű were published. Sándor Pethő's Szekfű Gyula Történetirása (The Historical Writing of Gyula Szekfű. Budapest: Lantos Könyvkiadó Vállalat, 1933) is an uncritical, adulatory review of the major works Szekfű published before 1933. Much more interesting, although no more objective, is a book written by the populist writer László Németh. In Szekfű Gyula (Budapest: Bólyai Kiadás, 1940) Németh attempted to prove that all of Szekfű's views--from Rákóczi to Széchenyi, from the Middle Ages to Liberalism and Dualism--were wrong. Németh was a witty and brilliant stylist and the book makes for lively and entertaining reading. It is primarily a Kuruc polemic attacking the Labanc point of view.

In 1943, on the occasion of Szekfű's Sixtieth birthday, the periodical Magyar Szemle, which Szekfű edited from 1927 to 1938, devoted an entire issue to the historian. Count István Bethlen wrote the preface and some of the foremost Hungarian historians and journalists of the period contributed articles on various aspects of Szekfű's career. These articles are interesting and informative, although no more critical than the usual writing in a Festschrift. There is, however, one common thread worthy of note running through every one of the articles: an emphasis on Szekfű's sense of responsibility as an educator of the nation.[3]

Post-World War Two articles on Szekfü have been understandingly ambivalent. The most extensive evaluation so far, an article by Gyula Mérei, "Szekfü Gyula Történetszemléletének Birálatához," (About the Evaluation of the Historical Views of Gyula Szekfü) appeared in Századok (XCIV, 1960, pp. 180-245). In it Mérei discussed Szekfü's historical method, the origin and the course of Hungarian Geistesgeschichte and the most important of Szekfü's books. Lavish praise for his meticulous scholarship, writing ability and his "accurate recognition of details" was mixed with disapproval for his harmful intellectual influence and for his responsibility for the counterrevolutionary political philosophy of the 1920's. Szekfü was charged with "incorrect interpretation of the whole" of Hungarian history wrongly deduced from "accurate evaluation of its parts."[4] The turning point in Szekfü's historical and political point of view came in 1941, according to Mérei.[5] A similar but brief evaluation of Szekfü's work appeared in József Szigeti's A Magyar Szellemtörténet Birálatához (About the Evaluation of Hungarian Geistesgeschichte. Budapest: Kossuth Kiadó, 1964), a book about the political implications of the Hungarian Geistesgeschichte. Two of the chapters of the book were originally published in 1952, at the height of the so-called "personality cult." Szigeti presented the thesis that Szellemtörténet was a weapon of political reaction directed against socialism and the Soviet Union. Szekfü's works, especially Három Nemzedék and Magyar Történet, were used as examples.

The difference between the Hungarian historical writings of the 1950's and the subtly changing attitude in the 1960's can be perceived when we compare Szigeti's and Mérei's work with that of a shorter article by Imre Lóránd. In "A Három Nemzedéktöl a Forradalom Utánig" (From Three Generations to After the Revolution, Világosság, VII, 1966, pp. 347-352), Imre Lóránd traced the changes in Szekfü's point of view during the period between 1920 and 1947. This article lacks the stridency of tone which characterized some of the historical works written in the 1950's. Lóránd examined the influence of Szekfü's writing and showed a keen insight into the complexities of the period. He found that Szekfü's Labanc revision of Hungarian history was, to a limited extent, salutory, for it brought a needed balance to the strongly anti-Habsburg historiography of the nineteenth century. In contrast to earlier Marxist views, Lóránd agreed with Szekfü on some of the advantages, (principly economic), of Dualism.

The most objective treatment of Hungarian historiography can be found in the writings of Ágnes Várkonyi. Unfortunately so far Várkonyi has not written specifically about Gyula Szekfü, but the latter figures peripherally in her Thaly Kálmán és Történetirása (Kálmán Thaly and his Historical Writing. Budapest: Akadémiai Kiadó, 1961).

This book contains the best account of the Szekfü-Thaly controversy which erupted in 1913 after the publication of Szekfü's book on Rákóczi. The appearance of Ágnes Várkonyi, <u>A Pozitivista Történetszemlélet a Magyar Történetirásban</u> (The Positivist View of History in Hungarian Historical Writing, 2. vols. Budapest: Akadémiai Kiadó, 1973) is an important addition to the literature of the history of Hungarian historical scholarship. Várkonyi discusses the origin and development of the positivist view of history, deals with European historians of the positivist school from August Comte to Herbert Spencer and evaluates the course of the positivist historiography in Hungary preceding World War I. According to Várkonyi, it was the controversy around <u>A Száműzött Rákóczi</u> which ended the positivist school of historical writing in Hungary. In a book written by Szekfü as an answer to his critics, Szekfü discredited both the romantic views of Thaly and those of the positivists.[6] Várkonyi considers Szekfü's <u>A Száműzött Rákóczi</u> and <u>Der Staat Ungarn</u> manifestations of a clear break with the previous schools of historical scholarship; they were the first products of the Hungarian <u>Geistesgeschichte</u>. Mérei and Szigeti, on the other hand, hold the view that this new school of historical scholarship was adopted as a tool of counterrevolutionary nationalism after the Revolutions of 1918-1919 and it was first employed by Szekfü in <u>Három Nemzedék</u>.

* * *

Because of the relationship between twentieth-century Hungarian history and Szekfü's political and historical points of view, Szekfü's work has to be examined in the context of Hungarian history. Since 1945, an impressive amount of historical scholarship produced a steady flow of published primary sources, comprehensive histories, monographs and articles on every aspect of Hungarian history, supplementing or replacing works written before the Second World War. Hungarian historical scholarship of the past fifteen years has been impressive in quality as well as in quantity; Marxist Hungarian historiography has become increasingly objective. A good general introduction to twentieth-century Hungarian historical scholarship is an article by Zoltán Horváth, "Hungary: Recovering from the Past," in <u>Contemporary History in Europe</u>, ed. by D. C. Watt (Frederick A. Praeger, New York, 1969). Horváth was imprisoned in 1949 and rehabilitated just before the Revolution of 1956. His article discusses the problem of the misuses of political power and its effect on historical scholarship and objectivity; he is highly critical of the one-sided, Hungarocentric historiography and of the interference of politics and ideology with the evaluation of the past. That such an article can appear abroad and its author can continue to be a historian of good standing in Hungary whose works are published, prove the extent of freedom of expression in Hungary today.

Published primary sources in the form of documentary collections consulted in the course of the preparation of this study include A Magyar Munkásmozgalom Történetének Válogatott Dokumentumai (Selected Documents of the History of the Hungarian Labor Movement). Budapest: Magyar Munkásmozgalmi Intézet, Szikra, 1951-1959; Az Ellenforradalom Hatalomrajutása és Rémuralma (The Achievement of Power and the Terror of the Counterrevolution), ed. by Dezsö Nemes. Budapest: Szikra, 1953; Bethlen István Titkos Iratai (The Secret Documents of István Bethlen), ed. by Miklós Szinnai and László Szücs. Budapest: Kossuth Könyvkiadó, 1963; Diplomáciai Iratok Magyarország Külpolitikájáról 1936-1945 (Diplomatic Documents about Hungary's Foreign Policy, 1936-1945), 4. vols. Budapest: Akadémiai Kiadó, 1952-1962; Horthy Miklós Titkos Iratai (The Secret Documents of Miklós Horthy), ed. by Szinnai Miklós and László Szücs. Budapest: Kossuth Könyvkiadó, 1963; Iratok a Magyar Nemzetiségi Kérdés Történetéhez (Documents Pertaining to the History of the Hungarian Nationality Question), ed. by Gábor G. Kemény, 3. vols. Budapest: Tankönyvkiadó, 1952-1964; Iratok az Ellenforradalom Történetéhez 1919-1945 (Documents Related to the History of Counterrevolutionary Regime, 1919-1945). Budapest Országos Levéltár, 1959; Magyarország és a Második Világháború: Titkos Diplomáciai Iratok a Háború Elözményeihez és

Történetéhez (Hungary and the Second World War: Secret Diplomatic Documents Related to the Events Before and During the War), ed. by László Zsigmond. Budapest: Kossuth Kiadó, 1961; Sorsforduló: Iratok Magyarország Felszabadulásának Történetéhez, 1944.szeptember-1945.április (Turningpoint: Documents related to the History of the Liberation of Hungary, September 1944-April 1945). Budapest, 1970; and Vádirat a Nácizmus Ellen: Dokumentumok a Magyarországi Zsidóüldözések Történetéhez (Indictment against Nazism: Documents Concerning the History of the Persecution of the Jews in Hungary). Budapest: Magyar Izraeliták Országos Képviselete, 1967.

There are many personal accounts and memoirs which shed light on the political and intellectual history of twentieth-century Hungary. Among them Dávid Angyal, Emlékezések (Remembrances. London: Szepsi-Csombor Kör, 1971), the memoir of a historian and former professor at the University of Budapest who, at one time, served as a tutor of Otto Habsburg, a son of the last Hapbburg ruler of Hungary, Charles IV. Wilhelm Böhm, Im Kreuzfeuer zwei Revolutionen (München: Verlag für Kulturpolitik, 1924), and Manó Buchinger, Küzdelem a Szocializmusért (The Struggle for Socialism. Budapest: Népszava, 1948), both deal with memories of the Hungarian Revolutions of 1918-1919. Oscar Jászi began to publish his memoirs in the last year of his life in a Hungarian journal published in Munich.

"Emlékeimből: Szülőföldemen; Egyetemi Évek" (From my Memoirs: In My Native Land; Student Years), "A Huszadik Század Elindul a Herbert Spencer Égisze Alatt" (The Huszadik Század Begins under the Aegis of Herbert Spencer) and "Elmélet és Gyakorlat Között" (Between Theory and Practice, Látóhatár, VIII (1956), pp. 59-70, 135-139 and 208-217), deal with the beginnings of an intellectual movement which was the basis of the Hungarian bourgeois radical politics preceding World War I. The Memoirs of Michael Károlyi: Faith Without Illusions. (London: Jonathan Cape, 1956), Miklós Horthy, Memoirs (New York: R. Speller, 1957), and Nicholas Kállay, Hungarian Premier (New York: Columbia University Press, 1954), present the recollections of three of the leading political figures in Hungary. Kállay's volume is an important source for Hungary's unsuccessful attempt to leave the German Alliance and make peace with the Allies during the Second World War. Vince Nagy, Októbertől Októberig (From October to October. New York: Pro Arte Publishing Co., 1960), contains the memoirs of one of the few democratic members of the Hungarian House of Representatives during the interwar period. Parts of Stephen D. Kertész, Diplomacy in a Whirlpool: Hungary between Nazi Germany and Soviet Russia (Notre Dame: University of Notre Dame Press, 1953), also utilized recollections of personal experiences. An interesting work dealing with the memoirs of anti-Communist Hungarian emigres needs to be mentioned here: in Emlékiratok és Valóság

Magyarország Második Világháborus Szerepéről (Memoirs and the Truth about Hungary's Role in the Second World War. Budapest: Kossuth Kiadó, 1964), György Ránki takes issue with the assertions of Horthy, Kállay, Kertész and others.

The best general history of Hungary is Erik Molnár et al. ed., Magyarország Története (The History of Hungary. Budapest: Gondolat Könyvkiadó, 1967), a two-volume history of Hungary from the ninth century to 1956. Written by eight historians, it emphasizes economic changes and a materialist view of history; it is nevertheless an example of sophisticated historical scholarship with a high level of objectivity. For a wealth of detail especially on political and intellectual history from the beginnings of Hungarian history to 1914, Bálint Hóman and Gyula Szekfű's Magyar Történet (Hungarian History, V. vols., Budapest, 1928-1932), is still useful.

Important monographs dealing with aspects of Hungarian history since the end of the nineteenth century include Iván T. Berend, A Magyar Gazdaság Száz Éve (One Hundred Years of Hungarian Economy. Budapest: Kossuth Kiadó, 1972), dealing with the development of Hungarian industry since the beginning of the Dualistic period. Fukász György, A Magyarországi Polgári Radikalizmus Történetéhez, 1900-1918: Jászi Oszkár Ideológiájának Birálata (On the History of the Bourgeois Radicalism in Hungary, 1900-1918: The Evaluation of Oscar Jászi's Ideology. Budapest: Gondolat Kiadó, 1960), is a close examination of the pre-1918 books, speeches and correspondence of Oscar Jászi. Péter Hanák, A Dualizmus Korának Történeti Problémái (The Historical Problems of the Dualistic Period. Budapest: Tankönyvkiadó, 1971), is a handbook for teachers and it examines the Dualist period from the sociological point of view. Zoltán Horváth, Die Jahrhundertwende in Ungarn: Geschichte der Zweiten Reform Generation: 1896-1914 (Luchterhand: Neuwied, 1966), illuminates the intellectual as well as the political development of an era which was one of political decline but literary brilliance. The traditional Hungarian, anti-Communist point of view about the Hungarian Revolutions of 1918-1919 is given in Gusztáv Grátz, A Forradalmak Kora: Magyarország Története 1918-1920 (The Age of Revolutions. The History of Hungary 1918-1920, 2 vols. Budapest: Magyar Szemle Társaság, 1934). A mildly critical but establishmentarian view of Hungarian society in the 1920's is presented in István Weis, A Mai Magyar Társadalom (Hungarian Society Today. Budapest: Magyar Szemle Társaság, 1930). The most important book on the anti-Fascist resistance during the Second World War is a book by Gyula Kállai, A Magyar Függetlenségi Mozgalom (The Hungarian Independence Movement. Budapest: Kossuth Kiadó, 1965). Kállai's membership in the Hungarian Communist Party dates from 1931. He was one of the organizers of the March Front and the Historical Memorial Committee.

    Literature containing a realistic treatment of the pre-World War I nationality problems began to be published in the 1920's. At the same time, a concern for the Magyar minorities in the succession states and the hope for the future revision of the Trianon borders gave rise to a new attitude toward the nationality areas of pre-war Hungary. Numerous articles concerning the nationality question appeared in the Bethlen-sponsored and Szekfü-edited Magyar Szemle. An example was László Ottlik, "Uj Hungária Felé," (Toward a New Hungaria, Magyar Szemle, IV (1928), pp. 1-9), discussing the possibility of autonomy of the non-Magyar peoples within Hungary, in the event of the revision of the national borders. István Bethlen, The Treaty of Trianon and the European Peace (London: Longman Greene and Co., 1933), contains Count Bethlen's four lectures presented in England; it was a more authoritative and detailed statement of the same proposal. Most of the articles Gyula Szekfü wrote on the nationality problems (discussed in Chapter Eight of this study) had originally appeared in the periodical Magyar Szemle which was a major forum of the nationality questions. Szekfü's articles were collected and published in book form under the title Állam és Nemzet (State and Nation. Budapest: Magyar Szemle Társaság, 1942). État et Nation (Paris: Les Presses Universitaires de France, 1945) is a slightly changed French version of this book.

Marxist treatment of the nationality problems include Erzsébet Andics, ed., A Magyar Nacionalizmus Kialakulása és Története (The Development and the History of the Hungarian

Nationalism. Budapest: Kossuth Könyvkiadó, 1964), a collection of essays dealing with nationalism in different historical periods. Zoltán Horváth, "The Rise of Nationalism and the Nationality Problem in Hungary in the Last Decade of Dualism," appeared in Acta Historica (IX, 1963, pp. 1-38), the foreign language journal of the Hungarian Historical Society; the emphasis of this article is on the socio-economic conflicts between the Magyar ruling classes and the non-Magyar peasants. Lóránt Tilkovszky, in Revizió és Nemzetiségpolitika Magyarországon, 1938-1941 (Revision and Nationality Policy in Hungary, 1938-1941. Budapest: Akadémiai Kiadó, 1967), shows that the autonomy advocated by Bethlen and others was not put into effect in the areas that were returned to Hungary as a result of the Vienna Decisions; the nationality policies of this period were as shortsighted and harmful as those of the Dualist era.

Finally, there are a number of books written in English and published in England and in the United States which are useful to the student of Hungarian history. An important source is C. A. Macartney's October Fifteenth: A History of Modern Hungary, 1929-1945, (Edinburg: University Press, 1956); it contains a wealth of details of domestic politics and diplomatic history. Reference to this book is often made by historians in Hungary writing about wartime diplomacy. A less important work by Macartney is Hungary and her

Successors: The Treaty of Trianon and its Consequences 1919-1937, (London: Oxford University Press, 1937), giving the interwar, Hungarian point of view in justifying the need for the revision of the Treaty of Trianon.

Paul Ignotus' Hungary (New York: Praeger Publishers, 1972), is a general work of twentieth-century Hungarian politics and Hungarian society. Now living in England, Ignotus is a member of a notable Hungarian literary family (his grandfather edited the Pester Lloyd and his father was one of the founders and the first editor of the literary monthly, Nyugat); the book is noteworthy for the special insight it provides for the intellectual and literary history of the twentieth century and their connection with political events.

In the United States, aside from the memoirs published by post-World War Two immigrants who played a role on the Hungarian political scene, there are a number of scholars of Hungarian origin contributing monographs and articles to the historical literature of Hungary. For example, George Barany, Stephen Széchenyi and the Awakening of Hungarian Nationalism, 1791-1841 (Princeton: Princeton University Press, 1968), is an excellent source of the history of Hungary in the Age of Reform. Iván Völgyes, ed., Hungary in Revolution, 1918-1919 (Lincoln: University of Nebraska, 1971), is a collection of scholarly and informative essays and Rudolf L. Tőkés, Béla Kun and the Hungarian Soviet Republic (Stanford: F. A.

Praeger, 1967), evaluates the role of Béla Kun and the significance of the first Communist Revolution of Hungary in 1919.

FOOTNOTES

[1] Personal information from Dr. Olga Pajkossy, librarian of the University Library of the Eötvös Lóránd University in Budapest. A former student of Szekfü, Dr. Pajkossy visited him regularly during the year the historian spent in hiding, delivering him mail and information.

[2] Csaba Csapodi, "Történészhagyatékok a Magyar Tudományos Akadémia Könyvtárának Kézirattárában" (Posthumous Papers of Historians in the Archives of the Hungarian Academy of Sciences), Századok, CVI (1972), p. 1372.

[3] The Gyula Szekfü memorial issue of the Magyar Szemle (XLIV, 1943, no. 5) was published in book form also. Emlékkönyv Szekfü Gyula a Történetiró és Nemzetnevelö 60. Születésnapjára (Memorial Volume for the Sixtieth Birthday of Gyula Szekfü, Historian and Educator of the Nation), (Regnum, vol. V., Budapest, 1943); in addition to the articles which appeared in the Magyar Szemle, it contained a bibliography of Szekfü's works written before 1943. The volume containing the partial bibliograply, however, was not available to this writer.

[4] Gyula Mérei, "Szekfü Gyula Történetszemléletének Birálatához," (About the Evaluation of the Historical Views of Gyula Szekfü), Századok, XCIV (1960), p. 181.

[5] Ibid., pp. 248-249.

[6] Várkonyi's reference was to Gyula Szekfü's Mit Vétettem Én? Ki Gyalázta Rákóczit? (Where Have I Sinned? Who Vilified Rákóczi?). Budapest: Dick Manó Kiadása, no date.

BIBLIOGRAPHY

BIBLIOGRAPHY

WORKS BY GYULA SZEKFŰ

Szekfű, Gyula. Adatok Szamosközy István Történeti Munkájának Kritikájához (Factors about the Evaluation of the Historical Works of István Szamosközy). Doctoral Dissertation, Budapest, 1904.

――――――― "Szamosközy Műve az 1594. Év Eseményeiről" (Szamosközy's Work about the Events of the Year 1594). Századok, XLII (1908), pp. 217-244.

――――――― "Gustav Wolf: Einführung in das Studium der Neueren Geschichte." Történeti Szemle, I (1912), pp. 114-121.

――――――― "Az Osztrák Központi Kormányszervek Történetének Irodalma" (The Literature of the Austrian Central Government Organization). Történelmi Szemle, I (1912), pp. 185-219.

――――――― Serviensek és Familiárisok. Budapest: A Tudományos Akadémia, 1912.

――――――― A Száműzött Rákóczi, 1715-1735 (The Exiled Rákóczi, 1715-1735). Budapest: A Magyar Tudományos Akadémia Kiadása, 1913.

――――――― "Két Historiographus Castaldo Erdélyi Seregében" (Two historiographers in Castaldo's Transylvanian Troops), Századok, XLVIII (1914), 17-35.

――――――― Mit Vétettem Én? Ki Gyalázta Rákóczit? (Where have I sinned? Who Vilified Rákóczi?). Budapest: Dick Manó Kiadása, no date.

――――――― "Ujabb Válasz Bírálóimnak" (Another Answer to My Critics). Történeti Szemle, III (1914), pp. 452-480.

Sándor Takáts and Ferenc Eckhardt. A Budai
Basák Magyar Nyelvű Levelezése (The Magyar
Correspondence of the Pashas of Buda).
Budapest: A Magyar Tudományos Akadémia,
1915.

Der Staat Ungarn: Eine Geschichtsstudie.
Stuttgart-Berlin: Deutsche Verlag Anstalt,
1917.

A Magyar Állam Életrajza (The Biography of
the Hungarian State). Budapest: Dick Manó
Könyvkereskedése, 1918.

Három Nemzedék (Three Generations). Budapest:
Királyi Magyar Egyetemi Nyomda, 1920.

Széchenyi Igéi (Széchenyi's Ideas). Budapest:
Pallas R. T., 1921.

"Faji sajátságosságaink a Gazdaságtörténet
Világánál" (Our Racial Characteristics in the
Light of Economic History). Minerva, 1922.

"A Magyar Bortermelő Lelki Alkata" (The
Psychological Make-up of the Hungarian Wine
Merchant). Minerva, 1922.

"Állam és Nemzetfenntartás" (The Maintenance
of State and Nation). Keresztény Politika,
1922.

"A Liberális Pártalakulás Társadalmi Alapjai"
(The Social Bases of the Formation of a
Liberal Party). Keresztény Politika, 1922.

"Fajbiológia vagy Történeti Egység" (Racial
Biology or Historical Unity). Keresztény
Politika, 1922.

"A Faji Kérdés és a Magyarság" (The Racial
Question and the Hungarians). Napkelet, II
(1923), pp. 801-820.

"Andrássy." Napkelet, I (1923), pp. 418-423.

"Negyvennyolcas Történetünk Mai Állása"
(Our History of 1848 Today). Napkelet, II
(1924), pp. 243-253.

"Egy Hetvenéves Történetíró. (Károlyi Árpád)"
(A Seventy-Year Old Historian (Árpád Károlyi).
Napkelet, II (1923), pp. 786-789.

"Petőfi-Centennárium" (Petőfi Centennial).
Napkelet, I (1923), pp. 21-31.

"Báró Wlassics Gyula: Deák Ferenc."
Napkelet, IV (1924), pp. 263-264.

"Magyarok Török Rabságban" (Hungarians in
Turkish Captivity). Napkelet, IV (1924),
pp. 266-268.

Történetpolitikai Tanulmányok (Historical-
Political Studies). Budapest: A Magyar
Irodalmi Társaság, 1924.

"Az Erdélyi Probléma" (The Transylvanian
Problem). Napkelet, V (1925), pp. 453-466.

"Széchenyi Ünnepe" (Széchenyi's Memorial).
Napkelet, VI (1925), pp. 347-351.

"Tomory." Napkelet, VIII (1926), pp. 585-594.

Iratok a Magyar Államnyelv Kérdésének
Történetéhez, 1790-1848 (Documents Pertaining to the History of the Magyar Language of
the State). Budapest: A Magyar Történelmi
Társulat Kiadása, 1926.

"Ruswarm gróf 'Gyáva' Magyarjai" (The "Coward-
ly" Hungarians of Count Ruswarm). Napkelet,
IX (1927), pp. 426-431.

"György Barát" (The Friar György). Napkelet,
X (1927), pp. 753-758.

"Álarcos Könyvek" (Masked Books). Napkelet,
VII (1927), pp. 255-261.

"A Magyar Folyóirat Problémája" (The Problem of the Hungarian Periodical). Magyar Szemle, I (1927), pp. 1-4).

"Kossuth Budapesti Szobrának Leleplezésekor" (At the Unveiling of Kossuth's Statue in Budapest). Magyar Szemle, I (1927), pp. 293-296.

"A Katolikus Történetirás Magyarországon" (The Catholic Historical Writing in Hungary). Magyar Katolikus Almanach. Budapest, 1927, pp. 685-700.

"A Mai Ifjuság Korosztályai" (The Age Divisions of Today's Youth). Magyar Szemle, III (1928), pp. 136-139.

"A Magyar Nagybirtok Történeti Szerepéről" (About the Historical Role of the Hungarian Latifundia). Magyar Szemle, II (1928), pp. 305-314.

and Bálint Hóman. Magyar Történet (Hungarian History). V. volumnes. Budapest: Királyi Magyar Egyetemi Nyomda, 1928-1933.

"A Turáni Szláv Parasztállam" (The Turan-Slav Peasant State). Magyar Szemle, V (1929), pp. 30-37.

"Négy Egyetem" (Four Universities). Magyar Szemle, VI (1929), pp. 322-331.

Bethlen Gábor. Budapest: Magyar Szemle Társaság, 1929.

"II.Rákóczi Ferenc." Napkelet, XVI (1930), pp. 813-821.

"Az Ifjuság Társadalmi Szemlélete" (The Youth's View of Society). Magyar Szemle, VIII (1930), pp. 207-214.

"Sufflay Milán Tragédiája" (The Tragedy of Milan Sufflay). Magyar Szelme, XI (1931), pp. 377-384.

"A Nemzeti Politika Tíz Esztendeje" (Ten Years of National Politics). Magyar Szemle, XI (1931), pp. 384-386.

"Trianon Reviziója és a Történetirás" (The Revision of Trianon and Historiography). Magyar Szemle, XII (1931), pp. 328-337.

"A Történet Mechanizálása" (The Mechanization of History). Magyar Szemle, XIII (1931), pp. 331-341.

"A Politikai Történetirás" (Political Historiography), in A Magyar Történetirás Új Útjai (New Path in Hungarian Historiography). Ed. by Bálint Hóman. Budapest: Magyar Szemle Társaság, 1932.

"Károlyi Árpád, a Történetiró" (Árpád Károlyi, the Historiographer), in Emlékkönyv Károlyi Árpád Születése 80-ik Fordulójának Ünnepére (Memorial Volume for Károlyi Árpád's Eightieth Birthday). Budapest: Sárkány Nyomda, Rt., 1933.

"Trianon Óta" (Since Trianon), in Három Nemzedék és ami Utana Következik (Three Generations and What Comes After). Budapest: Királyi Magyar Egyetemi Nyomda, 1933.

"Népiség, Nemzet és Állam" (Ethnicity, Nation and State). Magyar Szemle, XXII (1934), pp. 5-13.

"Bethlen István Gróf és a Magyar Szemle" (Count István Bethlen and the Magyar Szemle). Magyar Szemle, XXII (1934), pp. 285-288.

"Magyar Katolikus Történetfelfogás" (The Hungarian Catholic Historical Concept). Katolikus Irók Új Magyar Kalauza. Budapest: no date, pp. 396-418.

_____ ed., A Mai Széchenyi (Széchenyi Today). Budapest: Révai Kiadás, no date.

_____ "A Magyarság és Kisebbségei a Középkorban" (Hungarians and their Minorities in the Middle Ages). Magyar Szemle, XXV (1935), pp. 5-13.

_____ "Politikai Érzékünk Társadalmi Alapjairól" (About the Social Basis of our Political Sense). Magyar Szemle, XXVI (1936), pp. 297-306.

_____ "A Középosztály és a Választójog" (The Middle Class and the Franchise). Korunk Szava, December 15, 1936.

_____ "Schittenhelm Ede." Magyar Szemle, XXX (1937), pp. 223-231.

_____ "Az Irók Ellen Inditott Perekről" (About the Lawsuits against the Writers). Erdélyi Szemle, 1937, nos. 5-6, 8-9.

_____ "Magam és Mások Ügyében" (In My Own and in Others' Behalf). Korunk Szava, 1937, no. 24, pp. 707-712.

_____ "Szent István a Magyar Történelem Századaiban" (St. Stephen in Centuries of Hungarian History), in Emlékkönyv Szent Istvan Király Halálának 900. Évfordulóján (Memorial Volume on the 900th Anniversary of the Death of King St. Stephen). Budapest: Magyar Tudományos Akadémia Kiadása, 1938.

_____ "Nem Vagyunk Bujdosók" (We are no Wanderers). Magyar Szemle, XXXII (1938), pp. 391-396.

_____ "A Népi Elv Két Arca" (The Two Faces of the Ethnic Principle). Magyar Szemle, XXXV (1939), pp. 5-12.

_____ "Időszerű Történeti Munkák" (Timely Historical Works). Magyar Szemle, XXXV (1939), pp. 222-230.

"Lirai Történetirás" (Lyrical Historical Writing). Magyar Szemle, XXXVI (1939), pp. 297-306.

"Mégegyszer az Asszimilációról" (Once Again about Assimilation). Nyugat, XXXII (1939), pp. 1-3.

Mi a Magyar? (What is Hungarian?). Budapest: A Magyar Szemle Társaság, 1939.

"Az Elitélt Magyar Irók Mellett."(In Behalf of the Convicted Hungarian Writers). Magyar Nap, December 28, 1939.

"A Legújabb Nemzetiségi Javaslat" (The Most Recent Recommendation for a Nationality Law). Magyar Szemle, XXXIX (1940), pp. 5-10.

"Mégegyszer a Középkori Kisebbségeinkről" (Once Again about our Minorities in the Middle Ages). Magyar Szemle, XXXIX (1940), pp. 169-177.

"A Mátyás Emlékkönyv Tegnap és Ma" (The Memorial Volume of Mátyás Yesterday and Today). Magyar Szemle, XXXIX (1940), pp. 398-404.

"Messiási Szimbólum" (Symbol of Messiah). Magyar Nemzet, July 28, 1940.

"Népek Egymás Közt" (Nations Among Nations). Magyar Nemzet, October 13, 1940.

"Zűrzavar egy Lényeges Dologban" (Confusion in an Essential Matter). Magyar Nemzet, December 8, 1940.

"Az Uralkodó Osztály" (The Ruling Class). Magyar Nemzet, March 31, 1940.

"A Tévedés" (The Mistake). Magyar Nemzet, April 28, 1940.

"Akik Mérlegelnek" (Those who Weigh Things). Magyar Nemzet, September 29, 1940.

"Nehéz a Zavart Eloszlatni" (It is Difficult to Clear up the Confusion). Magyar Nemzet, December 25, 1940.

"Kevés a Melegség" (Too Little Warmth). Magyar Nemzet, January 5, 1941.

"A Türelem Útján" (On the Road of Patience). Magyar Nemzet, January 19, 1941.

"Kisebbségek a Többségi Társadalomban" (Minorities in a Majority Society). Magyar Nemzet, March 2, 1941.

"A Nehéz Kérdés" (The Difficult Question). Magyar Nemzet, March 15, 1941.

"A Szentkorona Eszme" (The Concept of the Holy Crown). Magyar Nemzet, March 20, 1941.

"Mi, az Utókor" (We, the Posterity). Magyar Nemzet, October 26, 1941.

"Népek Egymásközt a Középkorban" (Ethnic Relationships in the Middle Ages). Magyar Szemle, XVI (1941), pp. 225-233.

"Műveltség és Állam" (Education and the State). Magyar Nemzet, December 7, 1941.

"A Szabadság Eszméje" (The Concept of Freedom). Népszava, December 25, 1941.

"Egy Magyar Levéltárnok" (A Hungarian Archivist). Magyar Nemzet, January 18, 1942.

"A Parasztművelődés Két Útja" (Two Ways to Peasant-education). Magyar Nemzet, July 12, 1942.

Állam és Nemzet (State and Nation). Budapest: A Magyar Szemle Társaság, 1942.

"A Nemzetiségi Kérdés Rövid Története" (The Short History of the Nationality Question), in Állam és Nemzet. Budapest: A Magyar Szemle Társaság, 1942.

_____ ed., A Magyarság és a Szlávok (The Hungarians and the Slavs). Budapest: Budapesti Királyi Magyar Pázmány Péter Tudományegyetem Bölcsészeti Karának Magyarságtudományi Intézete, 1942.

_____ "Ma és Száz Év Előtt" (Today and a Hundred Years Ago). Magyar Szemle, XLV (1943), pp. 113-119.

_____ and Zoltán Tóth, Marczali Henrik. Budapest: Izraelita Magyar Irodalmi Társaság Évkönyve, 1943.

_____ "Valahol Utat Vesztettünk" (Somewhere We Lost Our Way). Magyar Nemzet, December 1943-January 1944.

_____ État et Nation. Paris: Les Presses Universitaires de France, 1945.

_____ Forradalom Után (After the Revolution). Budapest Cserépfalvi Kiadó, 1947.

_____ "Az Öreg Kossuth, 1867-1894" (The Old Kossuth, 1867-1894), in Emlékkönyv Kossuth Lajos Születésének 150-ik Évfordulójára (Memorial Volume on the 150th Anniversary of the Birth of Lajos Kossuth). Budapest: Magyar Történelmi Társulat, Akadémiai Kiadó, 1952.

_____ "Az Értelmiségiek Átállása a Felszabadulás Idején" (The Conversion of the Intellectuals at the Time of the Liberation). Csillag, IX (1955), pp. 1633-1639.

WORKS ABOUT SZEKFÜ

Bóka, László. "Szekfű Gyula." Válogatott Tanulmányok (Selected Studies). Budapest: Magvető, pp. 1054-1059.

Dezséri, György. "Magyar Kulturkrónika: Szekfű Gyula." Korunk, 1935, no. 7-8, pp. 523-527.

Erdélyi, László. "Szekfű Gyula: Serviensek és Familiárisok" Történelmi Szemle, II (1913), pp. 282-287.

Fehér, Pál E. "Kulturális Jegyzetek" (Cultural Notes). Népszabadság, May 23, 1973.

Féja, Géza. "A Történetiró mint Publicista" (The Historian as Publicist). Magyar Élet, 1943, no. 9, pp. 19-21.

Hatvany, Lajos. "Történelem Hamisitók" (Falsifiers of History), in Emberek és Korok (People and Ages). Budapest: Szépirodalmi Könyvkiadó, 1964, I, pp. 283-327.

Joó, Tibor. "Szekfű Gyula Új Könyve" (Gyula Szekfű's New Book). Magyar Szemle, XLIII (1942), pp. 1-9.

Kovács, Imre. "A Hónap Krónikája: Szekfű Gyula Tanuvallomása" (Chronicle of the Month: Gyula Szekfű's Testimony). Hid, 1937, no. 3-4.

Loránd, Imre. "A Három Nemzedéktől a Forradalom Utánig" (From Three Generations to After the Revolution). Világosság, VII (1966), pp. 342-352.

Mérei, Gyula. "Szekfű Gyula Történetszemléletének Birálatához" (About the Evaluation of the Historical Views of Gyula Szekfű). Századok, XCIV (1960), pp. 180-245.

Németh, László. Szekfű Gyula. Budapest: Bólyai Akadémia, 1940.

Ortutay, Gyula. "Szekfű Gyula." Csillag, IX (1955), pp. 1691-1692.

Pach, Zsigmond Pál. "Az Ellenforradalmi Történelemszemlélet Kialakulása Szekfű Gyula Három Nemzedékében" (The Development of the Counterrevolutionary View of History in Gyula Szekfű's Three Generations). Történelmi Szemle, V (1962), pp. 387-425.

Pamlényi, Ervin. "A Másik Szekfű" (The Other Szekfű). Magyar Nemzet, May 20, 1973.

Pethő, Sándor. Szekfű Gyula Történetirása (The Historical Writing of Gyula Szekfű). Budapest: Lantos Könyvkiadó, 1933.

Schöpflin, Aladár. "Asszimiláció és Irodalom" (Assimilation and Literature). Nyugat, XXXII (1939), pp. 281-293.

_____. "Mi a Magyar?" (What is Magyar?). Nyugat, XXXIII (1940), pp. 75-78.

_____. "Thaly Kálmán Reviziója" (The Revision of Kálmán Thaly). Nyugat, VII (1914), pp. 183-189.

_____. "Aforizmák a Szekfű Ügy Körül" (Aphorisms about the Szekfű Debate). Nyugat, IX (1916), pp. 503-506.

Szabó, Zoltán. "Naplójegyzetek: A Historikus Halálhirére Emlékek Elevenédnek" (Diary notes: The News of the Death of the Historian Evoke Memories). Látóhatár, VI (1956), pp. 15-21.

"Szekfű és Andrássy Gyula Gróf" (Szekfű and Count Gyula Andrássy). Huszadik Század, XXIX (1914), pp. 685-686.

Szekfű Gyula Emlékkönyv: A Történetiró és Nemzetnevelő 60. Születésnapjára (Gyula Szekfű Memorial Volume: On the 60th Birthday of the Historian and Educator of the Nation). Written by Count István Bethlen, Gyula Bisztray, Csaba Csapodi, Sandor Eckhardt, Lajos Gogolak, Domokos Kosary, Imre Kovács and Béla Zolnai. Budapest: A Magyar Szemle Társaság, 1943.

Tarnai, Andor. "Szekfű és a Nemzetietlen Kor Irodalmi Története" (Szekfű and the Literary History of the Anationalistic Age). Irodalom Történeti Közlemények, LXIV (1960), pp. 189-198.

Tilkovszky, Lóránt. "Bajcsy-Zsilinszky Önéletrajzi Vallomása Politikai Nézetei Fejlődéséről és a Szellemtörténethez Való Viszonyáról. Részletek Szekfű Gyulához Intézett 1942 Évi Vitairatából" (The Autobiographical Confessions of Bajcsy-Zsilinszky about the Development of his Political Views and his Relationship to Szellemtörténet. Portions of his Pamphlet of 1942 addressed to Gyula Szekfű). Századok, CV (1971), pp. 966-1001.

SELECTED BIBLIOGRAPHY ON THE HISTORY OF HUNGARY
SINCE THE END OF THE NINETEENTH CENTURY

I. Published Primary Sources

A Magyar Munkásmozgalom Történetének Válogatott Dokumentumai
(Selected Documents of the History of the Hungarian
Labor Movement). VI. vols. Budapest: Magyar
Munkásmozgalmi Intézet, Szikra, 1951-1959.

Benoschofszky, Ilona, ed. Vádirat a Nácizmus Ellen:
Dokumentumok a Magyarországi Zsidóüldözés Történetéhez
(Indictment against Nazism: Documents about the Persecution of the Jews in Hungary). 3. vols. Budapest:
A Magyar Izraeliták Országos Képviselete, 1967.

Bethlen István Titkos Iratai (The Secret Documents of István
Bethlen) edited by Miklós Szinai and László Szűcs.
Budapest: Kossuth Könyvkiadó, 1972.

Hetes, Tibor, ed. A Magyar Vörös Hadsereg, 1919. Válogatott
Dokumentumok (The Hungarian Red Army, 1919. Selected
Documents). Budapest: Kossuth Könyvkiadó, 1959.

Horthy Miklós Titkos Iratai (The Secret Documents of Miklós
Horthy). Edited by Miklós Szinai and László Szűcs.
Budapest: Kossuth Könyvkiadó, 1963.

Iratok az Ellenforradalom Történetéhez, 1919-1945 (Documents
to the History of the Counterrevolution, 1919-1945).
Budapest: Országos Levéltár, 1959.

Karsai Elek, ed. Fegyvertelen álltak az Aknamezőkön:
Dokumentumok a Munkaszolgálat Történetéhez
Magyarországon (They Stood Unarmed on the Minefields:
Documents about the History of the Labor Battalions
in Hungary). 2 vols. Budapest: A Magyar Izraeliták
Országos Képviselete Kiadása, 1962.

Kemény, Gábor, ed. Iratok a Magyar Nemzetiségi Kérdés
Történetéhez (Documents pertaining to the History
of the Hungarian Nationality Question). 3 vols.
Budapest: Tankönyvkiadó, 1952-1964.

Magyarország és a Második Világháború.Titkos Diplomáciai Iratok a Háború Előzményeihez és Történetéhez (Hungary and the Second World War. Secret Diplomatic Papers on the Development and History of the War). Edited by László Zsigmond. Budapest: Kossuth Könyvkiadó, 1961.

Nemes Dezső, ed. Az Ellenforradalom Hatalomra Jutása és Rémuralma Magyarországon; 1919-1921 (The Achievement of Power and the Terror of the Counterrevolution; 1919-1921). Budapest: Szikra, 1952.

Papers and Documents Relating to the Foreign Relations of Hungary. Budapest: Royal Hungarian University Press, 1939.

Ránki, György, Ervin Pamlényi, Lóránt Tilkovszky and Gyula Juhász, eds. A Wilhelmstrasse és Magyarország: Német Diplomáciai Iratok Magyarországról, 1933-1944 (Wilhelmstrasse and Hungary; German Diplomatic Papers about Hungary, 1933-1944). Budapest: Kossuth Könyvkiadó, 1968.

Sorsforduló: Iratok Magyarország Felszabadulásának Történetéhez, 1944 szeptember-1945 április (Change of Fortune: Documents on the History of the Liberation of Hungary, September 1944-April 1945). 2 vols. Budapest, 1970.

II. Memoirs

Angyal, Dávid. Emlékezések (Recollections). London: Szepsi-Csombor Kör, 1971.

Böhm, Wilhelm. Im Kreuzfeuer Zweier Revolutionen. München: Verlag für Kulturpolitik, 1924.

Buchinger, Manó. Küzdelem a Szocializmusért (The Struggle for Socialism). Budapest: Népszava Könyvkiadó, 1948.

Fenyő, Miksa. Az Elsodort Ország: Naplójegyzetek 1944-45-ből (The Drifting Land: Diary entries from 1944-45). Budapest: Révai Könyvkiadó, 1946.

Horthy, Miklós. Memoirs. New York: R. Speller, 1957.

Jászi, Oszkár. "Emlékeimből: Szülőföldemen; Egyetemi Évek" (From my Memoirs: In my Native Land; Student Years). Látóhatár, VIII (1957), pp. 59-70.

_____. "Emlékeimből: A Huszadik Század Megindul Herbert Spencer Égisze Alatt" (From my Memoirs: Huszadik Század gets Underway under the Aegis of Herbert Spencer). Látóhatár, VIII (1957), pp. 135-139.

_____. "Emlékeimből: Elmélet és Gyakorlat Között" (From my Memoirs: Between Theory and Practice). Látóhatár, VIII (1957), pp. 208-217.

Kállay, Nicholas. Hungarian Premier. New York: Columbia University Press, 1954.

Károlyi, Michael. The Memoirs of Michael Károlyi: Faith without Illusion. London: Johnathan Cape, 1956.

_____. Fighting the World: The struggle for Peace. London: K. Paul, Trench, Trubner and Co., 1924.

Nagy, Vince. Októbertől Októberig (From October to October). New York: Pro Arte Publishing Co., 1960.

Sulyok, Dezső. Zwei Nächte Ohne Tag. Zürich: Thomas Verlag, 1948.

III. Historiography (Hungarian)

Babits, Mihály. "Szellemtörténet" (Geistesgeschichte). Nyugat, XXIV (1931), pp. 321-336.

Borsody, Stephen. "Modern Hungarian Historiography." Journal of Modern History, XXIV (1952), pp. 398-405.

Csapodi, Csaba. "Történészhagyatékok a Magyar Tudományos Akadémia Kézirattárában" (Posthumous Papers of Historians in the Archives of the Hungarian Academy of Sciences). Századok, CVI (1972), pp. 1369-1389.

Domanovszky, Sándor. "A Magyar Történetirás Új Útjai" (New Paths in Hungarian History Writing). Századok, LXV (1931), pp. 273-279.

Horváth Zoltán. "Hungary: Recovering from the Past," in Contemporary History in Europe: Problems and Perspectives. Edited by Donald C. Watt. New York: Frederick A. Praeger, 1969.

Hóman, Bálint. A Magyar Történetirás Új Útjai (New Paths in Hungarian Historical Writing). Budapest: A Magyar Szemle Társaság, 1932.

_____. Történetirás és Forráskritika (Historiography and Source-criticism). Budapest: Magyar Történelmi Társulat, 1938.

Glatz, Ferenc. "A Kortörténetirás Kérdése a Magyar Polgári Történetirásban" (The Question of Periodization in Hungarian Bourgeois Historiography). Századok, CIV (1970), pp. 579-583.

_____. "Historiography, Cultural Policy and the Organization of Scholarship in Hungary on the 1920's." Acta Historica, XVI (1970), pp. 273-293.

Gunszt, Péter. Acsádi Ignác Történetirása (The Historical Writing of Ignác Acsádi). Budapest: Akadémiai Kiadó, 1973.

Hatvany, Lajos. "Szalay László," in Emberek és Korok (Men and Ages). Budapest: Szépirodalmi Könyvkiadó, 1964, I, pp. 600-606.

_____. "Az Egyik Horváth Mihály és a Másik" (The One Mihály Horváth and the Other), in Öt Évtized (Five Decades). Budapest: Szépirodalmi Könyvkiadó, 1965.

Léderer, Emma. A Korábbi Középkorra Vonatkozó Magyar Polgári Történetirás Birálata (Evaluation of the Hungarian Bourgeois Historiography about the Early Middle Ages). Budapest: A Magyar Tuc mányos Akadémia Társadalom-Történeti Tudományok Osztályának Közleményei, 1954.

Léderer, Emma. "Marczali Henrik Helye a Magyar Polgári Történettudományban" (The Place of Henrik Marczali in the Hungarian Bourgeois Historical Scholarship). Századok, XCVI (1962), pp. 440-468.

Lukács, Borbála. Szellemtörténet és Irodalom Tudomány (Geistesgeschichte and Literary Scholarship). Budapest: Akadémiai Kiadó, 1971.

Marczali, Henrik. "A Magyar Történetirás Fejlődése a Tizenkilencedik Században" (The Development of Hungarian Historiography in the Nineteenth Century), in Magyar Irodalomtörtenet (History of Hungarian Literature), ed. by Zsolt Beöthy, Budapest, 1900.

Molnár, Erik. "A Magyar Történetirás Fejlődése az Elmult Évtizedekben" (The Development of Hungarian Historical Writing in the Past Decades). Századok, XCIV (1960), pp. 45-58.

Ránki, György. Molnár Erik. Budapest: Akadémiai Kiadó, 1971.

Sőtér, István. "Kemény Zsigmond Történelemszemlélete" (The Historical Views of Zsigmond Kemény). Magyar Tudományos Akadémia Nyelv és Irodalomtudomány Osztályának Közleményei, XII (1961), pp. 47-100.

Szigeti, József. A Magyar Szellemtörténet Birálatához (About the Evaluation of the Hungarian Geistesgeschichte) Budapest: Kossuth Könyvkiadó, 1964.

Szűcs, Jenő. "A Magyar Szellemtörténet Nemzet-koncepciójának Tipológiájához" (On the Typology of the Nation-Concept of the Hungarian Geistesgeschichte). Történelmi Szemle, IX (1966), pp. 245-269.

Thaly, Kálmán. "Történetirodalmunkról" (About Our Historical Literature). Századok, VII (1874), pp. 295-300.

Thienemann, Tivadar. "A Positivizmus és a Magyar Történettudományok" (Positivism and the Hungarian Historical Sciences). Minerva, 1922.

Vardy, Stephen B. Hungarian Historiography and the Geistesgeschichte School. Cleveland, Ohio: An Árpád Academy
Publication, 1974.

Varga, János. "Magyar Szellemtörténet, Magyar Nacionalizmus"
(Hungarian Geistesgeschichte, Hungarian Nationalism).
Kritika, IV (1966), pp. 6-13.

Várkonyi, Ágnes R. A Pozitivista Történetszemlélet a Magyar
Történetirásban (The Positivist View of History in
Hungarian Historiography). 2 vols. Budapest: Akadémiai
Kiadó, 1973.

——————————. "Művelődéstörténeti Törekvések az Europai
és a Hazai Polgári Történettudományban" (Cultural
Historical Strivings in the Bourgeois Historical
Scholarship in Europe and at Home). Századok, CIV
(1970), pp. 136-148.

——————————. Thaly Kálmán és Történetirása (Kálmán
Thaly and his Historical Writing). Budapest:
Akadémiai Kiadó, 1961.

——————————. "Thomas H. Buckle és a Magyar Polgári
Történettudomány" (Thomas H. Buckle and the Hungarian
Bourgeois Historical Scholarship). Századok, XCVII
(1963), pp. 610-644.

——————————. "The Impact of Scientific Thinking on
Hungarian Historiography about the Middle of the
Nineteenth Century." Acta Historica, XIV (1968),
pp. 1-20.

IV. Historiography (General)

Aron, Raymond. Introduction to the Philosophy of History.
Boston: Beacon Press, 1961.

Barg, M. A. "A Módszer Problémája a Mai Polgári
Történetirásban" (The Problem of Method in Today's
Bourgeois Historiography). Századok, CVII (1973),
pp. 719-737.

Bloch, Marc. *The Historian's Craft*. New York: Vintage Book, 1953.

Carr, Edward Hallett. *What is History?* New York: Random House, 1961.

Dorpalen, Andreas. "The German Historians and Bismarck." *Review of Politics*, XV (1953), pp. 53-67.

Fitzsimmons, M. A. and A. G. Pundt. *The Development of Historiography*. Harrisburg: The Stackpole Co., 1954.

Halperin, S. William, ed. *Essays in Modern European Historiography*. Chicago: The University of Chicago Press, 1970.

Higham, John. "Beyond Concensus: The Historian as Moral Critic." *The American Historical Review*, LXVII (1962), pp. 609-625.

Holborn, Hajo. "Wilhelm Dilthey and the Critique of Historical Reason." *Journal of the History of Ideas*, XI (1950), pp. 93-118.

Kohn, Hans. *Reflections on Modern History: The Historian and Human Responsibility*. Princeton: D. Van Norstand Co., Inc., 1963.

_____. *The Mind of Germany: The Education of a Nation*. New York: Harper and Row, 1965.

Korniss, Gyula. "Dilthey Történetszemlélete" (Dilthey's View of History). *Történeti Szemle*, I (1912), pp. 480-527.

Kovács, Endre. "Ismeretelméleti Problémák a Mai Polgári Történetirásban" (Problems of the Theory of Knowledge in Today's Bourgeois Historiography). *Történelmi Szemle*, XI (1968), pp. 349-370.

Lee, Dwight E., and Robert N. Beck. "The Meaning of Historicism." *The American Historical Review*, LIX (1954), pp. 568-577.

Lukacs, John. Historical Consciousness or the Remembered Past. New York: Harper and Row, 1968.

Masur, Gerhard. "Wilhelm Dilthey and the History of Ideas." Journal of the History of Ideas, XIII (1952), pp. 94-107.

Mazlish, Bruce, ed. Psychoanalysis and History. N.J.: Prentice-Hall Englewood, 1963.

Pois, Robert. Friedrich Meinecke and German Politics in the Twentieth Century. Berkeley: University of California Press, 1972.

Rickman, H. P., ed. Wilhelm Dilthey: Pattern and Meaning in History. New York: Harper & Brothers, 1961.

Stern, Fritz. The Varieties of History. Cleveland: The World Publishing Co., 1965.

_____. The Politics of Cultural Dispair. Garden City, N. Y.: Doubleday and Co., 1965.

Thompson, James Westfall. A History of Historical Writing. New York: The Macmillan Co., 1942.

Walsh, W. H. Philosophy of History. New York: Harper and Row, 1960.

Watt, Donald C., ed. Contemporary History in Europe. New York: Frederick A. Praeger, 1969.

V. Secondary Works Consulted:

A. Széchenyi and the Age of Reform

Barta, István. "István Széchenyi." Acta Historica, VII (1960), pp. 63-102.

_____. "Széchenyi István: Halálának Századik Évfordulójára" (István Széchenyi: On the Onehundredth Anniversary of his Death). Századok, XCIV (1960), pp. 257-277.

Barany, George. Stephen Széchenyi and the Awakening of Hungarian Nationalism, 1791-1841. Princeton: Princeton University Press, 1968.

Haraszti, Éva H. "Széchenyi and England." The New Hungarian Quarterly, VIII (1967), pp. 156-164.

Horváth, Mihály. Huszonöt Év Magyarország Történelméből (Twenty-five Years of Hungarian History). 3 vols. Budapest: Ráth Mór Kiadása, 1883.

Kemény, Zsigmond. Összes Munkái (Collected Works). Vol. IX. Történelmi és Irodalmi Tanulmányok (Historical and Literary Studies). Vol. XII. Forradalom Után (After the Revolution). Budapest: Franklin Társulat, 1906 and 1908.

Kosáry, Domokos. "Kossuth Lajos Harca a Feudális és Gyarmati Elnyomás Ellen" (Lajos Kossuth's Struggle Against the Feudal and Colonial Oppression), in Emlékkönyv Kossuth Lajos Születésének 150-ik Évfordulójára (Memorial Volume on the 150th Anniversary of the Birth of Lajos Kossuth). Budapest: Magyar Történelmi Társulat, Akadémiai Kiadó, 1952.
_____. "Széchenyi in Recent Western Literature." Acta Historica, IX (1963), pp. 255-278.

Mályusz, Elemér. "A Reformkor Nemzedéke" (The Generation of the Age of Reform). Századok, LVII (1923), pp. 17-75.

Ortutay, Gyula. "The Living Széchenyi." The New Hungarian Quarterly, I (1960), pp. 36-49.

Sőtér, István. Eötvös József. Budapest: Akadémiai Kiadó, 1953.

Spira, György. 1848 Széchenyije és Széchenyi 1848-a (The Széchenyi of 1848 and Széchenyi's 1848). Budapest: Akadémiai Kiadó, 1964.

Varga, János. A Jobbágyfelszabadítás Kivívása 1848-ban (The Achievement of the Emancipation of the Serfs in 1848). Budapest: Akadémiai Kiadó, 1971.

Varga, Zoltán. "A Szabadságeszme a Magyarság Államszemléletében a XIX-ik Század Első Felében" (The Concept of Liberty in the Hungarian View of the State in the First Half of the Nineteenth Century). Századok, LXXII (1938), pp. 576-641.

B. Nationalism and Nationalities

Andics, Erzsébet, ed. A Magyar Nacionalizmus Kialakulása és Története (The Development and the History of Hungarian Nationalism). Budapest: Kossuth Könyvkiadó, 1964.

Asztalos, Miklós. A Nemzetiségek Története Magyarországon Betelepülésüktől Máig (The History of the Nationalities in Hungary from the Time of their Settlement to the Present). Budapest: Lantos Könyvkiadó, 1934.

Baloghy, Ernő. A Magyar Kultura és a Nemzetiségek (Hungarian Culture and the Nationalities). Budapest: Deutsch Zsigmond és Társa, 1908.

Barany, George. "The Awakening of Magyar Nationalism before 1848." Austrian History Yearbook, II (1966), pp. 19-50.

Bellér, Béla. "Az Ellenforradalmi Rendszer Első Éveinek Nemzetiségi Politikája" (Nationality Policy in the First Years of the Counterrevolutionary Regime). Századok, XCVII (1963), pp. 1279-1318.

Bethlen, István. The Treaty of Trianon and the European Peace. London: Longmans, Green and Co., 1934.

Grátz, Gusztáv. "Magyarország és a Nemzeti Kisebbségek" (Hungary and the National Minorities). Magyar Szemle, IV (1928), pp. 185-199.

Hanák, Péter. Die Nationale Frage in der Osterreichisch-Ungarischen Monarchie, 1900-1918. Budapest: Akadémiai Kiadó, 1966.

Horváth, Zoltán. "The Rise of Nationalism and the Nationality Problem in Hungary in the Last Decade of Dualism." Acta Historica, IX (1963), pp. 1-38.

Jászi, Oszkár, A Nemzeti Államok Kialakulása és a Nemzetiségi Kérdés (The Development of the Nation-states and the Nationality Question). Budapest: Grill Károly Könyvkiadó, 1912.

Joó, Tibor. Magyar Nacionalizmus (Hungarian Nationalism). Budapest: Athenaeum Rt. Kiadása, 1941.

Kann, Robert A. The Multinational Empire. 2 vols. New York: Rutgers University Press, 1950.

Katus, László. "A Tisza Kormány Horvát Politikája és az 1883. Évi Horvátországi Népmozgalmak" (The Croatian Policies of the Tisza Government and the People's Movement of Croatia in the Year 1883). Századok, XCII (1958), pp. 644-684.

Macartney, C. A. Hungary and her Successors: The Treaty of Trianon and its Consequences, 1919-1937. London: Oxford University Press, 1937.

Ottlik, László. "Új Hungária Felé" (Toward a New Hungary). Magyar Szemle, IV (1928), pp. 1-9.

Rónai, András. "A Nemzetiségi Kérdés Területi Megoldásai" (The Territorial Solution of the Nationality Question) Magyar Szemle, XXXI (1937), pp. 201-209.

Sugar, Peter F. "The Nature of non-Germanic Societies under Habsburg Rule." Slavic Review, XXII (1963), pp. 2-46.

Szabó, István. "A Nemzetiségek Térnyerése és a Magyarság" (The Expansion of the Nationalities and the Hungarians), in Magyar Művelődéstörténet, ed. by Sándor Domanovszky, Budapest, 1937.

Tilkovszky, Lóránt. "Volkdeutsche Bewegung und Ungarische Nationalitätenpolitik, 1938-1941." Acta Historica, XII (1966), pp. 59-110; 319-345.

Tilkovszky, Lóránt. Revízió és Nemzetiségpolitika Magyarországon, 1938-1941 (Revision and Nationality Policy in Hungary, 1938-1941). Budapest: Akadémiai Kiadó, 1967.

Tóth, Zoltán. I. "A Soknemzetiségű Állam Néhány Kérdéséről az 1848 Előtti Magyarországon" (About some Questions of the Multinational State in pre-1848 Hungary). Magyar Tudományos Akadémia Társadalmi-Történeti Tudományok Osztályának Közleményei, VII (1956), pp. 259-279.

_____. Az Erdélyi és Magyarországi Román Nemzeti Mozgalom, 1790-1848 (The Romanian National Movement in Transylvania and Hungary, 1790-1848). Budapest: Akadémiai Kiadó, 1959.

_____. "A Nemzetiségi Kérdés a Dualizmus Korában" (The Nationality Question in the Age of Dualism). Századok, XCI (1956), pp. 368-391.

C. The Jews

Braham, Randolph L. "Hungarian Jewry: An Historical Retrospect." Journal of Central European Affairs, XX (1960), pp. 3-23.

Dubnow, Simon. Weltgeschichte des jüdischen Volkes. vols. VIII and IX. Berlin: Jüdischer Verlag, 1929.

Katzburg, Nathaniel. "Hungarian Jewry in Modern Times: Political and Social Aspects." Hungarian Jewish Studies, I (1966), pp. 137-170.

László, Ernő. "Hungarian Jewry: Settlement and Demography, 1735-38 to 1910." Hungarian Jewish Studies, I (1966), pp. 61-136.

_____. "Hungary's Jewry: A Demographic Overview, 1918-1945." Hungarian Jewish Studies, II (1969), pp. 137-182.

Kann, Robert A. "Hungarian Jewry During Austria-Hungary's Constitutional Period (1867-1914)." Jewish Social Studies, VII (1945), pp. 357-386.

Lévai, Jenő. Zsidósors Magyarországon (Jewish Fate in Hungary). Budapest: Magyar Téka, 1948.

McCagg, William O. Jewish Nobles and Geniuses in Modern Hungary. New York: Columbia University Press, 1972.

Pach, Zsigmond Pál. "A Magyarországi Zsidóság Statistikájának Szembetűnő Jelenségei:Tanulmány" (The Striking Phenomena in the Statistics of Hungarian Jewry: A Study), in Maradék Zsidóság (Remnant Jewry). Budapest, 1946.

Scheiber, Alexander. "Recent Additions to the Medieval History of Hungarian Jewry." Historia Judaica, XV (1952), pp. 145-158.

Schickert, Klaus. Die Judenfrage in Ungarn. Essen: Essener Verlaganstalt, 1937.

Straus, Raphael. "The Jews in the Economic Evolution of Central Europe." Jewish Social Studies, III (1941), pp. 15-41.

Vágó, Béla. "Germany and the Jewish Policy of the Kállay Government." Hungarian Jewish Studies, II (1969), pp. 183-210.

Végházi, István. "The Role of Jewry in the Economic Life of Hungary." Hungarian Jewish Studies, II (1969), pp. 35-84.

Venetianer, Lajos. A Magyar Zsidóság Története a Honfoglalástól a Világháboru Kitöréséig (The History of the Hungarian Jews from the Magyar Conquest to the Outbreak of the World War). Budapest: Fővárosi Könyvkiadó R. T., 1922.

Zborovsky, Mark and Elizabeth Herzog. Life is with People: The Jewish Little Town of Eastern Europe. New York: International University Press, 1952.

D. Anti-Fascist Resistance

Baksay, Zoltán. "A Csepeli Munkásság Harca Magyarország Függetlenségéért. 1939-1944" (The Struggle of the Workers of Csepel for the Independence of Hungary. 1939-1944). Századok, CII (1968), pp. 991-1023.

Darvas, József. Város az Ingoványon (City on the Quagmire). Budapest: Szépirodalmi Kiadó, 1960.

Dernői Kocsis, László. Bajcsy-Zsilinszky. Budapest: Kossuth Könyvkiadó, 1966.

Johancsik, János. "A Magyar Nemzet 'Szellemi Honvédelme' és az Antifasiszta Függetlenségi Mozgalom. 1938-39" (The 'Intellectual National Defense' of the Magyar Nemzet and the Anti-Fascist Independence Movement, 1938-39). Századok, CIV (1970), pp. 97-117.

Kállai, Gyula. A Magyar Függetlenségi Mozgalom, 1936-1945 (The Hungarian Independence Movement, 1936-1945). Budapest: Kossuth Könyvkiadó, 1965.

Lackó, Miklós. "Az Uj Szellemi Front Történetéhez" (About the History of the New Intellectual Front). Századok, CVI (1972), pp. 919-985.

Pamlényi, Ervin. "A Függetlenségi Népfront Seregszemléje. Népszava, 1941. Karácsony" (A Look at the Independence People's Front. Christmas, 1941). Magyar Nemzet, December 25, 1971.

_____. "Petőfi Útján" (On the Path of Petőfi). Magyar Nemzet, March 15, 1972.

Pethő, Sándor. Csillagos Órák (Starry Hours). Budapest: Magyar Nemzet, 1939.

Pintér, István. "A Magyar Ellenállás és 1944. Október 15-e" (The Hungarian Resistance and October 15, 1944). Századok, CIV (1970), pp. 35-67.

_____. Magyar Kommunisták a Hitler-Ellenes Nemzeti Egységért (Hungarian Communists for Anti-Hitler National Unity). Budapest: Kossuth Könyvkiadó, 1968.

"Történelmi Tanuvallomások a Történelmi Emlékbizottságról" (Historical Testimonials about the Historical Memorial Committee). Magyar Nemzet, March 2, 1967.

E. General Books and Monographs

Berend, Tibor Iván and György Ránki. The Hungarian Manufacturing Industry; Its Place in Europe. 1900-1938. Budapest: Akadémiai Kiadó, 1960.

Berend, Tibor Iván. A Magyar Gazdaság Száz Éve (One Hundred Years of Hungarian Economy). Budapest: Kossuth Könyvkiadó, 1972.

Bóka, László. Válogatott Tanulmányok (Selected Studies). Budapest: Magvető, 1966.

Duczynszka, Ilona and Karl Polányi. The Plough and the Pen: Writings from Hungary, 1930-1956. London: Peter Owen, 1963.

Eckhardt, Ferenc. A Szentkorona Eszme Története (The History of the Concept of the Holy Crown). Budapest: Magyar Tudományos Akadémia, 1941.

Farkas, Gyula. Az Asszimiláció Kora Magyarországon (The Age of Assimilation in Hungary). Budapest: Magyar Történelmi Társulat, 1939.

Fehér, András. A Magyarországi Szociáldemokrata Párt és az Ellenforradalmi Rendszer (The Social Democratic Party of Hungary and the Counterrevolutionary Regime). Budapest: Akadémiai Kiadó, 1969.

Fukász, György. A Magyarországi Polgári Radikalizmus Történetéhez. Jászi Oszkár Ideológiájának Birálata (To the History of the Bourgeois Radicalism in Hungary. Evaluation of the Ideology of Oscar Jászi). Budapest: Gondolat Kiadó, 1960.

Galántai, József. Az 1867-es Kiegyezés (The Compromise of 1867). Budapest: Kossuth Könyvkiadó, 1965.

Grátz, Gusztáv. A Forradalmak Kora. Magyarország Története, 1918-1920 (The Age of Revolutions. The History of Hungary, 1918-1920). Budapest: A Magyar Szemle Társaság, 1935.

Hajdu, Tibor. Az 1918-as Magyarországi Polgári Demokratikus Forradalom (The Bourgeois Democratic Revolution of Hungary in 1918). Budapest: Kossuth Könyvkiadó, 1968.

Hanák, Péter. A Dualizmus Korának Történeti Problémái (The Historical Problems of the Age of Dualism). Budapest: Tankönyvkiadó, 1971.

Horváth, Jenő. A Milleniumtól Trianonig; Huszonöt Év Magyarország Történetéből, 1896-1920 (From the Millenium to Trianon; Twenty-five Years of Hungarian History, 1896-1920). Budapest: Szent István Társulat, 1939.

Horváth, Zoltán. Die Jahrhundertwende in Ungarn; Geschichte der Zweiten Reform Generation, 1896-1914. Luchterhand: Neuwied, 1966.

Jászi, Oscar. The Dissolution of the Habsburg Monarchy. Chicago: The University of Chicago Press, 1961.

_____. Revolution and Counterrevolution in Hungary. Westminster: P. S. King and Son, Ltd., 1924.

Juhász, Gyula. Magyarország Külpolitikája, 1919-1945 (The Foreign Policy of Hungary, 1919-1945). Budapest: Kossuth Könyvkiadó, 1969.

Karsai, Elek. A Budai Sándor Palotában Történt, 1919-1941 (It Happened in the Sándor Palace of Buda, 1919-1941). Budapest: Táncsics Kiadó, 1964.

Kelleher, Patrick J. The Holy Crown of Hungary. Rome: The American Academy in Rome, 1951.

Kertész, Stephen D. Diplomacy in a Whirlpool: Hungary Between Nazi Germany and Soviet Russia. Notre Dame, Indiana: The University of Notre Dame Press, 1953.

Király, J., L. Labádi, P. Hajdu, Z. Horváth and K. Lengyel. A Magyar Munkásmozgalom Története, 1867-1945 (The History of the Hungarian Labor Movement, 1867-1945). Budapest: Kossuth Kiadó, 1963.

Kun, Bela. A Magyar Tanácsköztársaságról. Válogatott Beszédek és Irások (On the Hungarian Soviet Republic. Selected Speeches and Writings). Budapest: Kossuth Könyvkiadó, 1958.

Lackó, Miklós. Nyilasok, Nemzetiszocialisták, 1935-1944 (Arrow-Cross Men, National Socialists, 1935-1944). Budapest: Kossuth Könyvkiadó, 1966.

Léderer, Emma. Az Ipari Kapitalizmus Kezdetei Magyarországon (The Beginnings of Industrial Capitalism in Hungary). Budapest, 1952.

Macartney, C. A. October Fifteenth. A History of Modern Hungary, 1919-1945. 2 vols. Edinburgh: The University Press, 1956.

Mérei, Gyula. Polgári Radikalizmus Magyarországon, 1900-1919 (Bourgeois Radicalism in Hungary, 1900-1919). Budapest: Karpinszky Nyomda, 1947.

Nagy, Zsuzsa L. A Budapesti Liberális Ellenzék, 1919-1944 (The Liberal Opposition in Budapest, 1919-1944). Budapest: Akadémiai Kiadó, 1972.

Nemes, Dezső. Az Ellenforradalom Hatalomrajutása és Rémuralma Magyarországon, 1919-1921 (The Achievement of Power and the Terror of the Counterrevolution in Hungary, 1919-1921). Budapest: Szikra Kiadó, 1953.

_____. Az Ellenforradalom Története Magyarországon (The History of the Counterrevolutionary Regime in Hungary). Budapest: Akadémiai Kiadó, 1962.

Ortutay, Gyula. Művelődés és Politika (Culture and Politics). Budapest: Hungaria, 1948.

Ránki, György. Emlékiratok és Valóság Magyarország Második Világháborús Szerepéről; Horthyista Politika a Második Világháborúban (Memoirs and Truth about the Role of Hungary in the Second World War; Horthyist Politics in the Second World War). Budapest: Kossuth Könyvkiadó, 1964.

Salamon, Ferenc. Budapest Történetéhez (On the History of
  Budapest). Budapest: Atheneum, 1885.

Sándor, Vilmos. Nagyipari Fejlődés Magyarországon. 1867-
  1900 (The Development of the Manufacturing Industry
  in Hungary). Budapest: Szikra, 1954.

Seton-Watson, Hugh. The East European Revolution. New York:
  Frederick A. Praeger, 1962.

Sőtér, István. Nemzet és Haladás (Nation and Progress).
  Budapest: Akadémiai Kiadó, 1963.

_____. Tanulmányok a Magyar Parasztság Történetéből
  (Studies from the History of the Hungarian Peasantry).
  Budapest: Teleki Pál Tudományos Intézet, 1948.

Szélpál, Árpád. Les 133 Jours de Bela Kun. Paris: Librairie
  Arthème Fayard, 1959.

Szilassy, Sándor. Revolutionary Hungary, 1918-1921. Behind
  the Iron Curtain Series. Astor Park, Florida:
  Danubian Press, 1971.

Tőkés, Rudolf L. Béla Kun and the Hungarian Soviet Republic.
  Stanford, California: F. A. Praeger, 1967.

Tömöry, Márta. "Új Vizeken Járok." A Galilei Kör Története
  ("I am Walking on Fresh Waters." The History of the
  Galilei Circle). Budapest: Gondolat Kiadó, 1960.

Tonelli, Sándor. Nagyapáink Pest-Budája (The Pest-Buda of
  our Grandfathers). Budapest: Athenaeum, 1944.

Varjassy, Louis. Revolution, Bolchevisme, Réaction. Histoire
  de l'Occupation Française en Hongrie (1918-1919).
  Paris: Jouve et Cie., 1934.

Völgyes, Iván. Hungary in Revolution, 1918-1919. Lincoln:
  University of Nebraska Press, 1971.

Weis, István. A Mai Magyar Társadalom (The Hungarian Society
  of Today). Budapest: A Magyar Szemle Társaság, 1930.

Weltner, Jakab. Forradalom, Bolsevizmus, Emigráció (Revolution, Bolshevism, Exile). Budapest: Weltner, 1929.

F. General Articles

Balázs, Béla. "A Horthy-Fasizmus Társadalmának és Ideológiájának Néhány Jellemző Vonása" (Some Characteristics of the Society and Ideology of the Horthy-Fascism). Magyar Tudományos Akadémia Társadalmi-Történeti Tudományok Közleményei, IX (1959), pp. 97-116.

Balogh, Sándor. "A Bethlen Konszolidáció és a Magyar Neonacionalizmus" (The Consolidation of the Bethlen Regime and the Hungarian Neo-nationalism). Történelmi Szemle, V (1962), pp. 426-448.

_____. "Az 1945. November 4-i Nemzetgyűlési Választások Magyarországon" (The November 4, 1945 Elections to the National Assembly in Hungary). Századok, CIV (1970), pp. 869-936, 1192-1239.

_____. Die Geschichte Ungarns nach dem Zweiten Weltkrieg in der Marxistischen Geschichtsliterature. Studia Historica, no. 81. Budapest: Akadémiai Kiadó, 1970.

Deák, István. "Budapest and the Hungarian Revolutions of 1918-1919." The Slavonic and East European Review, XLVI (1968), pp. 129-140.

Diószegi, István. "A Magyar Függetlenségi Ellenzék és a Monarchia Külpolitikája" (The Opposition Party of the Hungarian Independents and the Foreign Policy of the Monarchy). Századok, CVII (1973), pp. 3-24.

Hajdu, Tibor. "A Tanácsok Szerepe a Magyar Októberi Polgári Demokratikus Forradalomban" (The Role of the 'Soviets' in the October Bourgeois Democratic Revolution of Hungary). Századok, LXXXVIII (1954), pp. 245-265.

_____. "Michael Károlyi and the Revolutions of 1918-19." Acta Historica, X (1964), pp. 351-371.

Hanák, Tibor. "Vázlatok a Századelő Magyar Társadalmáról" (Outlines of the Hungarian Society in the Beginning of the Century). Történelmi Szemle, V (1962), pp. 210-245.

Incze, Miklós. "A Néptömegek Helyzete Magyarországon az 1929-1933 évi Gazdasági Válság Idején" (The Situation of the Masses during the Economic Crisis of 1929-1933) Századok, LXVII (1953), pp. 233-311.

McCagg, William O., Jr. "Hungary's Feudalized Bourgeoisie" Journal of Modern History, XLIV (1972), pp. 65-78.

Nagy, Zsuzsa L. "The Mission of General Smuts to Budapest, April, 1919." Acta Historica, XI (1965), pp. 163-184.

Nemes, Dezső. "A Magyar Tanácsköztársaság Történelmi Jelentősége" (The Historical Significance of the Hungarian Soviet Republic). Századok, XCIII (1959), pp. 1-48.

Pach, Zsigmond Pál. "A Dualizmus Rendszerének Első Évei Magyarországon" (The First Years of the Dualist Regime in Hungary). Századok, LXXXIX (1955), pp. 34-74.

Ránki, György. "Gondolatok az Ellenforradalmi Rendszer Társadalmi Bázisáról az 1920-as Években" (Thoughts about the Social Basis of the Counterrevolutionary Regime in the 1920's). Történelmi Szemle, VI (1963), no. 3-4.

Rozsnyói, Ágnes. "1944, Október 15. A Szálasi Puccs Története" (October 15, 1944. The History of the Szálasi Coup). Századok, XCIII (1959), pp. 373-403.

Szekeres, József. "Adatok az 1937. Évi Pécsi Éhségsztrájk Történetéhez" (Factors about the History of the Hunger-strike in Pécs in 1937). Századok, XCIII (1959), pp. 438-472.

Vincze, Edit S. "A Magyarországi Szocialdemocrata Párt Megalakulása és Tevékenysége" (The Establishment and the Activities of the Hungarian Social Democratic Party). Századok, XC (1956), pp. 126-166.

G. Histories

Asztalos, Miklós and Sándor Pethő. A Magyar Nemzet Története Ősidőktől Napjainkig (The History of the Magyar Nation from Ancient Times to our Own Day). Budapest: Dante Könyvkiadó, 1931.

Grátz, Gusztáv. A Dualizmus Kora: Magyarország Története, 1867-1918 (The Age of Dualism: The History of Hungary, 1867-1918). Two vols. Budapest: A Magyar Szemle Társaság, 1934.

Ignotus, Paul. Hungary. New York: Praeger Publishers, 1972.

Macartney, C. A. Hungary. London: Ernest Benn Ltd., 1934.

_____. The Habsburg Empire, 1790-1918. London: Weidenfels and Nicolson, 1968.

May, Arthur J. The Hapsburg Monarchy, 1867-1914. Cambridge, Mass: Harvard University Press, 1965.

Molnár, Erik, Ervin Pamlényi and György Székely, eds. Magyarország Története. Two vols. Budapest: Gondolat Könyvkiadó, 1967.

Pethő, Sándor. Világostól Trianonig (From Világos to Trianon). Budapest: Enciklopédia R. T. Kiadása, 1925.

Taylor, A. J. P. The Habsburg Monarchy. London: Hamish Hamilton, 1955.

H. Bibliographies

Braham, R. L. The Hungarian Jewish Catastrophe. A Selected and Annotated Bibliography. New York: Yivo Institute for Jewish Research, 1962.

Kosáry, Domokos. Bevezetés Magyarország Történetének Forrásaiba és Irodalmába (Introduction to the Sources and the Literature of the History of Hungary). Budapest: Tankönyvkiadó, 1970.

Magyar Tudományos Akadémia Történettudományi Intézete, A Magyar Történettudomány Válogatott Bibliográfiája, 1945-1960 (Selected Bibliography of the Institute of the Hungarian Historical Sciences). Budapest: Akadémiai, 1971.

Tezla, Albert. Hungarian Authors: A Bibliographical Handbook. Cambridge: Harvard University Press, 1970.

Varga, Rózsa and Sándor Patyi. A Népi Írók Bibliográfiája: Művek, Írók, Irodalom, Mozgalom (The Bibliography of the Populist Writers: Works, Writers, Literature, Movement). Budapest: Akadémiai Kiadó, 1972.

Völgyes, Iván. The Hungarian Soviet Republic, 1919. An Evaluation and Bibliography. Stanford: Hoover Institution Press, 1970.

For Product Safety Concerns and Information please contact our EU representative GPSR@taylorandfrancis.com
Taylor & Francis Verlag GmbH, Kaufingerstraße 24, 80331 München, Germany

www.ingramcontent.com/pod-product-compliance
Lightning Source LLC
Chambersburg PA
CBHW072131220426
43664CB00013B/2203